DIVIDED LOYALTIES

Divided Loyalties

CANADIAN CONCEPTS

OF FEDERALISM

Edwin R. Black

McGill-Queen's University Press   MONTREAL AND LONDON 1975

© McGill-Queen's University Press 1975
International Standard Book Number 0 7735 0230 0 (cloth)
International Standard Book Number 0 7735 0238 6 (paper)
Legal Deposit 1st Quarter 1975
Bibliothèque nationale du Québec

Printed in Canada by John Deyell Company

This book has been published with the help of a grant
from the Social Science Research Council of Canada using
funds provided by the Canada Council.

For Anne,
who, even now, may not believe
the book is *really* finished.

CONTENTS

PREFACE   xi

1. Confederation's Competing Images: Sorting them out   1

    Principled Politics and Federalism   3
    Problems of Definition   7
    The Purposes of Federal Structuring   10
    Methods of Problem-Solving   11
    The Question of Majorities   13
    The Five Concepts   15

2. The Centralist Concept   21

    The Centralism of Macdonald   28
    Crisis Centralism   40
    Finance Centralism   54
    Cultural Centralism   56
    Summary   59

3. Administrative Federalism   63

    Federal-Provincial Activities   66
    Interprovincial Equalization   86
    Technical Committee Collaboration   89
    The Federal-Provincial Conference   94
    Horizontal Collaboration   98
    Interdelegation of Powers   103
    Exposition and Examination   104
    Summary   110

4. The Coordinate Concept   113

    The Sirois Commission   114
    The Legal View of Federalism   119

Disallowance and Reservation   132
A Procedure for Constitutional Amendment   135
A Movement Toward Coordinate Federalism   141
Conclusion   144
Summary   146

5. The Compact Theory   149

Development of the Theory   151
Altering the Compact   157
Compact Federalism in Practice   164
Criticism of the Compact Theory   168
Conclusion   170

6. The Dual Alliance   173

Schools and Conscription   176
La Crise du Fédéralisme   178
The Tremblay Commission   182
Law and the Constitution   187
Dualism on the Left   189
Dualism on the Right   192
Criticism of the Dual Alliance   196
Conclusion   200

7. The Deux Nations Controversy   203

8. Two Nations or More?   217

Reflections on the Methodology   218
The Factors of Change   221
The Institutional Dimension   223
Implications for the Future   226

NOTES   235
TABLE OF MAJOR CASES   263
INDEX   265

TABLES

TABLE 1:–Conditional Grants and Shared Cost Programs 1971   74-77
TABLE 2:–Policy Limitation Index   83
TABLE 3:–Finance Dependence Index   88
TABLE 4:–Major Federal Expenditure Estimates for 1973-74 under
       Joint Programs   99
TABLE 5:–Differentiating Criteria and Five Concepts   220

CHART

CHART:–Time Lines for Concepts of Federalism   225

PREFACE

This book reports on an inquiry into Canadian ideas about federal government. Those ideas have not always been easy to specify, for political speculation in this country has been more practical than abstract. We have worried more about how to get along and how to continue doing public business with each other in a mutually satisfying way than we have about ideal forms of governance for mankind. Our political thought is implicit, not explicit. It must be inferred from what we do in and through governments rather than expounded from the texts of founding manifestoes and revolutionary pronouncements. In place of an authoritative charter myth, Canada has charter groups of people, and it is in their perceptions and actions that we find the best evidence of our political philosophies.

This book results from an inferential exercise; it seeks to delineate the major perceptions of society which underlie political activity affecting the federal form of government. The range of thought and action scrutinized is intended to be illustrative, never comprehensive. Despite the plethora of examples suggesting the continuing vitality of most of the major concepts of federalism, the events of the sixties and early seventies have been sketched in only lightly, as lightly as those of Confederation's other decades. The body of the work consists of an introduction together with one chapter devoted to each of the five major concepts. The *deux nations* controversy of 1967 and 1968, posing as it did one of the few occasions in which the shape of the federal structure was itself an important topic of general public debate, is given particular examination in another brief chapter. The final chapter considers the methodology employed in the study, looks at the implications of federalist jargon on the country's politics and attitudes, and offers some suggestions.

Since the word Dominion has fallen into disfavour for reference to the central government, the word "federal" has been substituted, despite the occasional ambiguity this might present to foreign readers.

Accordingly, the "federal government" means the central as distinct from the provincial governments. Similarly, "Parliament" means the body at Ottawa, except for a reference or two to Westminster which is made explicit. "Legislature" or "legislative assembly" refers to the provincial houses, whatever their official variants; "prime minister" means the leader of the federal government and "premier" the head of a provincial cabinet, even though official usage varies on that point as on others. "Confederation" refers to the union as a whole and not to the loose alliance of sovereign states which a rigorous foreign political scientist might well assume it to be.

Since the original investigation made more than a dozen years ago, the literature has increased enormously, although few works apart from those of Professor Donald V. Smiley have been comprehensive. While historians have been especially productive during this period, little reference to their recent work will be found in the footnotes; the reason lies in the rather particularistic nature of much of it. A notable exception is Professor Ramsay Cook's excellent study, *Provincial Autonomy, Minority Rights and the Compact Theory, 1867-1921* (Ottawa, 1969). Consequently this study has been chiefly in terms of political events and developments rather than of literature.

While legal writers and economists have also devoted some attention to the subject, the most important change in the materials available has been the tidal wave of government documents—a natural reflection of the intense changes during the 1960s. Popular commentary on this flood and on the outpourings of bodies like the Royal Commission on Bilingualism and Biculturalism has been plentiful. Most of it appears simply to confirm the general thesis of the work— that five major conceptions of the federal structure underlie and inform much of the political thought and action in the country. Consequently, a decision was taken not to clutter the text and footnotes with endless further illustrations. Most controversial in this respect is, perhaps, the decision not to deal with the Report of the Royal Commission on Bilingualism and Biculturalism. The various reports and research studies undoubtedly related to an aspect of Canadian life that is intimately linked to our conceptions of federalism. The public hearings which the Commission held elicited as well a variety of popular views impinging on the concerns of this book. Once, however, it has been said that bilingualism constitutes one component, but only one of the many components of a particular conception of federalism, there is little more to be said which is immediately relevant here.

The generosity of Duke University made this study possible in the first instance. Especial gratitude is due Professor R. Taylor Cole; somehow, while bearing the onerous duties of Provost of the University, he found the time and good-humoured patience to supervise a student who was not always as tractable as he should have been.

While I was on the faculty of the University of British Columbia, considerable intellectual debts to Professors Donald V. Smiley and Alan C. Cairns were incurred. For the unconscious but undoubted plagiarism that took place as a result of that association, I am most grateful—but above all for their friendship and encouragement.

Others who have contributed to this work have been students, some of whom helped with research and more of whom, recklessly perhaps, encouraged their professor to get it down in book form. Among others who assisted at various times were: William S. Livingston, University of Texas; Frank R. Scott, J. R. Mallory, and Michael Oliver, all at that time of McGill University; Alexander Brady, University of Toronto; H. B. Mayo, now of Carleton; and P.-E. Trudeau, then of Université de Montréal and now of other parts. The staffs of four university libraries—Duke, British Columbia, Queen's, and Exeter—did much to facilitate the research and writing. Particular debts are also owed to Queen's University which granted the needed sabbatical year and to Exeter University in Devon, where Professor A. D. Birch and his colleagues not only made me welcome but put up with me good-naturedly throughout the academic year 1972-73. Only their families can appreciate the debts which academic writers incur in terms of support, love, and tolerance—all of which and more are gratefully acknowledged by a frequently impatient and too busy father and husband.

EDWIN R. BLACK

Queen's University
Kingston, Ontario

CHAPTER

(1)

Confederation's Competing Images: Sorting Them Out

For the Canadian state the politics of federalism are the politics of survival. The continued vigour of her federalism, however, is probably responsible for the stillbirth of Canada as a nation-state; the most conspicuously missing ingredient in this political system has been any sign of an overarching nationalism. In no other mature country does it seem likely that political figures concentrate so much on the geographic distribution of public power to the apparent neglect of debate over the ends and purposes toward which authority is organized. Even the socialists, the most avowedly ideological of the major parties, have found their attempts to educate the voters about the "real" issues of politics repeatedly blunted and turned aside by problems reflecting the country's federal nature.

In the middle of the nineteenth century, the northern British American colonies rejoiced in their individuality and independence. While the forces impelling them toward union were varied—economic, military, political crisis, and so on—they did not include love of each other. Most explicitly they agreed to federate to avoid being swallowed up in a foreign political system—the American. Federation offered the only hope of survival then and so it has appeared for a century since. But the degree of local control and community identity that would be willingly surrendered to the centre has never been without limit. Even today the Canadian people remain to be persuaded that their political system can be more highly centralized without inspiring Quebec, British Columbia, or some other province to seek secession. The greatest "statesman" has been he who best recognized and reconciled the dominant centralizing and decentralizing forces of his time.

Federal or provincial responsibility? That question has distinguished Canada's domestic politics even more than the relationship with the United States has marked her foreign politics. Federal or provincial responsibility is much the same question as "to be, or not to be," for it together with its many responses illuminates the country's character just as the soliloquy does Hamlet's. To understand federalist politics, we must discriminate clearly between the different answers given to what seems initially to be a simple question of legal jurisdiction. To make the necessary distinctions is not always easy. Many times what appears to be the same problem gives rise to quite diverse responses because the participants in public debate often choose to deal with different questions and frequently disagree fundamentally about what constitutes the right question. At heart, the questions and answers are usually inspired by different images of what Confederation is all about, or ought to be. The resulting confusion is enormous, and it produces public argumentation of such complexity that few laymen can comprehend it. In consequence, the public and its commentators usually end up by dismissing the whole proceeding as yet another meaningless shadow game played by and for lawyer-politicians. Yet large issues are at stake, significant questions about who will get, or keep, what share of the public purse and public power.

Disentangling the issues from the confusion is essential if we hope to make sense of the political system. In this study the major approach has been to seek out and identify the basic images Canadians hold of their federal system, then to elucidate and analyze them. The first chapter grapples with the problems involved in distinguishing one such concept of federalism from another and suggests a feasible method. That method of analysis is employed in the remainder of the study first to outline and then to explore in succeeding chapters each of the five major conceptions of the federal system. How these rival images came into being, what sustains them, and what leads to their decline are concerns taken up in the conclusion. There, in addition to other matters, we inquire into the political consequences of structuring political discourse in these peculiarly Canadian terms rather than in those employing images and vocabularies originating in foreign cultures.

The prime importance of federal questions is manifested in a myriad of speeches, innumerable conferences, legal articles and academic books, and even in occasional semi-popular discussions in the mass media. This attention does attest to the widespread interest in federalism, but, more importantly, it reveals the lack of any general agreement about Confederation's essential nature either in fact or fancy. Indeed, the two states of "is" and "ought" are often much confused in contemporary disquisition. Trying to isolate the key qualities of any political system is difficult enough even for fairly dispassionate scholars. The problem is magnified immensely when the discussants are commonly politicians on a public stage (or similarly committed advocates of particular views), and when the framework for discussion involves: (1) two linguistic groups frequently and consciously at odds; (2) a federal division of powers, which is necessarily legalist; (3) a state with heterogeneous socio-economic regions; and, (4) political cultures weakly shared at the bottom which depend critically on customary practices but which are increasingly influenced by documentarian-constitutionalist ideas from abroad.

While the Fathers of Confederation had a clear conception of the type of state they sought, its constitution, like that of other states, has been considerably changed by judicial review, social change, and the course of political events. In 1865, both friend and foe of the Quebec Resolutions were agreed that, if these principles were embodied into law, they would lead to a highly-centralized state; they differed chiefly on the desirability of that outcome. Ever since, history has given evidence that different actors in Canadian politics have been devoted to conflicting sets of principles for organizing the state.

PRINCIPLED POLITICS AND FEDERALISM

That philosophies, or ideas in any structured sense, might characterize their politics might be thought by many to be so atypical as to be ludicrous. One of the most enduring of national images comprises a politics totally bereft of ideological content and conducted by mediocrities purged of all principles; while premiers and prime ministers squabble endlessly about constitutional irrelevancies, bureaucrats and businessmen are thought to be conspiring in secret to take all the important decisions of state to the benefit of their private power and purse. Such is a popular picture. Neither its persistence nor its perverse attractiveness makes it faithful to life; it is distorted and misleading. Canadians spend as much or more time as do other peoples in major debates about ends and means, about the rich and the poor, about freedom and equality, and about change and the status quo. But they do so in the strange vocabulary of the political élites, in terms of changing the structures and responsibilities of their systems of government—in short, in terms of different concepts of federalism.

Misunderstanding of the peculiar jargon of federalist ideologies is commonplace, as is the picture of an unprincipled politics—a picture which probably owes its persistence to at least two types of sources.

On the one side, some advocates of change refuse to accord the legitimacy of "principles" to all who wage politics in any terms other than those approved by the critic-advocate. On another side are the many who will label as "principled" or "ideological" only those debates carried on in what are essentially European terms.* No country can conduct politics at a complex level without developing its own images and vocabularies, and none should be surprised that Canadian political élites have largely abandoned European idioms for their own. These idioms are usually manifested in election campaigns chiefly as different stands on what is called the "constitutional issue."

In discussing constitutional issues affecting the nature of their federal union, Americans often begin by reexamining the intentions of the Framers of the Constitution and trying to reinterpret these in light of current conditions. A similar approach to the Canadian case would encounter serious difficulties. While one such obstacle is posed by the lack of records,[1] the most serious problem lies in the wide divergence of constitutional development from that expected by the Fathers of Confederation. Respect for the founding fathers' wishes is clearly greater in the United States than in Canada, and American constitutional interpretations are studded with legitimizing quotations from the "intentions of the Framers of the Constitution." Corresponding quotations are conspicuously absent from Canadian legal decisions; the long-established British courts which interpreted Canadian statutes had no need of resorting to such extraneous supports for their authority. References to the Canadian Fathers' wishes can be found, but chiefly in the writing of academic partisans of one or another interpretation of the balance of powers, as Professor A. C. Cairns has demonstrated.[2] The greatest problem in seeking guidelines for the present by appealing to the past lies in the popular perception of the utter irrelevance of the exercise. Little connection is seen between the contemporary situation and that with which the men of Charlottetown and Quebec were grappling over a century ago.

Confederation[3] was born in pragmatism without the attendance of a readily definable philosophic rationale. While, according to Professor A. R. M. Lower, it is reasonable to view the American union as one resting on the natural rights of philosophy of the eighteenth century, its northern neighbour was "quite without a comparable

---

*A country of immigrants, Canada has in its fairly open political system an astonishing number of political participants who are the products of foreign socialization processes. The consequences of this have not been much explored as yet. While many of these individuals may profess no concern or even have much knowledge of the contemporary problems of their birthplace, they cannot readily escape the continual screening of all political reality which their childhood images provide throughout much of their lives. A strong tendency to denigrate the quality of Canadian politics may well be one result of such foreign socialization.

ideological foundation in writing."[4] Perhaps the reason for this apparent lack of ideology lies in the absence of popular involvement in the federation's creation (there were no revolutionary troops or populations who had to be told what they were fighting for). We can also point, as Professor Gad Horowitz has, to the presence of organic conservatism as well as liberalism in the creative process, and to the relatively small number of issues which had to be decided at Quebec City.[5] There had been no war for independence; at times Britain seemed eager to be rid of the troublesome British American provinces. The Confederation Fathers had only three sets of decisions to take:

1. How best to improve their facilities for self-government within the British Empire;
2. How to defend the country against American annexation; and,
3. How best to annex the prairie empire of the Hudson's Bay Company before the Americans did it.

At no time, from the first stirrings of Confederation until the Second World War, did challenges arise which would force Canadians to debate, to haggle, perhaps even to draw blood, and eventually to reach some consensus on the whole range of questions about man's public relations with man. In consequence, Canadians were seldom if ever impelled during their country's first century to debate what it was they sought in terms of a state.[6] Some have seen a distinct benefit in this absence of official ideology and philosophical speculation. Professor W. P. M. Kennedy, for example, argued that Canada had thereby been saved from much emotional challenge, from the so-called invasion of sacrosanct instruments, and from "any attempt to confine [constitutional] interpretations within a preconceived Canadian notion of the essence of the Canadian system."[7] Where in the United States a particular version of liberalism developed into what Horowitz has called "an official American ideology," nothing of the sort occurred in Canada during the federation's founding decades. Not nearly so democratic as the American, politics in Canada remained largely a recreation of the élites who needed little more than a spoils system to provide a rationale for the enterprise. Those élites were themselves divided into groups defining themselves in the competing terms of British identity, canadienne survivance, and the parochialism of frontier agricultural communities. The greatest commonalty lay in their joint participation in Canada as essentially an unAmerican activity. Apart from John A. Macdonald and his close associates, few of the élites had enough involvement in the Canadian national enterprise to make necessary or profitable the development of competing national ideologies. So far as images were constructed and manipulated, they were more complementary than competitive: the benefits of local community, the building of a nation, and identification with the glories of

Empire. Rival politicians might emphasize one or the other image at any time or place but seldom did they deny the validity of the other images as part of the complete picture—unless they were appealing to French-speaking voters. The economic fates conspired with the decline of Macdonaldism to make advocacy of the local and the imperial more attractive than that of nation-building during much of half a century. Although minority communities became increasingly unhappy with the situation during the nineteen-thirties, general acceptance of the fundamental arrangements of the state without public challenge or debate remained the case until the death of the Mackenzie King régime in 1957.

So isolated from each other and relatively homogeneous have they been that provincial communities have long provided the most convenient focus for organization and action. Political discourse has almost invariably centred on problems of federalism, usually in terms of the management or mismanagement of three sets of relations, those between: (1) the centre and the peripheries, or Inner and Outer Canada; (2) the French-speakers and the English-speakers; and, (3) Canada and the United States. A certain prescription for political crisis in Ottawa is to confront the federal government with difficult problems involving two of these sets of relationships simultaneously.[8] Disputes about tariff levels and reciprocity represented struggles by the central regions to win advantages which the western and eastern regions would pay for, or vice versa, chiefly because of the coincidence of regions with economic interest groupings. Educational and religious issues could scarcely ever be debated without reference to the federal division of powers and the distribution of English and French speakers. So too with all the issues associated with the welfare state, the egalitarian inspiration of which was in direct conflict with the espousal of the values of local participation. Interjurisdictional clashes of interest were inevitable during the nineteen-sixties, given the competing concerns for: (a) better management of both inflation and unemployment; (b) rapid development of local resources regardless of investment costs; and (c) reduction of the U.S. threat to domestic economic sovereignty. Given an extensive body of federal problems as all embracing as that suggested, we might deduce from the thought behind it some of the basic attitudes toward fundamental political issues. Unfortunately, the plethora of problems does not imply the existence of a comparable body of thought. What there is has existed for much of the country's history only in the work of historians, some judges, and the work of a few other scholars. To understand Canadian federalism, one must examine, besides the material mentioned, the speeches and activities of politicians, the work of legislative bodies and the public services, the decisions of courts, recommendations of royal commissions, and ideally, distributions of public opinion about the federal system. To analyze these data, two questions might be asked: (1) What are the major modes in which Canadians have conceived their federal system? and (2) In what significant ways do these concepts differ from and resemble each other? Among other things, we should also like to know who held or holds the various concepts, and with what effect; while some slight beginning can be made in this study, much of such problems must be left to future work.

PROBLEMS OF DEFINITION

Attempts to differentiate the various ideas of federalism bring us to problems of definition. Concepts of government like federalism achieve precise meaning only through being used in similar ways over time and by a variety of people. Precision of meaning is impaired, however, whenever somebody tries to use such concepts to promote a particular political view—whether for ideological or programmatic reasons. The phrase "cooperative federalism" has particularly suffered debasement in this way. Much political debate in Canada has evolved around the real meaning of federalism, a generally fruitless enterprise, because what most disputants have in mind is the ideal structure of the Canadian state; the "real meaning" of federalism or Confederation has been of interest only to the extent to which it justifies or discredits particular policy preferences. Among the factors which have inhibited general agreement on the federation's nature have been: (a) its cultural dualism and its desirability; (b) the lack of an overarching nationalism; (c) a scholarly and popular tradition of ignoring political implications of differences in the regional subcultures of English-speaking Canada; and (d) a number of fictions arising from the combination of two divergent theories of constitutional authority.[9]

The body of constitutional law does provide a fairly clear definition of federal government for Canada although some scholars dislike its implications on policy grounds and seek to deny its validity in legal interpretation. While detailed in some respects, the British North America Act does not deal with federal government in general. The only broad statement is found in the preamble which recites the desire of the British North American provinces to be "federally united into one Dominion under the Crown of the United Kingdom of Great Britain and Ireland, with a Constitution similar in Principle to that of the United Kingdom." An authoritative definition of federal government for Canada was laid down by the Judicial Committee of the Privy Council in a series of late nineteenth century judgements. In 1892, Lord Watson said in the *Maritime Bank* case; "The object of the Act was neither to weld the provinces into one, nor to subordinate provincial governments to a central authority, but to create a federal government in which they should all be represented, entrusted with the exclusive administration of affairs in which they had a common interest, each province retaining its independence and autonomy."[10] This view of federalism was amplified by the *Local Prohibition* case some four years later and confirmed by Lords Haldane and Atkin in twentieth century judgements such as the *Initiative and Referendum Act* (1919) and the *Labour Conventions* case (1937). Although critics such as Professor V. C. Macdonald believe this definition to be foreign to the British North America Act and improperly impressed on it, the more persuasive argument is that of Professor G. P. Browne who demonstrated that a scheme of strict or classical federalism inheres in the provisions of the Act and is quite logically derivable from it.[11] Canadian political scientists have generally adhered closely to this legalist definition. R. MacGregor Dawson, for example, wrote that: "The pure federal form is one in which the component local units are of equal or coordinate rank with the central government," and also that "A federal system implies by its very definition an aggregation of local governing units, each exercising its own separate powers apart from those which are in the hands of the central or federal government."[12] J. A. Corry identified "classical federalism in the Anglo-American case . . . [as] general and regional governments of co-ordinate authority, each independent of the other in its appropriate sphere, ruling over the same persons and the same territory under the benign surveillance of a court."[13] Contemporary students such as D. V. Smiley and R. L. Watts have usually adopted similar definitions of the legal structure of federal governments.[14]

Legal approaches, however, "are of value only in the solution of legal problems, and federalism is concerned with many other problems than those of a legal nature."[15] Federal governments are expected to promote a great many ends and their decentralized structure simply facilitates some of those ends rather than others; one's preference for more or less centralization of the structures of government is often governed by the order of competing values promoted by the existing structure. So great is the attention customarily devoted to this question of structures that one authority on federalism, Professor R. Taylor Cole, warns us not to focus so much attention on structure that we neglect the dynamic processes of the system. Indeed, for some purposes he even defines federalism as "the process by which, under the impact of centrifugal and centripetal forces, a continuing adjustment is made in the relationships between the central government and the regional governments of the constituent units of a political system."[16] Having heeded his warning, we must still remember that it is the very structure of federal governments which distinguish them from others. Professor W. R. Lederman reminds us that whatever may be the behaviour in reality of political parties and of diplomats engaged in intergovernmental negotiations, the legal distribution of powers and the institutions of arbitration remain "a primary element in defining the bargaining power of the federal government on the one hand and the provincial governments on the other."[17] Many forms of reorganization have been suggested by political reformers in Canada; not all of them have been federalist in nature and those that are not are excluded from consideration here. To distinguish between the federalist and non-federalist, we shall use the following as a working definition:

> Federalism is a form of constitutional organization which unites a number of diverse political units into one state for some important public purposes but preserves their independence of political action in certain matters defined as being of particular regional concern.

This definition specifies neither a fixed structure nor a fixed division of powers. It accommodates the idea that institutions and social forces affect each other, that neither is wholly dependent as an effect of the other, and that modern society is both dynamic and diversified. Modern states incorporate not only centralizing but decentralizing tendencies, tendencies which at one and the same time influence and are influenced by the formal structures among which power is distributed. The act of organizing Canada as a federal type of state not only recognized the previous vitality of decentralizing forces but instituted structures and processes which would sustain and stimulate such forces. Where a country enjoys a reasonably responsive political system, we may expect the federal distribution of powers to correspond, at least roughly, to the prevailing pattern of the regional and national self-identifications of the citizens. Changes in that pattern may be expected to generate pressures leading to changes in the federal organization of power as well. Challenges to the federalist structure are challenges to the basic systems of influences to which governments are responding and to the resulting effects of those interactions.

Despite this extended discussion of process and social change within federations, there exist stable elements which differentiate federal forms of government from others. The most common characteristics of federal régimes include:

1. A written constitutional document which distributes significant powers between two sets of territorial governments, co-equal in the exercise of their exclusive jurisdictions.
2. A method of authoritative interpretation of the constitutional division of powers.
3. Dual citizenship, which implies that both sets of government have dealings with the people in respect of some important areas of life.

4. Some representation of the provinces as provinces in the central legislature.
5. A federalized executive, either in composition or in appointment.

Taken collectively, these five characteristics constitute the "syndrome of federalism," to borrow a medical concept. Just as a particular set of symptoms found collectively suggests to a physician the presence of a particular medical condition, so the syndrome of federalism helps us to distinguish concepts of federal government from other forms of state organization. Of these characteristics, the fourth—manifested usually in a second chamber such as a Senate of the states or provinces—is a common though not an essential condition of federalism. One might even question whether giving provincial representatives either membership or some say in determining the composition of the central executive is a necessary condition, but the point need not be debated here. If regional groups should lack altogether any way of exerting power in the making of major national policies, it is unlikely the federation will endure for very long. The utility of the syndrome is chiefly in the readiness with which it helps us to determine the federal or non-federal quality of the various conceptions of how Canadian government should be organized. More precise indicators than this rough yardstick will then be required to differentiate the various concepts of federalism which have been isolated.

Federalism is generally acknowledged to be one of the most complicated forms of government in use. The active involvement of all governments in many new forms of activity has greatly increased the complexity of federal régimes since the nineteenth century. Only a politically sophisticated population can keep a federation working and we might reasonably expect political argumentation in a modern federation to appear especially labyrinthian and obscure to the outsider —particularly when some of the debaters are all the while urging that subtle changes should be made in the whole structure of federalism. Sorting out the body of argumentation, analysis, action, and advocacy bearing on Canadian federalism requires us to ask the right series of questions if we are to distinguish the chief notions of federalism.

THE PURPOSES OF FEDERAL STRUCTURING

Disputes about the nature of Confederation often arise from basic disagreement about the reason for federalism's continued existence in Canada. Two kinds of goals may be postulated for the federal arrangement. The first is monist or unitary in nature. People oriented in this way argue that while a federal structure may have been necessary a century ago, it is undesirable as a permanent arrangement, and that Canadians should work toward eliminating regional particularities and similar social impediments to unity. This means, of course, the early disappearance of the provinces and their integration into the central government. Other people, those who expect Canada to remain a pluralist society for some time, argue that pluralism is healthy, that federalism promotes it better than unitary governments, and that democratic participation is made more meaningful thereby. Pluralists expect politicians, ideally, to work to strengthen both provincial and central governments, encouraging that which is diverse and valuable in the belief that healthy cultural differences enrich the whole society. This pluralist or federalist group comprises both those who wish essentially to maintain the status quo and those who would modify the status quo by more extensive encouragement for the development and expansion of both linguistic cultures. In opposition to both sets of pluralist views are those who believe federal arrangements weaken the country in many ways and those who fear that federalism both permits fewer democratic practices in public policy processes and promotes unjust inequalities among the people. Those advocating the undesirability of continued federalism clearly have social values divergent from those who support continued federalism. General acceptance of either the unitary or pluralist goal for the federal arrangement as a whole requires assigning to the central government different powers and responsibilities. It thus becomes pertinent for the student to inquire into the particular attitude toward the future of federalism which is postulated or implied by the schools of thought or advocacy under study.

METHODS OF PROBLEM-SOLVING

People seldom state a conception of the purpose of federalism as explicitly as the preceding paragraph might appear to assume. But, because different goals are often visible from the pathways followed, we can often deduce a group's concept of the purpose of the federal arrangement from the solutions it proposes for various public problems. Categorizing the variety of procedures proposed for problem-solving, or public policy-making, furnishes a second set of useful reference points. The issues may relate to economic controls by the centre over the provinces, to the amount and kinds of political initiatives assigned to the provinces, or to the preferred locus of responsibility for certain culturally-related activities. The safeguards for the provinces' independence and territorial integrity constitute another set of critical indicators of attitudes toward federalism, all of which merit further discussion.

1. The system of public finance is a good indicator of the authority structure of a state, an even more accurate indicator than is the constitutional distribution of legislative authority. If provinces are to fulfil assigned constitutional roles they require financial resources—but whence is the money to come? If its financial resources, however secured, are adequate only in the short run, a government cannot be assured of its long range independence. To have meaningful autonomy, provincial cabinets must be able to give their policy decisions sustained financial support over a protracted time period. The ultimate power of the central régime is assured should all public taxes be collected and disbursed by the national government; total economic control by the centre puts the provinces at its mercy. It is possible, however, to centralize the *collection* of taxes (as being distinct from the *levying* of taxes), and to decentralize some or all of the spending authority. Such a system gives the federal capital a considerable economic lever but might deny it complete control.

The provinces could be given long term financial support for their policies through a number of methods but in Canada discussion has involved only two basic types of arrangements, those of fiscal autonomy and of financial independence. Both methods contemplate provincial governments being free to spend their funds without central controls, but there they part company. Inherent in the notion of fiscal autonomy is a substantial—perhaps constitutional—guarantee of a province's right to levy taxes which will raise enough revenue to meet its needs. The usual proposal has been to give the provinces exclusive rights to some particular, specified tax fields. Financial independence, however, envisions guarantees that the provincial treasuries will always receive certain minimum revenues; these might consist entirely of federal subsidies or result from a combination of federal subsidies and provincial tax levies. The concentration of all taxation rights in the federal capital would, of course, debar the possibility of fiscal autonomy for the provinces but would not rule out their being financially independent.

2. Guarantees of political independence are also important. While we may assume that the courts will keep the independence of both orders of government within legal bounds, the degree of effective independence of the various cabinets might vary widely. At one extreme, the provinces might exercise their constitutional powers in a manner like that of fully sovereign states. At the opposite extreme, provinces might exercise power only under the supervision of the central administration which might be able to require the subordinate government to perform duties they had either neglected or refused to carry out. Between these extremes is the current situation of the Canadian provinces. For all practical purposes they are independent and exercise initiatives in a variety of fields, yet they remain subject to the federal government's legal but seldom-used rights of vetoing provincial legislation and taking over public works in the general interest. We can formulate these ideas as political criteria denoted as (a) essentially *integrative,* where legislative initiatives are the prerogative of the central legislature; (b) *supervisory* in character, where the provinces retain some initiatives subject to the exercise of central vetoes or directed remedial legislation; or (c) *autonomist,* where each government exercises its "sovereign" powers under no other supervision than that of an independent court.

3. Cultural concerns and divergent governmental approaches to them were among the reasons Canadians adopted a federal form of government. Since Confederation, many English-speaking persons have argued in favour of centralizing authority over cultural subjects such as education. Others have opposed the idea vigorously. The range of disputed issues in Canada includes language rights, civil liberties, labour, social welfare, and education. In most cases, the choice seems to have been whether Ottawa or the provincial capitals should have responsibility and ultimate authority for each or all of these culturally-related activities.

THE QUESTION OF MAJORITIES

The final set of indicators or criteria to be discussed relates to the safeguards of the power and very life of the provinces, that is, the method of amending the federal constitution. Canada has not yet taken possession of full domestic authority to amend the British North America Act; in particular, that part of it dealing with the distribution of powers between provincial and federal governments remains with the United Kingdom Parliament which acts at Canada's request. Much agitation has been expressed about "nationalizing" or "domesticating" the amending power fully and in the process a great deal has been said about federalism.

That the constitutional amending procedure forms a critical hinge in the system's working seems obvious; if any single body possesses the absolute right to decide what, if any, shall be the effective powers of another government, then that body holds a life and death authority over the other government. Great alarm was expressed in some quarters when the Parliament of Canada in 1949 obtained the exclusive power to amend the B.N.A. Act in respect of nearly all central government activities. In no similar federation does the central régime have comparable authority, because the states or their representatives almost invariably have an effective voice in all constitutional amendments. Amending proposals therefore merit particular attention, especially when one recalls the vagueness of the B.N.A. Act about residual powers and when one recalls how other governments have exploited apparently insignificant powers to magnify their claims to certain jurisdictional areas.

The case of Canada, as K. C. Wheare has pointed out, "raises in the extreme form the argument used against the amending processes in a federal system—that they make it possible for the will of a majority to be obstructed by a minority." But, as he goes on to suggest, federal government is based on the idea that government by a bare majority of people is "not the only way in which to govern well and in some cases is equivalent to bad government."[18] Canadians have accepted majority rule in principle but they are far from agreed on what the principle means in practice. Many disputes about French-English relations or those between the provinces and the federal government are, at heart, disputes about the appropriateness of resolving certain questions according to the wishes of a national majority instead of a provincial majority, or vice versa. In all cases, it would be more accurate to refer not simply to majorities but, rather, to governments representing different majorities. The questions then become: "Should this issue be decided by governments representing a national majority?" and "What kinds of issues should be settled by each of the provincial and federal orders of government?" (Referring to governments representing majorities rather than speaking loosely about popular majorities deciding such questions, it should be noted, changes the emotive context of the issue.)

Without delving further into these questions, the assumption is made here that the federal principle is best observed by a constitutional amending process which requires the consent of both linguistic groups and of every major region before proposed amendments can take effect. This would be a Canadian version of the American concurrent majorities idea. On one side of this position is the essentially *confederal* requirement that every proposed change be subject to the necessary approval of the federal legislature and of every province. On the other side is the essentially unitary principle implicit in national majoritarianism: constitutional changes of any sort may be made so long as they have the approval of a majority of those voting, regardless of sectional, linguistic, ethnic, or any other kind of ballot distribution. We can pick out three basic positions around which are focused constitutional aspects of federal discussions:

(i) Amendments approved by national majority (either by referendum or vote in Parliament).

(ii) Amendments requiring approval by major groupings in the country: the primary examples discussed in Canada are the

Fulton-Favreau formula of the nineteen-sixties and the Trudeau-Turner formula of the seventies.*

(iii) Amendments approval confederally—by the unanimous consent of the legislatures of all constituent governments (thus giving a veto power to both large and small provinces.)

Employment of the differentiating criteria which have been outlined helps us to distinguish and identify five fairly distinct ways in which Canadians think of their federal arrangements. Common to all five concepts of federalism are two assumptions: (1) That whatever form of federal change is adopted, there would be continued respect for the established privileges of French- and English-speaking minorities; and (2) That the present institutional structure of the central government would continue largely intact except, possibly, for the Senate which some reformers would abolish while others would reconstitute, and for the Supreme Court of Canada in whose appointments the provinces would be given some voice according to some proposals.

THE FIVE CONCEPTS

The major sets of ideas, denominated here as centralist, administrative, coordinate, compact, and dualist, are represented schematically in Table 5 and described briefly below.

The Centralist Concept

The centralists view Confederation as an experiment in nation-building, a project which will only reach completion when the country has been unified enough to permit reduction of the provinces to administrative units of the central régime. Until this occurs, the centralist usually favours vigorous exploitation of all the potentialities for control inherent in Ottawa's virtually unrestricted spending powers and sometimes even the resurrection of Ottawa's obsolescent constitutional powers of supervising the provincial governments to make their policies harmonize with those of Ottawa. Responsibility for all policy

---

*The Fulton-Favreau plan divides the constitution into different sections, some of which can be amended by simple vote of the central Parliament; others require unanimous consent from the federation's various legislative bodies. See Guy Favreau, *The Amendment of the Constitution of Canada* (Ottawa, 1965). The Trudeau-Turner proposal, also called the Victoria Charter, took a different approach. For most changes passage of an amendment required the approval of Ottawa, Ontario, Quebec, any two of the four Atlantic provinces, and two of the four western provinces with at least 50 percent of the western population. Changes of interest to several provinces only could be made by those provinces and Ottawa in concert, and the federal and provincial governments individually could amend their own constitutions.

innovation would pass to the House of Commons, but most important of all, the central régime's controls over the whole society would be vastly enhanced by concentrating in Ottawa the full range of financial, fiscal, and other economic powers employed by modern states. The concept envisions the formal constitution being amended in virtually all respects by action of the central Parliament, although some advocates of centralization favour a procedure calling for national referenda.

At the heart of this concept is the notion that the whole of the Canadian people constitutes the only legitimate source of sovereign authority and that a government enjoying the support of a Canadian majority must be supreme over all other governments. The centralist is almost without exception of English expression and the concept has been beset from time to time by racist connotations. While devotion to the centralist idea was for decades an essential ingredient of socialist ideology, Canadian nationalists of a conservative bent have been hardly less devoted to the idea.

The Administrative Concept

Administrative federalism, sometimes called executive or cooperative federalism, is more of a general approach than a developed scheme involving final goals. Its advocates assume the long term continuance of the provincial governments but emphasize the necessity and desirability of expanding the tradition of intergovernmental cooperation without the antagonistic flaunting of sovereign rights and privileges. The major institution of collaborative federalism is the intergovernmental conferences—especially at bureaucratic levels. Close and frequent consultations largely outside the arenas of close public scrutiny have enabled officials of the different governments to establish an extensive network of joint programs. Through such joint endeavours, advocates of this approach hope to realize some of the efficiencies of the unitary state while retaining advantages of the federal.

The centralization of fiscal powers in Ottawa combined with provincial financial independence typifies the collaborative attitude. Although national administrative standards are often proposed in matters like education, and have even been initiated on a limited scale, this school of thought is usually content to leave the substance of school curricula to provincial authorities. In many ways the administrative concept of federalism reflects the large scale bureaucratization of public life. In the conferences of premiers and prime ministers, we witness the most publicly partisan of all politicians—the party leaders —subordinating their partisan concerns to the bureaucratic goals of greater rationality and convenience in the administration of similar programs across the country.

The Coordinate Concept

The strengthening of both orders of government, fiscal and financial independence, autonomy of the provinces within their assigned constitutional spheres, and the restriction of the federal government to its explicitly designated areas of jurisdiction characterizes coordinate federalism in most of its Canadian forms. The juridical view of Confederation does, however, acknowledge the *legal* right of the central government to veto provincial legislation and to protect some minority language and school rights. The experience of the past quarter century together with explicit declarations by federal prime ministers confirm the effective repudiation of these legal powers by customary practice, bringing the Canadian version more into line with international understanding of the "classical" form of federalism.

Both orders of government are recognized as having responsibility for different aspects of civil liberties, and the provinces are seen as the exclusive authorities in general education matters. In reducing the number of federal programs within provincial jurisdictions during the late sixties, the Liberal governments began moving more firmly toward coordinate federalism under the influence of Pierre-Elliott Trudeau. Both Parliament and the provincial legislatures are seen as having legitimate and independent authority to amend different parts of the B.N.A. Act. Advocates of coordinate federalism favour schemes such as the Fulton-Favreau or the Trudeau-Turner proposals for amending the federal constitution.

The Compact Theory

The Canadian union has been conceived by some to be a league of states which by solemn compact delegated certain powers to a newly-constituted central government. Compact theorists asserted that the central government ought accordingly to regard itself as a creature of the provinces. (Provinces admitted or created after 1867 are usually accorded status equal to that of the original members, New Brunswick, Nova Scotia, Ontario, and Quebec.)

Inherent in this is the notion that every province is sovereign within its appointed jurisdiction and that each province must assent before the constitutional compact can be changed. Financial and sometimes fiscal independence is held to be essential to the vitality of the provinces, and some compact theorists would assert that Confederation involved an implicit understanding that the partners would share equally in the benefits of union, but there is less accord on this point which, in any case, is virtually impossible to put into mutually agreed economic terms. Civil liberties, language rights, social services, and school matters are thought to be of exclusive provincial concern except where the B.N.A. Act specifies otherwise (e.g. Sec. 93). The compact theory seems to have been the working assumption of most politicians and governments during the first three decades of this century and it still appears occasionally in some official briefs. Expression of the idea might be found as well in the widespread agreement throughout the negotiations that the consent of every province would be required before Canada could adopt a procedure providing for the full domestic amending of the formal constitution.

The Dualist Concept

The idea that Confederation comprises two races, two linguistic groups, and two cultures provides the foundation of the dualist concept, which is sometimes called the two nations theory (although the latter has one quite divergent interpretation from the general trend in this concept). Dualists argue that Confederation should be dedicated primarily to promoting and extending the welfare of the two co-equal founding cultures—English and French. To this aim are united demands for fiscal and financial independence of the provinces. While advocates believe that education and civil rights are generally provincial responsibilities, they look to Ottawa to persuade English-speaking citizens to accord to French-speaking minorities everywhere the facilities they require to permit formation of a real bicultural society across the country. The Fulton-Favreau formula was drafted to provide in part for some of these viewpoints in the field of constitutional change; a number of dualists would argue, however, that French-speaking representatives should have an equal voice with the English-speaking in amendments touching culturally significant matters. While the clearest expression of the dualist concept of federalism is found in the 1956 report of the (Quebec) Royal Commission of Inquiry on Constitutional Problems, others were evident in briefs presented to the Royal Commission on Bilingualism and Biculturalism, in the editorial policies of *Le Devoir,* and to some extent in the deliberations of the Montmorency conference that preceded the 1967 leadership conventions of the Progressive Conservative Party. Federal government policies to extend French as a working language within its own administrative departments have been a similar manifestation, although it should be noted that the Trudeau government's policy was to regard Canada as a bilingual, multicultural state.

Allied to the dualist concept were the demands made by some that the province of Quebec be granted *statut particulier* within the federation, that is, certain federal powers would be reassigned to the Quebec government with respect to residents of that province while Ottawa continued to exercise that jurisdiction over other Canadians. The "associate statehood" advocated by others for Quebec envisioned that province assuming virtually full sovereignty and instituting a new confederal relationship with the remainder of Canada. This proposal of the mid-sixties was much more *séparatiste* than federalist.

As the federation was embarked on what optimists called its second century, not one of the five concepts sufficed as a model of the system. The centralist concept might have done as a rough abstraction of the federation during its first decade, and the compact theory appears to have been the working model from the turn of the century to the nineteen-thirties. A period of centralization during the nineteen-forties and early fifties was inspired by war and egalitarianism, following which there developed a more mixed federal system. Analyzing it presents difficulties. The political system was in crisis because of its inability to handle simultaneously two closely related but distinct problems: the management of relations between the centre and the dissimilar peripheries, and the demand for new relationships between English-speaking and French-speaking. Public discussion was further confused, first because of the intermixing of the two issues just mentioned and secondly because political élites charged with resolving the country's difficulties were debating the appropriate content and implications of "Canadian" citizenship on the basis of differing concepts of Canadian federalism. Complicating the matter further was a revival of economic nationalism; this took the form of demands for the simultaneous curbing of foreign capital investment and the stimulation of employment in the less industrialized regions of the country.

A combination of the concepts is required to characterize Canadian federalism at this time. The federation is chiefly coordinate in its political essentials, largely collaborative at the senior levels of the public bureaucracies, and tending to adopt linguistic cultural aspects of the dualist concept. Traces of the compact theory were represented in the constitutional amendment movement, but little evidence was to be found of the centralist concept in any influential circles.

While representation of the centralist and compact concepts may be found in the country's history, we can find no working models of the other three concepts delineated. This phenomenon serves simply to emphasize the point that concepts are abstractions, mental constructs, whose utility to the student of politics is not to be measured in terms of the precision with which they resemble reality. Rather, the concepts should be assessed in the more modest terms of the degree to which they permit us to describe, to analyze and thus to understand a little better the system under study. That the concepts discussed in the present instance also serve as normative or ideal goals for important figures in the political area adds further weight to their utility to the student of Canadian government.

CHAPTER

$$2$$

The Centralist Concept

The degree to which powers should be concentrated in authorities at one territorial head is a universal problem in politics, and is of especial importance in constitutional régimes which are federally organized. Records of the conferences that designed the federal structures of Australia, Canada, and the United States of America demonstrate that the most difficult negotiations concerned the degree of centralization of political authority. Once this question had been settled, the negotiators' tasks were considerably simplified.

Contemporary discussions of centralization contend with semantic difficulties fostered by the word's illiberal connotations. To many Canadians, these connotations include that of the submergence of minority cultures. Professor Frank R. Scott has commented that centralization "To certain sections of the population . . . carries a particular menace; for most Quebecers it suggests the loss of their provincial autonomy to Ottawa, centre of British influence and Protestant majorities, while for the business community, fearful of an expanding welfare state with its increased taxation and controls, the word seems a signpost on the road to serfdom."[1] Representatives of French Canada are prone to attach the tocsin word "centralist" to anything that may threaten their culture. The term is an epithet in some arenas. To certain English-speaking cultural extremists—found notably in organizations like the Orange Lodge, the United Empire Loyalists, and the Imperial Order of the Daughters of the Empire—centralization is a higher value to be pursued vigorously. It has been argued that only through centralization can there be built a "truly Canadian" nation.

Consideration of the centralist concept before the others is suggested by four factors: (1) Its perceived natural appropriateness for many in the general public, and especially for those who have been socialized in countries with unitary governments; (2) the primacy of the question of centralization for federal states generally; (3) provisions of the British North America Act, 1867, which appear to subordinate the provinces to the central government; and (4) reactions to centralism which inspired the concepts of the dual alliance and the compact theory. This discussion will focus on ideas and proposals that would effectively concentrate ultimate political authority at the centre at the expense of the provinces.

Pre-Confederation Proposals

The rudiments of the B.N.A. Act have been discerned in the various plans put forward during the ninety years following the Conquest of 1760. But virtually all constitutional thought of this period was concerned with constructing a British Canadian nation, and seldom, if ever, did it venture into discussing arrangements that would subdivide the sovereignty of the Queen between the colonies. The first significant project submitted from Quebec was drafted by the chief justice of the colony, William Smith. The governor, Lord Dorchester, sent the plan[2] to the Colonial Office in February 1790, along with his message concerning the Constitutional Act, then in bill form. The chief justice, who was a United Empire Loyalist, mentioned a governor general, a legislative council consisting of a minimum number of persons from each province appointed by the Crown for life, and a general assembly whose members would be elected by each of the provincial assemblies. Apparently only a simple majority of votes was to be needed for assent in the council, but approval in the assembly would be "by such and so many Voices as will make it the Act of the majority of the Provinces."[3] The executive was to make laws, in the name of the monarch, for the "peace, welfare and good Government of all or any of the said Provinces and Dominions," which would have included all British North America. Assemblies for these various provinces were mentioned but there was no discussion of their proposed role. One presumes the provinces were to have duties of a municipal nature. Nothing else came of this plan, although there is evidence that it was considered by the Colonial Office. The proposal was revived a quarter of a century later by Smith's son-in-law, Jonathan Sewell, who was also chief justice of Quebec, but no further details were given than in the original plan.[4]

Projects for unifying the provinces were often suggested, particularly by people in Upper Canada, and by the minority English elements in Lower Canada. John Beverley Robinson also suggested that "perhaps, it would not be found impracticable to group the colonial

possessions of the Empire into six or seven confederates . . . , and
to allow each of these confederacies a representative in Parliament."[5]
Although the term federation was used frequently at this time, it
usually denoted a proposed fusion of political entities rather than
their perpetuation in a federal union with coordinate governments.

Before serious consideration could be given to federalism, the
country had to digest Lord Durham's *Report,* experience the difficulties of trying to govern the two Canadas united into one Province of
Canada, and then incorporate into this structure the principle of responsible cabinet government. The ruling Tories became committed
to an expansionist viewpoint which accepted the likelihood of an
imperialist struggle with the Americans for the riches of the western
lands. To attain this, the Tories adopted as fundamental political
principles the desirability of centralized control and assimilation of
the French.[6]

A century before the shattered Southern Confederacy was subjected to "reconstruction," the *Canadiens* were subjugated by British
arms and forced to undergo the harassment of carpet-baggers who
were not only complete foreigners, but carpet-baggers who believed
that they were the bearers of the "true faith," of a higher civilization,
and a superior tongue. The *Canadiens'* battle to survive began in
1760 and is today in its third century.

It is in Lord Durham's *Report* that the French Canadian finds the
devil's handbook, for in it "Radical Jack" gave complete expression
to the objective toward which English Canadians have always been
striving in the eyes of Quebeckers. Durham had looked at the situation in Louisiana, found the tendencies there to be good, and urged
adoption of a régime that would bring about the gradual disappearance of New France and its distinctive culture. These were the terms
in which Durham saw the problem:

> The fatal feud of origin, which is the cause of the most extensive
> mischief, would be aggravated at the present moment by any
> change which should give the majority more power than they have
> hitherto possessed. A plan by which it is proposed to assure the
> tranquil government of Lower Canada must include in itself the
> means of putting an end to the agitation of national disputes in the
> legislature, by settling once and for ever the national character of
> the province. I entertain no doubts as to the national character
> which must be given to Lower Canada; it must be that of the
> British empire; that of the majority of British America; that of the
> great race which must, in the lapse of no long period of time, be
> predominant over the whole North American continent. Without
> effecting the change so rapidly or roughly as to shock the feelings
> and trample on the welfare of the existing generation, it must

henceforth be the first and steady purpose of the British Government to establish an English population, with English laws and language, in this Province, and to trust its government to none but a decidedly English Legislature.[7]

Durham had begun his mission with a predisposition for federation, but his inquiries persuaded him that any thought of a British North American federation would have to await the absorption of the French. This assimilation was, and is, seen by French Canadians as the real objective of any proposal to increase central powers; their battles against *les centralisateurs* has always been intimately linked to the saga of *la survivance*.

Public attention was first directed to federation as a possible solution for current difficulties in 1849. Many in the Province of Canada faced ruinous prospects as Great Britain started to dismantle the colonial trading system. The minority English-speaking element comprised large numbers of American immigrants with no great love for unprofitable English attachments. Radical and Grit political fortunes thrived as annexation sentiments grew in importance. Many of the conservative members of Montreal's business community had succumbed to the political heresy of the Annexation Manifesto. Tory politicians desperately needed a dramatic alternative. John A. Macdonald told his official biographer that he had been pressed to sign the manifesto, but refused, and "advocated the formation of the British America League as a more sensible procedure."[8] Representatives were summoned from all the English parts of the province for a convention of the league at Kingston. The first resolution of the meeting upheld the British connection, and then, as Macdonald told it:

> the second proposition was that the true solution of the difficulty lay in the confederation of all the provinces. The third resolution was that we should attempt to form in such confederation, or in Canada before confederation, a commercial national policy. The effects of the formation of the British North America League were marvellous. Under its influence the annexation sentiment disappeared, the feeling of irritation died away, and the principles which were laid down by the British North America League in 1850 [*sic*] are the lines on which the Conservative-Liberal party has moved ever since.[9]

The Kingston convention appointed a committee to discuss the project with representatives of the Maritime provinces. Joseph Howe, of Nova Scotia, was interested in the possibilities. He wrote:

> We desire free trade among all the Provinces, under our national flag, with one coin, one measure, one tariff, one Post Office. We

feel that the courts, the press, the educational institutions of North America, would be elevated by union; that intercommunication by railroads, telegraphs and steamboats would be promoted, and that, if such a combination were achieved wisely and with proper guards, the foundations of a great nation, in friendly connection with the mother country, would be laid on an indestructible basis.[10]

Talks between representatives of the British North America League and of New Brunswick were followed by a riotous meeting of the League in Toronto in which a "torrent of vague, grandiose, irresponsible constitution-making was immediately unloosed," followed by demands for a general convention of the people of British North America to discuss a federal union.[11] These projects did not mature of themselves but were, rather, in the nature of seeds cast in fertile soil. There had been present economic crisis, political disruption, and community determination to maintain political individualism, but at mid-century British North America lacked most of all a foreign threat to spur the process of nation-building.

United Canada: A Federal Policy

The most significant forerunner of the centralist idea of federalism was the method of conducting public business in the legislature of the Province of Canada. The Act of Union of 1840 had united Upper and Lower Canada to give effect to Durham's recommendations, a move which was supposed to promote assimilation of the French. But from the first the governors found themselves forced to solicit the support of the various French legislative blocs, which used their strength to purchase a decisive voice in all matters affecting the French interests. The inauguration, in 1849, of a system of responsible cabinet government made support of the French even more of a necessity for no one English person could gain majority support in the legislature. The ministries of the day were known by double-barrelled titles—the "Baldwin-Lafontaine" cabinet—derived from the names of the leaders of the English and French groups supporting the executive. The Baldwin-Lafontaine ministry in 1849 enjoyed strong majorities in both Canada East and Canada West; these majorities were agreed upon the chief issues of the times and decided to forego inquiry into local matters about which the other majority felt strongly. Yet, as Dr. O. D. Skelton has pointed out, the very composition of this ministry showed how incomplete was the union. Each wing of the governing coalition party was distinct in organization and leaders. "There were virtually two premiers, though one was given titular precedence over the other," said Dr. Skelton, "and there was both an Attorney-General West and an Attorney-General East."[12] The judicial and legal systems of the sections remained separate and at every session laws were passed which applied only to one section of the province.

Early in the eighteen-fifties a new ministry sought to amend the school legislation of Canada West. A majority of the Upper-Canadians opposed the amendment because it permitted the establishment of separate schools. The ministry ignored these protests and used the French-speaking majority to help get the bill through the legislature. When similar incidents recurred, it became apparent that party discipline would not stand the strain of having local legislation imposed on recalcitrant members with votes from the other language group. This realization led to the adoption by John Sandfield Macdonald and Joseph Cauchon of the "double majority" principle. In practice, this principle required a ministry to have a majority in each of the two sections. No legislation affecting one section alone was passed without that section's majority assent, and premiers resigned whenever they lost the majority support of their section, regardless of their overall strength in the legislature.[13] John A. Macdonald endorsed the principle in 1856 when, during a ministerial crisis, he sought to have the legislature support a motion formally recognizing the convention.

Here, then, was a scheme in which all matters of purely local concern required the assent of a majority of the local representatives, and a scheme in which the legislature acted as a whole only in those areas of concern to both sections of the province.[14] The objections to the plan were clearly set forth in a memorial from the Canada East opposition group in 1859. It pointed to the obvious difficulty of distinguishing clearly the cases to which the double or single majority should apply, and to the difficulty of persuading the members of the validity of each judgement. Even had these things been possible, the policy forced majorities gravely opposed to each other on principle to unite, thereby extinguishing the two minorities' possible influence. Each majority had to take care that it never trespassed upon the other's concerns in order that each section might be effectively governed by a majority of its representatives. "On many questions," said Dr. Skelton, "this could not be carried out without alternately forcing the majority of the representatives of each section of the province to abstain from voting, or to declare themselves in favour of measures which their judgment or conscience would disavow."[15] The system demanded the application of the federal principle to a single legislature, an application that could not, and did not, last long without precipitating serious difficulties.

The British Government, ignoring Durham's advice, had sought to ensure an English majority in the legislature by dividing the province into eastern and western sections and assigning forty-two representatives to each. At first, Canada East was greatly under-represented, but her legislators made no real objection. Soon, however, English-speaking immigrants began filling the once-empty western lands and by 1850 Canada West was under-represented. A number of Canada West politicians began to decry the "domination" of the French and began their famous "rep. by pop." agitation. These Radicals sat on the opposition benches, however, and they were unable to persuade the conservative ministry to adopt population as the representational base. The second line of attack of the English minority group was to move for repeal of the union. The leader of the French minority group, A. A. Dorion, agreed that change was needed but proposed a federal union of the two sections. He argued in the legislature that:

> It is our duty to see whether there is not some other way to meet the difficulty, which lies in the nature of the existing legislative union. . . . There would be no difficulty in getting the people of Upper and Lower Canada to set up a general legislature with control of Commercial interests, railway interests, public works and navigation, while at the same time education and matters of local character might be left to local legislatures.[16]

He did not think a wider union was practical.

Three years after Dorion made this speech in 1855, a ministry was formed that included the Quebec financial figure, A. T. Galt. His entry into the cabinet was conditional upon its making his proposals for a general British North American union the government's official policy.[17] Neither John A. Macdonald nor the British authorities displayed much initial enthusiasm for Galt's federation ideas; the enthusiasm came later with changes in political circumstances.[18] Galt elaborated his ideas in Britain when he, John Ross, and G.-E. Cartier made a trip to sound out the government on federation and on guarantees for an inter-colonial railway. Further details were suggested in a letter sent by the delegation to the Colonial Secretary on October 25, 1858.[19] The delegates took pains to stress that their plans conformed with British constitutional history and exhibited no "slavish adherence" to the American design. Their letter continued:

> It will be observed that the basis of Confederation now proposed differs from that of the United States in several important particulars. It does not profess to be derived from the people but would be the constitution provided by the imperial parliament, thus affording the means of remedying any defect, which is now practically impossible under the American constitution. The local legislature would not be in a position to claim the exercise of the same sovereign powers which have frequently been the cause of difference between the American states and their general government.[20]

The Colonial Office chose not to approve the Canadians' project at this time and several more years passed before federation was again taken up in earnest.

THE CENTRALISM OF MACDONALD

It is not proposed to detail the origins of each clause of the British North America Act. The federal design of the statute of 1867 is so close to the conceptions underlying the Quebec Resolutions of 1864 and the London Resolutions of 1866 that such close examination of the act would not be warranted. Our inquiry centres on the Quebec conference which brought together representatives from Canada, Nova Scotia, New Brunswick, Prince Edward Island, and Newfoundland. The Canadian delegation had a clear advantage—it was composed of the province's executive council whose members represented a coalition of the major party leaders formed to achieve a federal union. The Canadians were also united on an agreed plan for federal union, a plan that conformed closely to that which Galt had tried to promote in 1858. While it was true, as Professor Creighton points out, that "the plan was a Canadian one, the submission of the Canadian Cabinet as a whole," it was John A. Macdonald who ran the conference; "he alone, of all the ministers, seemed to have a truly architectonic view of the entire structure."[21] The broad outline of the proposed federation had been settled earlier at Charlottetown and the Quebec meeting assembled primarily to hear details of the Canadians' project. The minutes of the proceedings at Quebec City and the fragmentary record of discussions made by Colonel Hewitt Bernard[22] show that no rival schemes were considered or even brought forward. At one time, Macdonald had hoped to see a "legislative union" but he dropped this notion at Charlottetown where it was evident that the Lower Provinces would have no part of it. The Quebec discussions are thus presented, not as a battle of forces between rival plans for union, but as three weeks of negotiation on legislative detail and financial settlements.

The chief political struggle was waged by the Maritime Provinces which were disadvantaged in having already conceded that the lower house should be elected on the basis of population, and that provincial equality in the upper house would be most impractical. Because there was a distinct and immediate prospect of Maritime union, the Canadian proposal had grouped British North America into three sections for upper house representation, namely, Ontario, Quebec, and the Maritimes. To each was assigned twenty-four members. This arrangement left the Maritime representatives most unhappy; they dearly wanted more members in the second chamber. "And yet—in somewhat the same fashion as the Canadians," according to Professor Creighton, "they did not think in terms of the Philadelphia precedent, and they did not dream of asserting their demand for larger representation based on provincial sovereignty."[23] Macdonald made one minor concession to these complaints—Newfoundland would be assigned four members by itself apart from the twenty-four for the Maritime section—but otherwise the provision stood as proposed.

Few voices at Quebec favoured making the upper house elective. The Province of Canada had been electing its legislative council for ten years and the distress that campaigning caused to the semi-retired "elder statesmen" stood as a horrible example to the politicians at Quebec City. Two additional reasons militated against elections for the second chamber: it had long been British colonial custom to leave legislative council nominations to the governor and his advisers; and, perhaps more importantly, it was agreed as a matter of tactics that support for the federal scheme could be improved by constituting the first senate through nomination of members of the provincial legislative councils then in existence. Several of the Maritime speakers wanted the nominations to be made by the provincial government, but the Canadian representatives insisted upon nomination by the central government, a device which, as it turned out, practically ended the federal character of the Senate.

There was little sentiment for universal suffrage when discussions turned to the lower house. At first, the provincial voting qualifications were to be used for federal elections, and the provincial legislatures were to draw the boundaries for the federal ridings. It was soon realised, however, that these provisions would give a hostile provincial legislature an unhealthy hold on federal members, and the Commons was empowered to determine its own constituencies after the first House had been constituted.[24] Provincial suffrage qualifications continued in use, despite Macdonald's opposition, until 1885 when he fought a federal franchise bill through the Commons amid a rising tide of provincial autonomy. "I consider the passage of the Franchise Bill the greatest triumph of my life," he wrote to Sir Charles Tupper.[25]

Macdonald outlined the Canadian proposals giving all the "chiefest and most important matters of government" to the general legislature and apparently encountered no serious objection. Galt set forth the projected financial arrangements. All were agreed that the central government should subsidize the provincial governments; but few were agreed about how much money this would require. The subsidy issue was one of the most difficult problems of the conference. After Galt had spoken, Oliver Mowat presented a list of sixteen powers to which the local legislatures were to be restricted. Up to this point all had been going well for the Canadians who had been encouraging the elaboration of a scheme as similar to the desired legislative union as possible without neglecting provision for the "peculiar institutions" of the several provinces, and particularly Quebec. Now, George Coles, of Prince Edward Island, proposed to amend Mowat's motion so "That the Local legislatures shall have power to make all laws not given by this Conference to the General Legislature expressly."[26]

Here was the bogey that Macdonald was determined to avoid, for he was convinced that in leaving the residue of powers to the states and to the people, the American Union had grievously erred.[27] Most of the discussion, however, turned not on the principle, but on whether the Quebec conference was not already committed by the Charlottetown decisions to assign the residual powers to the central government. Apparently it had been so settled and the objectors were talked down. The capstone to the Macdonald argument was furnished by a New Brunswick delegate, Colonel Gray, who closed the debate:

> The power flows from Imperial Government. We proposed to substitute the Federal Government for the Imperial Government. . . . And as to the policy of the thing, I think it is best to define the powers of the Local Governments, as the public will then see what matters they have reserved for their consideration, with which matters they will be familiar, and so the humbler classes and the less educated will comprehend that their interests are protected.[28]

Such was the extent of the debate over the principles of Confederation. They were principles that the Prince Edward Island delegates did not like and to which they refused to subscribe, but at no time do they appear to have put forward an alternate plan. Neither the islanders nor the Nova Scotians were happy with the financial proposals but revising the agreement placated the Nova Scotians present. Of the conference's work, Professor Kennedy observed that, "in less than eighteen days seventy-two resolutions were agreed upon, which practically became the British North America Act of 1867."[29]

The London conference endorsed the Quebec Resolutions in most essentials but, for students such as the late R. MacGregor Dawson, "there is no doubt that the seven draft bills (resulting finally in the British North America Act) were founded on the London and not the Quebec Resolutions."[30] The most significant change was the extension to all provinces of the protection for religious minorities. Where local minorities felt oppressed by provincial education laws they would have the right of an appeal to the governor general: the central legislature was also empowered to pass remedial legislation to assist such minorities. Galt drafted this clause to protect Quebec Protestants, who never had to use it, but it later became a guarantee of sorts for the rights of Roman Catholic minorities in other provinces. In the other changes, authority over penitentiaries was given to the federal government; statistics became a stated federal topic; solemnization of marriage was given to the province; jurisdiction over sea coast and inland fisheries was removed from the concurrent powers and assigned exclusively to the federal authorities. Provincial subsidies were increased and construction of the Intercolonial railway was made a binding condition of union. The pardoning power of the lieutenant-governor was altered and finally abolished altogether. Arrangements were made for reapportionment of the Maritime senators should Prince Edward Island later agree to confederation; the imperial authorities insisted on a provision so that a possible Senate deadlock could be broken by the appointment of a limited number of senators equally from each section.[31] During the drafting, the "technical" changes already referred to were made in respect of the property and civil rights clause.

Virtually from genesis to legal birth, this constitutional document had been the carefully nursed child of Macdonald and Galt,[32] and both were in London early in 1867 to see Parliament pass the British North America Act. It was given royal assent on March 29, proclaimed on May 22, and brought into force July 1, 1867.

Intentions of the Fathers

Records of the Quebec and London conferences make it plain that the participants thought they were creating a highly-centralized federation, an impression generally confirmed by examination of the statute. Such has been the course of political dispute, however, that these intentions must be examined a little more closely, although it is not intended once again to dissect the arguments that the founding fathers' intentions were something quite contrary to all their public professions.[33] *The Confederation Debates* record the discussions in the Provincial Parliament of Canada on the Quebec Resolutions and constitute the most complete documentation on what the founders had in mind. While these debates represent only the Canadians' views, the records of conferences and the leaders' correspondence indicates that the Maritime confederationists agreed with the Canadians in what was sought.[34]

Members of the cabinet at Quebec were most explicit in declaring that the plan would create a highly-centralized state. Macdonald had made his views very clear at the Quebec conference. He argued that:

In framing the constitution care should be taken to avoid the mistakes and weaknesses of the United States' system, the primary error of which was the reservation to the different States of all powers not delegated to the General Government. We must reverse this process by establishing a strong central Government, to which shall belong all powers not specially conferred on the provinces. Canada, in my opinion, is better off as she stands than she would be as a member of a confederacy composed of five sovereign States, which would be the result if the powers of the local Governments were not defined.[35]

Leading off the debate in the Provincial Parliament, Macdonald admitted he would have preferred a legislative union (*i.e.,* a unitary government) but had been forced to settle for the next best thing, a centralized federation. The new federal union would not suffer from "mistakes" similar to those made at Philadelphia. In his view,

> We have strengthened the General Government. We have given the General Legislature all the great subjects of legislation. We have conferred on them, not only specifically and in detail, all the powers which are incident to sovereignty, but we have expressly declared that all subjects of general interest not distinctly and exclusively conferred upon the local governments and local legislatures, shall be conferred upon the General Government and Legislature. . . . This is precisely the provision that is wanting in the Constitution of the United States. It is here that we find the weakness of the American system—the point where the American Constitution breaks down.[36]

Galt, Cartier, George Brown, and other government supporters spoke similarly throughout the long debate in which the question of centralization received an unusual amount of attention, due possibly to the widespread Radical and Conservative support for a completely unitary form. Charles Tupper declared that he saw only one other reason besides Quebec's "peculiar condition" for preserving the provincial governments in the Maritimes, and that was because those sections did not have a developed municipal system.[37]

Opposition to the Quebec Resolutions, which came chiefly from the Rouges of Canada East, was focussed on the tendency of the project to reduce the legislatures to little more than municipal councils. Their financial autonomy would vanish, it was argued, for all the important revenue sources were being turned over to the federal government. The provinces were to have only the right to direct taxation which, at that time, meant realty taxes of the type levied by municipal corporations.[38] J. B. E. Dorion attacked the plan of federation because it provided for "local parliaments which will be simply nonentities, with a mere semblance of power on questions of minor importance."[39] The proof was in their lack of financial resources. A. A. Dorion returned again to make the point that the project was ill-conceived because it "gives all the powers to the Central Government, and reserves for the local governments the smallest possible amount of freedom of action."[40] The characterization of the provincial legislatures as lesser bodies was not disputed by Macdonald. In concluding the cabinet's argument, Macdonald said that adoption of the plan of union would provide "a powerful Central Government, a powerful Central Legislature, and a decentralized system of minor legislatures for local purposes."[41]

Devices of Central Control

The British North America Act, 1867, provided precise controls to assure dominance by the centre. It granted to the provinces only those powers which were considered to be of local concern while the federal authority was vested with control even over matters such as criminal law, marriage, and divorce, which had been reserved to the states in the American union.[42] All unassigned legislative powers went to the central government whose executive was authorized to disallow any new act of the provincial legislature. The lieutenant-governor was a federal officer, expected to follow the federal cabinet's direction. Appointments to all important judicial posts in the provinces were put in federal hands. The most important concerns left to the provinces were those relating to education and local government, and these did not bulk nearly so large in public attention as they do today.

Sections 58, 59, and 90 of the Act specify the manner of central supervision of the provinces, and sec. 95 provides for federal law to prevail over provincial in the (then) two concurrent fields of jurisdiction. Section 91 gave the central government authority "to make laws for the Peace, Order, and good government of Canada," in respect of all matters not assigned exclusively to the provinces. The import of these words was pointed out by the Royal Commission on Dominion-Provincial Relations:

> "Peace, order and good government," and the variations, "peace, welfare and good government" were the phrases habitually used by the British Colonial authorities in vesting colonial legislatures with the full range of their legislative powers. . . . As imperial control in the internal affairs of the colonies was mainly exercised through the power of disallowance, these phrases carried complete internal legislative competence.[43]

The conferral of provincial jurisdiction over "Property and Civil Rights in the Province" in sec. 92.13 was not limited in the way originally planned but it was tempered by the possibility of applying sec. 94. This clause empowered Parliament "to make Provision for the Uniformity of all or any of the Laws relative to Property and Civil Rights in Ontario, Nova Scotia, and New Brunswick," if the provinces should give their consent. Under sec. 101 there was established (in 1876) the Supreme Court of Canada, one that was not simply a national court, but one whose federally-appointed personnel would be the arbiters of the interpretation of provincial constitutions and statutes. Section 93 restricted provincial freedom in education and gave the federal government ultimate authority in matters affecting aggrieved religious minorities—a not inconsequential right in light of the importance of religious matters in education.

Provincial influence in the Senate was avoided by the workings of secs. 24, 29; while any hope the provinces might have of autonomy through the purse was made unlikely by sec. 91.3. That section conferred on the central government the ability to raise money "by any Mode of Means of Taxation." However unintended during the 1860s, the central government was thereby enabled to infringe at will on the provinces' fiscal resources; the subhead may even have opened the way to further federal "encroachment" on local concerns through the apparently unrestricted spending power.* The main source of provincial revenues was to be the federal subsidies set forth in sec. 118 (which has since been repealed and replaced by the federal Provincial Subsidies Act). The whole economy was to be under federal control according to secs. 91.2, 91.10, 91.12, 95, and the clauses of 92.10 which enabled the central government to take over virtually any public works by declaring them to be "for the general Advantage of Canada or for the Advantage of Two or more of the Provinces."

Execution of the Centralist Concept

Macdonald moved on from the task of chief architect and pilot of the constitutional statute to become the engineer whose task it was to animate and govern the new state. Attention will be concentrated on the prime means of direct control: the office of lieutenant-governor and the disallowance and reservation of provincial statutes.

There was no mistaking the intention that the lieutenant-governors should be central government agents; Macdonald had pointed out that "as this is to be one united province, with the local governments and legislatures subordinate to the General Government and Legislature, it is obvious that the chief executive officer in each of the provinces must be subordinate as well."[44] Such was to be the province's degree of tutelage that the first draft of the B.N.A. Act referred to the executive head as the Superintendent.[45] The extent to which the provinces were supervised at first is well illustrated by the work of Sir Hastings Doyle, the former governor of Newfoundland who became Nova Scotia's first lieutenant-governor. In office from 1867 to 1873, he was "perhaps the most active Lieutenant-Governor in the federal cause," in the judgement of Professor John Saywell. The prov-

---

*"At first glance it seems extraordinary that no one has challenged the constitutionality of the assumed spending power before the Supreme Court. It accounts for a very large portion of the heavy taxation about which everybody groans. Yet a little reflection will show that proof of the unconstitutionality of federal spending for objects outside federal legislative power would prove far too much for anybody's comfort." J. A. Corry, "Constitutional Trends and Federalism," in A. R. M. Lower, *et. al., Evolving Canadian Federalism* (Durham, N.C., 1958), p. 119.

ince was in the grip of a violent secessionist movement. Doyle laboured mightily on the union's behalf and placed every possible impediment in the way of his secession-minded ministry, even to the point of prohibiting any mention in the Speech from the Throne of the very policy on which his government had been elected.[46] The governors in the West were also consistently active in carrying out Ottawa's policy as these comments by Professor Saywell suggest: "Throughout his term Archibald represented just about all there was of federal authority in Manitoba and was virtually Manitoba's representative in Macdonald's cabinet. In his instructions Archibald was asked to investigate the land problems, . . . to establish contact with the Indians, . . . to report on the state of the Hudson's Bay Company, and immigration."[47]

The office was also useful for party purposes. Macdonald used his power of appointment both to compensate important political figures who had been denied an expected cabinet post and to create needed cabinet vacancies. The prime minister looked, as well, to the needs of the provincial wing of the party, whether it formed the government or sat in opposition. The post was no sinecure—services were required. So well was this understood that when the Conservative, Macdonald, appointed William Howland for Ontario, the Liberal government there fully expected him to work against its partisan interest. The impression was generally held at Toronto, according to Professor Saywell, that Howland might call on a Conservative to form a cabinet in 1872 when the Liberal premier, Edward Blake, resigned and turned over the party reins to Oliver Mowat.[48] Such anticipations were usually well-founded, for the lieutenant-governors were men who had belonged to the governing party at Ottawa, and frequently they had pursued their party careers in the very province to which they were appointed. Alexander Mackenzie followed Macdonald as prime minister but neither he nor Macdonald's colleagues who succeeded him deviated from his partisan practices, although, as time wore on, the growing autonomy of the provinces made such tactics difficult to exercise.

Appointments were held "during the pleasure" of the governor general and could not be terminated within the first five years "except for Cause assigned," according to sec. 59 of the B.N.A. Act. Ottawa's "pleasure" came to a sharp end once during Macdonald's tenure of office. Just before the critical federal election of 1878—which returned the Conservatives from the Opposition to the Treasury benches—the Liberal lieutenant-governor of Quebec, Luc de Letellier de St. Just, dismissed his provincial ministry led by the Conservative de Boucherville. This cabinet still enjoyed large majorities in both branches of the legislature but was accused by the lieutenant-governor of "deliberate and contemptuous neglect" of its office.[49] More important than majorities were the fruits of office which the Liberals' campaign required. Letellier called upon a Liberal, who failed to form a ministry enjoying the legislature's confidence, and the house was dissolved. These activities incurred the wrath of the Quebec Conservatives who, upon riding back into federal office with Macdonald, were able to effect the dismissal of Letellier.[50]

Control over a province may be exercised by the lieutenant-governor through his right to be informed of all government affairs and to advise on them, through his exclusive power to summon persons as ministers of the Crown, and through his right to deny validity to the legislature's bills. This latter power had been the most important one in practice. Its method of exercise has been described in this way: "[A] lieutenant-governor may do one of three things with a bill which has passed through all its stages in the legislature and is presented to him for royal consent so that it is transformed into an Act of the legislature; he may signify that he assents to the bill in the Queen's name; he may withhold his assent; or he may reserve the bill so that it may be considered by the governor general."[51] In 1882 Macdonald tried to prevent provincial governments from recommending reservation of bills; he instructed lieutenant-governors to reserve only on Ottawa's instructions. It seems, however, that of the fifty-nine bills reserved before 1900, only five were reserved on definite instruction. The others were reserved at the discretion of the lieutenant-governor acting as a high political officer of the government of the day. Bills were properly reserved, in Macdonald's eyes, if the lieutenant-governor considered them to be *ultra vires* or in conflict with federal policies or interests.[52] In such cases the federal cabinet would recommend appropriate action (*i.e.,* assent or refusal of assent to the bills) to the governor general. Of these fifty-nine bills reserved prior to 1900, only five were permitted to become law during Macdonald's tenure, and another nine during Liberal régimes.

The most important way in which the federal government directly intervened in provincial affairs was through the power of disallowing provincial legislation. Macdonald exercised this right five times during his first term of office and forty-one times from 1878 to 1891 when the provinces were beginning to assert their claims to co-ordinate status with the federal government. A leading student in this area has observed: "In so far as disallowance is concerned, judges have, from the early days of Confederation, repeatedly stated that in point of law the authority is unrestricted even with respect to statutes over which the provincial legislatures have complete jurisdiction, and whatever doubts there may have been on the subject were set at rest by the reference to the supreme Court on disallowance and reservation in 1938."[53] During the early days after confederation, Ottawa relied chiefly on the ground that provincial statutes (to be disallowed) were either *ultra vires* or in conflict with federal or imperial statutes. After the "National Policy" election of 1878, the most frequently used reason for disallowance was that the provincial statutes conflicted with federal policies or interests, whether or not the legislation was validly enacted. Some statutes were also disallowed because they were believed to be contrary to sound principles of legislation, an abuse of power, or unjust in their action.

Macdonald's free use of these controls over provincial legislative efforts is best illustrated by the Manitoba railway dispute. A fixed resolution of the Conservative administration was that nothing must be allowed to hinder the government's encouragement of the Canadian Pacific Railway which was a vital instrument of the Conservative national economic policy. Manitoba railway building, if "premature" in traffic terms, or headed for an American railway connection, invariably qualified for federal disapproval. Ten Manitoba railway statutes were disallowed, and royal assent was denied to four railway bills. Manitoba land legislation was disapproved on a similar scale.[54]

Macdonald's quarrel with Mowat affords a similar example. Each year during the three year period from 1881 to 1883, the Ontario Liberal ministry led by Oliver Mowat passed "an Act for protecting the Public Interests in Rivers, Streams and Creeks," and each year Macdonald's administration disallowed the statute. The act was retroactive in effect, and overrode a decision of a competent court, but it was *intra vires* the Ontario legislature. The statute also invaded the private property rights of a Conservative timber operator by permitting another person, a Liberal, to use those rights. This battle was eventually won by Mowat who persisted in a fourth attempt, at which point Macdonald gave up the struggle.[55]

George Brown, the embattled Toronto democrat, had highly approved of control by the federal government over provincial legislation because he believed that by "giving a veto for all local measures, we have secured that no injustice shall be done without appeal in local legislation."[56] Between the years 1867 and 1881, statutes were not invalidated as being unjust, unwise or impolitic, but the assent of the governor general was refused to a number of reserved bills for these reasons. After 1881, reservation or disallowance of provincial measures believed to be *ultra vires* fell into disuse except where it was thought immediate harm or damage might result from inaction, and the question was left to the courts' determination. Disallowance was still readily resorted to whenever provincial measures clashed with Ottawa's legislation, interests, or politics.[57]

In 1868 the new prime minister had clearly been in possession of substantial legislative powers, but they were not quite complete. Control over property and civil rights in the English provinces remained in their jurisdiction until the various provincial laws on these matters had been codified under provisions of sec. 94 of the B.N.A. Act. Once this had taken place, property and civil rights could, with the consent of the provinces concerned, be transferred to the federal Parliament. Macdonald was eager to make this transfer.[58] So pressing had been the need to pacify Nova Scotia, launch the new nation on its path, and deal with the places of Prince Edward Island and Manitoba in the union, that Macdonald had been unable to realize his ambition of unifying the common law system. Neither had he been able to establish the supreme court provided for in the B.N.A. Act. Suddenly, scandal discredited the Conservative administration and Macdonald was forced to resign in 1873. The onset of an economic recession, combined with the sectional politics of the 1874 campaign, had sent local patriotisms soaring at the expense of the new nation. Macdonald was relegated to opposition and all his hopes for the assimilation of laws relating to property and civil rights had to be postponed. The project was never resuscitated and the section is now considered a "dead letter."[59]

Further potentialities for central control of the provinces might have been realized through the Supreme Court of Canada.[60] This body was organized by the federal executive and vested with authority (a) to review provincial legislation, including provincial constitutions over which the provinces had exclusive amending power save for the office of lieutenant-governor; and (b) to render advisory opinions at the request of the governor in council. In practice, the court's bench was appointed without apparent reference to the judges' views concerning the sovereign pretensions of the provinces; and the court played no deliberate role, so far as can be determined, in the efforts of prime ministers to restrain the local units.

Another potential control which Ottawa could exercise over the provincial governments related to public works. In this respect, Bora Laskin, now chief justice of the Supreme Court of Canada, has commented: "It is an extraordinary power that the Parliament of Canada possessed under s. 92 (10) (c) of the B.N.A. Act to bring within its legislative jurisdiction 'such works as, although wholly situate within the Province, are before or after their execution declared by the Parliament of Canada to be for the general advantage of Canada or for the advantage of two or more of the Provinces.' "[61] The extrinsic clues as to the Fathers' intentions respecting this phrase suggest it was meant only to give Ottawa controls over works such as the Welland or St. Lawrence canals, but, read literally, the power is very broad. The limits depend on the definition of a "work" and what is required to make a valid "declaration." Use of such power, or its threatened use, might permit the federal authority virtually to control public works programs throughout the country. These provisions have led to Parliament's exclusive jurisdiction over interprovincial railways, grain elevators, atomic energy, telephone and telegraph companies and other similar works and undertakings.[62] No evidence has come to light that federal governments during the nineteenth century employed this section of the act in opposition to provincial policies.

The leading cases interpreting this section were decided within this century during which the Ottawa authorities have not hesitated to use the power even where it meant trenching, perhaps incidentally, on a local area of competence. The Judicial Committee of the Privy Council has upheld Parliament's right to exempt a telephone company from provincial legislation,[63] to authorize the use of Crown lands vested in the province by an interprovincial railway company,[64] to control radio broadcasting stations whose operations were wholly within one province,[65] and to regulate—to the exclusion of the province—an interprovincial bus line in its operations as a carrier over public highways wholly within one province.[66]

Many advocates of a centralized scheme found their justification in sec. 91 where it is declared that the Queen-in-Parliament shall have power "to make laws for the Peace, Order, and good Government of Canada, in relation to all Matters not coming within the Classes of Subjects by this Act assigned exclusively to the Legislatures of the Provinces." And truly was it said by the deputy attorney-general for Canada that this "residual power, originally thought of as providing for a strong general Parliament . . . has had the most troubled history of any provision in the British North America Act."[67] It is not certain that either Macdonald or Mackenzie, both of whom were among the Confederation Fathers, relied on this clause when attempting to implement their centralist views. The classic case of *Russell* v. *The Queen*[68] was decided on the basis of the peace, order, and good government phrase, but there is ground for believing that the Liberal government that passed the statute at issue—the Canada Temperance Act—may have been relying on the federal government's trade and commerce jurisdiction.

The *Sirois Report* stated that during the eighteen-eighties "there was the conception of federal dominance which the Dominion Government tried to enforce and which was strongly supported by powers of reservation and disallowance."[69] The practice· of the early prime ministers strongly suggested that it was through these two powers and the lieutenant-governorship that Ottawa attempted to ensure its dominance over the provinces. Fittingly enough, says Professor Creighton: "In the end, the [Tory] party was defeated on an issue which directly involved those superintending powers which Macdonald had claimed for the Dominion. The Conservatives were jockeyed into an attempt to protect the claims of the Roman Catholics in Manitoba by remedial legislation in respect of separate schools; and the Liberal party rode into power at Ottawa as the champion of provincial rights."[70]

CRISIS CENTRALISM

National crises bring demands for federal government action regardless of the legal division of responsibilities. Those making such demands insist that the constitution is not supposed to paralyze the state in times of crisis but rather to facilitate attainment of the common good. Attaining this objective might require greater concentration of authority at Ottawa. If so, according to proponents of the centralist thesis, legal support for increased federal powers can be found through a restrictive reading of the provinces' property and civil rights clause and a liberal interpretation of the federal jurisdiction conveyed by the peace, order, and good government phrases and the trade and commerce section.

Manifestation of this crisis philosophy of the constitution may be observed in the action of the federal government at the turn of the century when it sought to avert the dangers of civil strife arising from the conflict between industrialists and organized labour. W. L. Mackenzie King, who became the first deputy minister of labour at Ottawa, had reported in connection with an Alberta coal dispute that:

> Organized society alone makes possible the operation of mines to the mutual benefit of those engaged in the work of production. A recognition of the obligations due society by the parties is something which the State is justified in compelling if the parties are unwilling to concede it. . . . Clearly, there is nothing in the rights of parties to a dispute to justify the inhabitants of a province being brought face to face with a coal famine in winter conditions, so long as there is coal in the ground and men and capital to mine it.[71]

King then drafted an "Act to aid in the Prevention and Settlement of Strikes and Lockouts in Coal Mines, and Industries connected with Public Utilities,"[72] a bill which passed the Commons in 1907 as the Industrial Disputes Investigation Act. The Lemieux Act, as it was popularly known, made it illegal for anyone to declare either a strike or a lockout until governmental investigation had taken place and a report been issued. This statute gave Ottawa wide controls over labour disputes wherever they might occur, although the legislation was initially restricted in its application. In introducing the bill, the Laurier government appears to have felt the presumed social crisis was adequate justification. The parliamentary debates showed no evident concern for provincial rights in labour matters, and the minister of labour seems to have relied on the omnibus clause for the bill's legal footing. Although operation of the act was extended during the First World War, it was not until the Judicial Committee's decision in

Toronto Electric Commissioners v. *Snider*[73] that the legislation's unconstitutionality was established. In its opinion, the Judicial Committee said that only the existence of an "emergency putting the national life of Canada in peril" would have justified federal trenching on provincial jurisdictions by legislation like the Lemieux Act. The Government reenacted the statute to limit its application to a much narrower sphere.

Reference has been made to the troubled course of the peace, order, and good government provision. The leading case adduced in its support for many years was *Russell* v. *The Queen* on the principle of which the courts supported the central government over the provincial for almost two decades. A broad interpretation of the peace, order, and good government clause regards the enumeration in sec. 91 as being solely for illustration of the general power conferred by the introductory phrases; the federal government is thereby given all powers not reserved to the provinces in sec. 92. Professor Kennedy's comments illustrate this widely-held viewpoint:

> The federal powers are wholly residuary for the simple reason that the provincial powers are exclusive; and the twenty-nine "enumerations" in Section 91 cannot add to the residue; they cannot take away from it. . . . They can have no meaning except as examples of the residuary power, which must be as exclusive as is the grant of legislative powers to the provinces. The enumerated examples of the residuary power cannot occupy any special place; they cannot be exalted at the expense of the residuary power, for that would "restrict the generality" of that power. It all looks reasonably simple, and Sir John A. Macdonald was perhaps justified as he looked at the scheme in hoping that "all conflict of jurisdiction" had been avoided.[74]

This interpretation of sec. 91 numbers among its adherents justices of the Supreme Court of Canada and of the superior provincial courts, many professors of law at leading universities, and a large number of practising constitutional lawyers, all of whom realize that this interpretation did not prevail with the Judicial Committee of the Privy Council during the last sixty years in which it heard Canadian appeals.[75]

Wartime Centralism

While the Judicial Committee of the Privy Council was unable to interpret the peace, order, and good government clause into complete oblivion, it was able to limit greatly the peacetime application of the clause by discovering that in these words "lurked a comprehensive emergency power" which came into play only in perilous times. On such rare occasions, the general clause has been held to dominate any or all of the provincial powers obstructing the national interest. This interpretation permitted the federal government to assume almost unlimited authority during the war in Korea, during the world wars, and for short postwar periods. Most controversial of all such exercises was the federal government's assumption of special powers in October 1970 to deal with terrorism in Quebec.

In August, 1914, Parliament passed The War Measures Act, 1914, which empowered the Governor in Council to do "such acts and things, and to make from time to time such orders and regulations, as he may . . . deem necessary or advisable" for the national security. The statute was without limitation in respect to time or effect on either persons or property and resulted in vesting almost unrestricted powers in the central authorities. The provinces cooperated fully in the effort to coordinate national resource utilization. Virtually the only demurrer heard came in 1918 when the cabinet prohibited provincial borrowing,[76] but even in this instance the provinces soon acquiesced. Throughout the war period the provinces acted as federal agents—administering national labour, price, food, fuel, and other economic regulations. Civil liberties, which were the special preserve of the provinces according to sec. 92, were completely subject to the central government during the war; restrictions were placed on speech, publication, assembly, organization, personal movements, labour, and even loafing.[77]

Ottawa's actions during the war and immediate postwar periods were upheld in *Fort Frances Pulp and Power Company* v. *Manitoba Free Press*. To quote from a recognized authority:

> Here, the War Measures Act was in question by which Parliament absorbed practically the whole legislative field of the provinces for the purpose of the conduct of the First Great War. It would, it appears, have been perfectly capable for the Board to hold that this legislation was authorized by the express language of the introductory part of section 91 . . . but the Board chose another line, namely, to invent an implied power in the case of an emergency.[78]

Although the *ratio decidendi* of this case has been criticized, its support of unlimited war powers for the federal authorities has been confirmed and solidly established. Lord Wright observed in the *Japanese Canadians* case that Parliament has authority during "a sufficiently great emergency such as that arising out of war" to deal as best it can to protect the country's interest and that "what those interests are the Parliament of the Dominion must be left with considerable freedom to judge."[79]

During the second war, the Canadian federation became even more of a unitary state than it had been in the first, due, no doubt, to the much more intensive mobilization of resources. The War Measures Act of 1914 had not been repealed and the federal government moved quickly in 1939 to impose comprehensive controls over many aspects of life where jurisdiction was normally vested exclusively in the provinces. To the War Measures Act were added various transitional measures which, by virtue of parliamentary declaration that an emergency state still obtained, carried the centralized controls of wartime over into the era of reconstruction.

The extent of federal assumption of provincial competences was suggested in 1945 by Maxwell A. Cohen, a Montreal legal scholar, in a discussion of powers which Ottawa would have to return to the provinces at war's end. His list included price control, wage and salary ceilings, working conditions, movement and control of labour supply within the country, collective bargaining and other labour matters (except in those few utilities and industries normally under federal jurisdiction), rationing of industrial stocks and consumer goods, agricultural and industrial production controls, rentals, exploitation of natural resources, housing programs, and "treaty-making powers with authority to pass implementing Legislation putting into effect international agreements, having intra-provincial consequences" (other than those passed under imperial treaties).[80] There can be little quarrel with Professor Wilfred Eggleston's observation that "in 1914-19 and again in 1939-45 . . . the emergency provisions of the constitution turned Canada for the time being into a unitary state."[81] Save for the restriction of personal liberties and great economic controls, the wartime constitution is an embodiment of the centralist concept of federalism carried to an extreme.

The only meaningful limitations to the enormous potential for centralization inherent in the War Measures Act are those imposed by the (federal) Bill of Rights, 1960, and by customary political practice. Briefly, the Bill of Rights provided that if the federal cabinet caused regulations to be enacted under the War Measures Act then the federal legislature was to be given an early opportunity at its next meeting to debate the emergency and, if it so desired, to repudiate the legal force of the federal executive's actions under the act. Whatever the actions taken, there was no provision for the association of provincial governments in the declaration or discussion of the emergency. While both the War Measures Act and the B.N.A. Act mention conditions of "war, invasion, insurrection, real or apprehended," customary practice had presumably restricted application of the emergency powers to war-related situations. That apparent limitation vanished when, in response to terrorist activities in Quebec, Prime Minister Trudeau invoked the emergency powers on October 16, 1970 and successfully defended his actions before Parliament and the country.[82] The extent of the federal invasion of provincial jurisdiction is debatable and chiefly centres around the declaration that membership in certain (terrorist) associations was illegal and around the suspension of certain provincially-governed judicial procedures. This issue has not been much analyzed, probably because the government of Quebec had requested such action, which, in practice, increased rather than diminished the powers exercised by the Quebec government through its attorney general (who is responsible for the administration of justice in the province). Theoretically, because all that is required in law is a governor-general's declaration that an insurrection is "apprehended," or feared, the way is open in Canada to development of central interventionist powers comparable to those in the quasi-federations such as India.[83] The major inhibition to the use of the emergency power in Canada must now be found in the political culture rather than in the law.

Economic Crisis

The advent of the economic depression in the nineteen-thirties brought calls for government action. Primary responsibility for relief and welfare measures was constitutionally that of the provinces, but they were unable to cope with the problem financially. Demands arose that the federal government intervene regardless of the legal distribution of powers. Spokesmen for important segments of the population began to hearken back to the centralist designs of the state's founders. A Liberal-Conservative summer school was told in 1933 that the Fathers of Confederation had aimed at, and thought they had achieved, through the B.N.A. Act, "a form of government which, while preserving some of the visible emblems of autonomy in the provinces, would actually be a strong centralized government," with virtually unlimited powers to deal with crises. The same speaker, Professor Norman A. Mackenzie, said:

> I believe it is possible and necessary to work out a method for more rapid common action in many fields of legislation and government. . . . The simplest device is to give the Dominion the temporary or permanent power to legislate in regard to any matter of national concern, save for a few excepted subjects, like education and language.
>
> . . . .
>
> In addition, the Act should be amended so as to give the Dominion full powers in regard to the making of treaties and conventions and the enacting of the legislation necessary to carry out such treaties.[84]

Mackenzie King, the opposition leader, spoke of the unarguable necessity of Ottawa's assuring the enjoyment of a national minimum standard of living. Toward this objective, his party proposed creation of a national commission to direct all relief work. It also promised, if elected, that the government would undertake rigorous supervision of provincial spending of federal relief funds. "As to permanent measures," said King, "the Liberal party is pledged to introduce policies which will serve to provide employment by reviving industry and trade, and to introduce a national system of unemployment insurance," and to set up a closely controlled central bank under federal ownership.[85] Such measures, if inaugurated in time, "would have enabled Canada to meet the economic crisis with an organization and a will to victory such as was characteristic of national effort during the Great War,"[86] according to one of King's biographers. The Liberal leader recognized the constitutional problem. He observed: "I think the British North America Act is a marvellous achievement. I think it served its purpose well, but it requires amendment. It should be changed in many particulars."[87]

The Conservative prime minister, R. B. Bennett, fought strongly against the centralists' stand. He asserted that centralization was constitutionally impossible and continued to channel relief measures through the provinces. Then, as the 1935 election neared, Mr. Bennett announced what was for many observers an astonishing *volte-face* on his part: that the time had come for "a radical change in the policy of the Administration." A measure of government control of the economy was needed, he said, and outlined a legislative program on which his opponent, Mackenzie King, congratulated him—not, however, without disputing its constitutionality. Mr. Bennett's legislation was enacted promptly. It included a Trade and Industry Act, the Employment and Social Insurance Act, the Minimum Wage Act, the 48-Hour Week Act, the One Day's Rest in Seven Act, and the Natural Products Marketing Act. The prime minister felt that this legislation had sound legal footing. He claimed, in substance:

> Ratification of six Draft Conventions of the General Conference of the International Labour Organization of the League of Nations in accordance with the Labour Part of the Treaty of Versailles were authorized by Resolutions adopted by Parliament during the 1935 Session. This action was regarded as necessary in order to give warrant for invoking Section 132 of the British North America Act which, the Prime Minister (Mr. Bennett) contended, conferred upon the Dominion Parliament authority to legislate and to give effect to obligations incurred in international conventions.[88]

These measures sought to consolidate in federal hands certain powers which traditionally had been judicially assigned to provincial areas of authority. The *Aeronautics* and *Radio* cases, however, had given the prime minister reason to believe the Judicial Committee might well rule in Ottawa's favour.

On winning power in 1935, the Liberal government submitted eight of the Conservative reform measures to the Supreme Court for an advisory opinion. Some of the Supreme Court justices decided parts of the legislation were valid through the operation either of the implied emergency powers doctrine of Lord Haldane, or simply through the peace, order, and good government provisions. But the majority of the Canadian jurists agreed, as did the Judicial Committee on the appeals, that the bills were *ultra vires* the federal Parliament. The measures could not be comprehended by sec. 132 (the treaty clause), and the exclusivity of provincial jurisdiction under sec. 92 precluded the legislation from being solidly footed in sec. 91.[89]

Presentations made to the Royal Commission on Dominion-Provincial Relations evidenced the widespread support for a centralist view of confederation. In the prairie provinces, both official government briefs and private representations expressed the view that the duties and taxing powers of the federal authority should be greatly expanded. Westerners said that only Parliament could effectively deal with the legislative problems of relief, social insurance, and regulation of wages and hours. The gist of the submission from the centralist-minded provinces was that confederation was designed to give the federal government, along with the most important revenue sources, all the important and expensive duties, and that those tasks which had been insignificant in 1867 but were now large national problems should be transferred to the central legislature.[90]

Except for those from Quebec, the private citizens who testified before the commission were centralist almost unanimously, and particularly was this view held by the businessmen who thought centralized government could cut costs and reduce taxes. The Vancouver Board of Trade urged that a plebiscite be held in each province on the question of abolishing the legislature in favour of an Ottawa-appointed and controlled commission. The Canadian Legion demanded that the federal government be given jurisdiction in all matters of national importance "even though to do so it is necessary to encroach upon property and civil rights, or other powers delegated to the provinces." The Native Sons of Canada suggested that the purpose of Confederation was to "establish a national unit" and to "obliterate the provincial boundaries and fuse the colonial units" then existing.[91]

There was little question during the nineteen-thirties about the existence of an economic crisis, but the issue has never since been so clear cut. Objective definition is impossible today, so much have modern governments accepted responsibility for the performance of the economy. The definition of an "economic crisis" is now almost entirely a political act. The inflation and unemployment of 1970-74 provides us with a curious exception to the Canadian practice of debating major issues in federalist terms if it is at all possible as it certainly was here. The increases in prices, wage rates, and unemployment of the early seventies was thought by many to constitute an economic crisis and the parliamentary debates of those years are filled with demands that the Ottawa government remedy the situation. The most hotly discussed "remedy" related to the imposition of a federal regime of price and wage controls. Few politicians, whether those demanding such action or those refusing to take it, seem to have asked whether the federal government had the constitutional powers to impose a universal, compulsory scheme of controls. While Ottawa operated such a system during the world wars, its exercise of these powers was exceptional, temporary, and needed the justification of the famous emergency doctrine. Without such an emergency, sec. 92.13 of the B.N.A. Act gave the provinces exclusive jurisdiction over most contracts and hence, of price and wage controls if they chose to exercise them. The prime minister of the day, P.-E. Trudeau, was probably the most legalist-minded of all politicians. Although he did not wish to adopt such control schemes, he said he would do so "if necessary" but never did he suggest in what way Ottawa could assume such authority from the provinces. Under normal circumstances, the constitutional issue will be raised by the provinces. That did not happen here. Not only were the provincial governments also exercised about the unemployment issue, but they were particularly concerned that Ottawa be seen to be responsible. One can only speculate that a federal government seeking to impose price and income controls would do so either hoping to escape legal challenge altogether, or gambling that centralist-tending judges of the Supreme Court would sustain such action under the general clause and the trade and commerce power.

Centralism for Planning
Among the most strident centralists of the nineteen-thirties were the socialists. The Regina Manifesto,[92] adopted at the first national convention of the Co-operative Commonwealth Federation in 1933, remained the party's ideological foundation for a quarter-century. The Manifesto declared that "what is chiefly needed today is the placing in the hands of the national government of more power to control national economic development," which was to be achieved through the adoption of a flexible constitution. It proposed a national labour code to guarantee the workers full social welfare benefits, freedom of association, and effective participation in the management of industry. Article 7 said: "The labour code should be uniform throughout the country. But the achievement of this end is difficult so long as jurisdiction over labour legislation under the B.N.A. Act is mainly

in the hands of the provinces. It is urgently necessary, therefore, that the B.N.A. Act be amended to make such a national labour code possible." All public financing had to be brought under central control, for none was to be permitted "which facilitates the perpetuation of the parasitic interest-receiving class"; public works would be directed by a national planning commission and financed by the central government's credit resources. (Art. 11.) All health services would be brought under the one government. The Senate would be abolished, for it had even failed in its original duty of protecting the provinces (so ran the argument) and was now "the bulwark of capitalist interests." All important means of production, especially those in which workers might be exploited, were to be put under social ownership; the agency might be municipal, provincial, or national, depending upon administrative convenience. The whole constitution was to be brought into line with "the increasing industrialization of the country and the consequent centralization of economic and finance power." What the Regina Manifesto socialists proposed, among other things, was a virtual return to Macdonald's conception of what the federal union should be.

The inadequacy of provincial resources was no excuse for the non-provision of necessary services, the socialists argued. The federal government had been given authority over "the raising of money by any mode or system of taxation," so it must provide the necessary services. Conditional grants were opposed. Federal subsidies for provincial services were wrong because the principles of political responsibility demanded that the taxing agency be the spending agency. The greater efficiency gained by national initiation and direction was expounded. If the development of provincial individuality is thought valuable, let it be achieved through a national policy backed by the country's concentrated resources, equitably shared. Provincial autonomy actually inhibits regional development; central authorities could organize the prosperity of each region through complementary developmental programs. These views were not held solely by C.C.F. members; Brooke Claxton, later an important Liberal party cabinet minister, warned in 1935 that the nation laboured under a constitution which was beginning to be, "not an Act of Union but [one] which, if present tendencies continue, may well be the means of developing on the northern half of this continent several distinct economic and social orders in active competition, if not conflict with one another."[93]

The intellectual heart of the early socialist movement was the Research Committee of the League for Social Reconstruction, which was to the C.C.F. what the Fabian Society once had been to the Labour Party. Its members included Eugene Forsey, Leonard Marsh, Frank R. Scott, Frank H. Underhill, J. King Gordon, J. R. Parkinson, and Graham Spry. They were the principal authors of a thorough exposition of the Canadian socialist viewpoint,[94] *Social Planning for Canada,* which applauded the idea of cabinet government if it was in proper hands. It noted, however, that in Canada the cabinet was "federal rather than unitary in character," thereby resulting, at the very least, in some inefficiencies. An inner cabinet was proposed in which "obviously, the selection of the senior secretaries of state would be primarily based upon the capacity of the members of Parliament under consideration, and as little as possible upon the plan of giving representation to sections of the country."

The provincial governments were to be reduced to a thoroughly subordinate role, as these quotations will suggest:

> While the provinces, and for that matter, all the organs of regional government can play their part in economic planning, it is essential that the Dominion Government, in the final analysis, should have full control. . . . The Dominion Parliament must be supreme. (p. 231)

> The [National Investment] Board would formulate and assist in plans for the nationalization of provincial and (through the provinces) municipal finances. . . .

> Finally, the Board would exercise a strict control over all foreign borrowings of public and private agencies. . . . (p. 313)

> The reforms we advocate in this field [workmen's compensation] are the extension of the existing system to all workers, making benefits more generous, and transferring administration from the provinces to the Dominion. (p. 383)

> . . . the Dominion must assume a general responsibility to see that the standards of services with which people are provided are adequate in all parts of Canada. (p. 406)

Civil liberties and the special minorities guarantees were to be made meaningful by making them Parliament's especial concern, while the provincial regulation of labour, education, health, and welfare would be subject to Ottawa's guidance. "The problem of financial relations between the Dominion and the provinces is too complex to be dealt with fully here," the League said,[95] but at the same time it suggested that the provincial financial difficulties would disappear under a socialist régime because all the expensive jurisdictions would be the concern of Parliament, not of the provinces.

Not only did the C.C.F. frown upon the country's provincial organization but also upon the "natural" sections as well: "In the past generation Canada has been torn by yet other divisions—the divisions between east and west, between the Maritime Provinces and Central Canada, between English-speaking and French-speaking Canadians." There was no sound reason, the party said, why the country should lack unity, for "these divisions, too, are unnecessary and are the result of the inherent contraditions of capitalism."[96]

The socialists did not greatly modify their views during the prewar years, but some began to admit the imperative of providing some place for the provinces if ever they hoped to win power. Thus, in 1943, the C.C.F. leaders asserted that "the last thing desired is complete centralization. Side by side with the National Planning Commission will be established provincial and municipal planning bodies in order to achieve the greatest degree of citizen and local participation."[97] The role of the provinces was to be "even more essential and important than it is today"; not only would they have their functions in private law and education, but new fields of activity were mentioned. Nearly all of these new activities envisioned the provincial governments as administrators of socialized enterprises under Ottawa's ultimate control; the rhetoric had changed, but not the substance.

The virtues of decentralized administration were noted in the wartime literature but there was little or no suggestion of the virtues of political independence. A section in the book *Make This Your Canada* touched on constitutional amendment but it did not even mention the provinces. The party's national leader, M. J. Coldwell, warned that the C.C.F. must start "with the very clear understanding that any attempt by the national Parliament of Canada to secure control of education as a federal function would not only be doomed to failure but would destroy any hope of national unity in other respects."[98] He suggested that socialists could achieve their objectives in educational matters by having Parliament accept its "major responsibility" in promoting higher standards of education. "The Dominion authority would thus first lay down in agreement with the provinces certain minimum requirements which all the provinces must fulfil, raising these standards progressively and periodically as the provinces responded."[99] He assumed for the federal government another burden, that of assuring that the country's natural resources were not squandered but safeguarded and used in the common interest. Nowhere did he hint what would be done about sec. 109 of the B.N.A. Act, which grants to the provinces the exclusive care of all natural resources within their borders.[100]

During the war, the Liberal Cabinet commissioned a former member of the League for Social Reconstruction to draft a federal program of social services to be implemented after the war. The *Marsh Report*,[101] as it is known, proposed that the country's various social services be over-hauled, rationalized, and unified under the federal government's aegis. Matters comprehended by the *Report* included national social minimum standards; a national employment, training, placement, readjustment and job insurance program; coverage for the "universal risks" of mankind—sickness, death expenses, disabilities, retirement—and children's allowances, survivors' insurance, and mothers' allowances. "The significance of such a system for the citizen body generally, and the magnitude of the sums involved are so great, however, that a paramount consideration is the constitutional freedom of the federal government to lead and coordinate." The important task was to visualize the system as a whole "and to integrate the component units with proper regard for regional and administrative decentralization." The *Marsh Report* gave some unenthusiastic attention to the possible role of the provinces; if the provinces were to be used, then the grant-in-aid device was favoured. Doubt was cast upon the special advantages that provincial administration was supposed to have. The *Report* contended that:

Decentralized or regional administration is *prima facie* just as feasible through Dominion as through provincial administration; and incidentally is not a constitutional question. Much depends on practice and personnel, of course, if local administration is to be flexible and sound. But there is no reason why officers of the Dominion government with good local knowledge should not be as effective, and as considerate of provincial rights, as provincial or municipal officers.[102]

The most recent significant work in which centralist concepts were upheld was a series of essays,[103] edited by a McGill professor of political science who was elected first president of the New Democratic Party after is formation in 1961. The distance socialists had traversed between 1931 and 1961 was evidenced in the book *Social Purpose for Canada*. During the early thirties, said Dean Frank R. Scott in an essay, "all were agreed that there must be more central authority, for reasons obvious to anyone faced with the conditions in Canada at the time. But this was centralization for planning's sake, not for centralization's sake."[104] In 1961, the "need" for central authority was not nearly so important, for younger socialists saw possibilities of planning through the provinces if their governments were controlled by "right-minded" people. One essay in *Social Purpose for Canada,* "The Practice and Theory of Federalism," is notable for its attempt to reconcile socialist objectives with provincial autonomy. The author was Pierre-Elliott Trudeau, later a Liberal prime minister. He asserted that socialists should cease their objections to the country's federal structure and begin to exploit the opportunities inherent in the existence of diverse governments. Many reforms could be accomplished through control of the provincial governments, he said, and pointed out that socialists probably had better chances of coming to power in the provincial capitals than they had in Ottawa. Both Messrs. Trudeau and Scott, who discussed "Social Planning and Canadian Federalism" in the same volume, emphasized the advantages of "cooperative federalism"—the coordination of the policies and administrations of the various governments. While Dean Scott placed more stress on the possibilities of enlarging the federal area of jurisdiction than did the other essayists, even his opinions illustrated the increased attention that the provincial governments were beginning to receive from the socialists. This attention contrasts sharply with the thorough-going centralist attitudes that characterized the left-wing during the nineteen-thirties.

A Centralized Amending Process

In the same year that the C.C.F. was born, 1933, a constitutional lawyer, Professor Norman MacKenzie, expressed the opinion that from a legal point of view the British North America Act could be amended by Parliament without consideration of the opinions of the provincial governments.[105] Another constitutional lawyer from the University of Toronto, Professor W. P. M. Kennedy, took the same position during his testimony before a House of Commons committee set up in January, 1935, to inquire into possible procedures for Canadian amendment of the B.N.A. Act. It might be healthy in political terms to consult the provinces, said Professor Kennedy, but, legally, there was no obligation.[106] During a Commons debate in 1949 over redistribution, the then minister of justice, Louis St. Laurent, denied that Parliament was under any juridical obligation to consult with the provinces in matters of constitutional amendment. A Conservative member from Calgary, Arthur Smith, asked whether this applied as well to the language guarantees to Quebec. St. Laurent replied: "The hon. gentleman asked, what about section 133. . . . Can that be dealt with without the consent of the provincial legislatures. Legally I say it can." He said this was also the opinion of his advisers in the Department of Justice.[107]

The League for Social Reconstruction had earlier taken note of the view of some people that in ordinary federations the amending process necessarily involved a vote by the constituent states. "But," said the League, "Canada is not an ordinary federation," as any look at the B.N.A. Act's centralist features would demonstrate. These socialist writers contended, in short, that:

> The present feeling of Canadians that they have a weak central government, produced by long years of planned inactivity on the part of Liberal and Conservative governments, would rapidly give way to a truer appreciation of the wisdom of the Fathers of Con-

federation if ever a socialist government began to carry out the wishes of an electorate asking for change.

．　　．　　．　　．　　．　　．　　．　　．

It is therefore in keeping with Canadian political tradition that the process of amendment for the future should be as it has been in the past—by action of the Dominion Parliament. Parliament alone represents all provinces, speaks for every Canadian, and should properly be held responsible for a matter of such national importance.[108]

The first socialist administration to come to power in Canada was that of T. C. Douglas in Saskatchewan. Throughout the constitutional conferences, his government fought to prevent the adoption of an amending system that deferred to provincial wishes in economic matters. This attitude stemmed from C.C.F. fears that a socialist government at Ottawa might be thwarted in its efforts to inaugurate social reforms by provincial regimes controlled by the "capitalist" parties. In the conferences, Douglas promoted the advisability of entrenching minority rights in a federal bill of rights and giving Parliament virtual *carte blanche* to amend the rest of the B.N.A. Act. Unable to prevail with this argument, Saskatchewan sought continuously to reduce the areas in which unanimous provincial consent would be required to make constitutional amendments effective, and to enlarge the number of provisions which would require approval of a simple majority of the provinces.[109]

"Green Book" Centralism

While scholars have devoted much attention to the findings of the Royal Commission on Dominion-Provincial Relations, relatively little study has been devoted to the proposed scheme contained in the federal government's "Green Book" of submissions to the 1945 Dominion-Provincial Conference on Reconstruction.[110] This plan was more representative of the thinking of the government of the day, and possibly of popular attitudes toward central controls, than the *Sirois Report* recommendations ever were. Ottawa's reconstruction proposals rejected the equalization principles and the concept of effective provincial autonomy which had animated the Sirois inquiry, and urged sweeping changes in the structure of the federation. While amendment of the B.N.A. Act was not believed essential, the federal minister of labour did think it would be desirable for the provinces to concede a delegation power to authorize federal action in industrial relations. Hopefully, he added: "It is suggested that an amendment of this nature would be non-controversial and, if framed in general terms, would have useful application to many other matters of joint Dominion-provincial character."[111]

In introducing this blueprint for the postwar era, the minister of justice, Louis St. Laurent, pointed out that it assumed a broad federal responsibility for establishing and maintaining high employment and income policies, and support of national minimum standards of social services. Measures were outlined for the transitional period and for veterans' rehabilitation, and the necessity of concluding new fiscal arrangements was discussed briefly. At the heart of the project was a public investment policy which would attempt to mitigate ill-effects of economic cycles through the timing of public works. Participating local governments would receive considerable technical assistance and twenty-five percent of the costs of programs whose concept, timing, and standards of execution met Ottawa's approval.

The social security section began with a comprehensive national health scheme which offered grants for a staged health insurance plan and for hospital construction. In addition, almost fourteen million dollars would be granted to meet the cost of a wider range of public health services, tuberculosis treatment, assistance for crippled children, and mental health treatment. The central government would assume the entire cost of a universal pension plan for those over seventy, and would contribute fifty percent of the cost of pensions, administered with a means test, for those between sixty-five and sixty-nine. Unemployment insurance, vocational retraining, and employment service plans were to be extended. Also contemplated were grant-in-aid programs for housing projects, slum clearance, community planning, and agricultural price and marketing schemes.

The financial proposals were the key to the government proposals.[112] The cabinet urged that all provinces agree to forego the imposition of the three most important revenue sources—personal income taxes, corporation taxes, and estate duties—as well as all the statutory subsidies. In return, the provinces were offered one large, unconditional subsidy calculated on the basis of one of several alternate formulae, which would guarantee to the provinces absolute minimum payments (corresponding roughly to the estimated current worth of those tax fields to the provinces). These payments would be increased as the gross national product increased. The whole scheme was to be tried out for three years on the basis of voluntary agreements. According to Professor Dawson, "the most casual scrutiny will show that [the proposals] involved a very substantial change in the federation terms, and the general intent was certainly to enhance the federal power enormously."[113]

FINANCE CENTRALISM

Constitutionally, the provinces enjoy a high degree of independence from the central government in that they have full authority to borrow on the provincial credit, limit their expenditures in whatever way they see fit, and raise revenue through a variety of means. In practice, however, the provinces are at times seriously restricted by the exercise of some of the federal government's unlimited powers of taxation. A particular tax field, even if constitutionally open to the provinces, may be effectively closed to them if the central authority levies a similar impost at a certain level.

The history of federal-provincial relations is a history of hard bargaining between premiers and prime ministers. Professor Maxwell, who favoured a rationalized scheme of grants-in-aid, called these negotiations a "shameful history of unconditional subsidies."[114] In 1867, the confederation arrangements had assigned the most lucrative tax fields to the federal government and gave, in place of these, certain unconditional subsidies to the provinces. But while Ottawa's financial resources grew faster than did its spending liabilities, the situation was reversed in the provinces, and local treasuries were frequently in a parlous state. In consequence, there arose many demands for "better terms"—an argument which justified a province's claim to higher subsidies on the ground that the existing terms did not fulfil the bargain agreed upon at confederation.

"Better terms" were often granted, both on their own merits and for outright partisan advantage. In 1930, for example, Prime Minister Mackenzie King had to deal with provincial demands for help in meeting the unemployment and social welfare problems. The prime minister also had to face a general election that year, and the provincial governments were largely in hostile hands. In his capacity as prime minister, the Liberal chieftain told Parliament: "So far as giving money from this federal treasury to provincial governments is concerned, in relation to this question of unemployment as it exists to-day, I might be prepared to go to a certain length possibly in meeting one or two of the western provinces that have Progressive premiers at the head of their governments . . . but I would not give a single cent to any Tory government."[115] As one student observed, the "main political effect of the financial system has been to make the defence of provincial claims and rights an important campaign issue."[116] While most governments have been able to agree that alterations in the country's financial relationships were required, never have they been able to progress beyond measuring reform proposals in terms of immediate and local monetary advantage.

One result of the federal-provincial negotiations was to make the provinces suspicious of any attempt by the central government to impose conditions in connection with its grants. Such suspicion was sometimes rooted in the involvement of parties at two different, and often, contending, levels of government. Federal funds with "strings attached" were also viewed as infringements of provincial "sovereignty" likely intended to lead to another attempted invasion by Ottawa of an additional field of exclusive provincial jurisdiction. Properly exploited, the grants-in-aid could be an important weapon with which to achieve greater centralization. Many of the political decisions which provincial governments make are economic in nature and depend upon the financial resources available; subversion of the budgetary independence of a provincial government could lead to the erosion of essential characteristics of the federal system.

That some of Canada's financial arrangements during this century have been essentially centralizing seems clear even though ready characterization of particular features is not always easy. From the thirties until the early sixties, the federal conditional grant system was centralist in direction and possibly in intention as well. Whatever the apparent legal loophole, in point of political practice, provincial governments did not have the alternative of non-participation and were forced to fall in with Ottawa's plans and programs. Immediately following the Second World War, the federal government was able to effect its own goals in a large number of areas constitutionally assigned to provincial jurisdictions. This centralizing aspect of the joint pro-grams largely disappeared with "opting out," a policy device that had a tentative beginning under J. G. Diefenbaker's Progressive Conserva-tive regime and full scale development under the Pearson Liberal regime. Allowing provinces to "opt out" of shared cost programs without incurring financial penalty transformed the political and fed-eralist character of conditional grants. Although the various devel-opment stages of the grants might logically be dealt with in different chapters here, for convenience, the general discussion of conditional grants has been concentrated in the chapter following. Undoubtedly, Canada-wide uniformities were also produced, and deliberately, by the development of the wartime finance arrangements into a central-ized taxation scheme for both federal and provincial governments. During the past two decades, these arrangements have undergone radical changes in character, the discussion of which has also been concentrated in the following chapter on collaborative federalism.

CULTURAL CENTRALISM

The Second World War brought more than changes in financial arrangements in its wake; it also brought changes in feeling. English Canadians expressed concern that their country's distinctiveness was threatened by the increasing pervasiveness of influences from the neighbouring American society and the federal government decided that it was "in the national interest to give encouragement to institu-tions which express national feeling, promote common understanding, and add to the richness and variety of Canadian life."[117] A Royal Commission on National Development in the Arts, Letters, and Sciences was established under the chairmanship of Vincent Massey. The commission conducted its extensive inquiries in an atmosphere of cultural crisis and made recommendations designed to secure Canadian culture from being submerged. In consequence of the Massey commission's *Report* and the philosophy which illuminated it, the central administration's involvement in cultural affairs was greatly extended.

The commission had justified its recommendations in this negative fashion: "If the Federal Government is to renounce its right to associate itself with other social groups, public or private, in the general education of Canadian citizens, it denies its moral and intellectual purpose, the complete conception of the common good is lost and Canada, as such, becomes a materialistic society."[118] The B.N.A. Act, however, had done that very thing—excluded the government at Ottawa from any jurisdiction over educational matters, and probably from cultural matters as well. Except for the minority guarantees, education had been given into the exclusive care of the provinces. Nonetheless, the Massey commission proposed what one writer has called "almost a new dimension in the responsibilities of the federal authorities" with its wide-ranging suggestions for federal involvement in cultural affairs. At its instigation, the Canada Council was established and substantial grants were made to universities and other education groups. The sequel was seen in the complaints which broke out afresh on the subject of Ottawa's centralizing proclivities and "unconstitutional" activities. An extensive catalogue of "invasion" complaints relating to the cultural field was compiled and published in the Report of 1956 of the Quebec Royal Commission of Inquiry on Constitutional Problems. During the sixties, the Pearson government implemented a program of federal loan funds for university students which was seen by some as additional evidence of Ottawa's determined "cultural imperialism." The "opting out" provisions averted serious difficulties here.

Television is a growing irritant between federal and provincial governments. Although Quebec had protested Ottawa's radio broadcasting policies for some years, it was largely ignored while serious problems had been avoided elsewhere by the circumspection of the Canadian Broadcasting Corporation which worked closely with provincial authorities in producing their educational broadcasts. During the sixties, Canadian politicians (like others) discovered television and decided it had enormous cultural implications of decided interest to the federal government. A direct federal-provincial clash arose from the growing interest of both Ontario and Quebec in educational television in combination with the widespread development of cable systems for television reception. Both provincial governments established educational television authorities and that in Quebec had wider cultural pretensions as well. The federal government argued that it had complete and exclusive occupancy of the field and that no provincial agency could properly be licensed or be given the power to regulate others. The federal case rested on the aberrant decision of the Judicial Committee of the Privy Council, *In re Regulation and Control of Radio Communication in Canada* (1932, A.C. 304). Provincial spokesmen argued that however sound (or otherwise) that decision might have been for radio, it did not deal with television broadcasting, that it could not override the specific education authority of the provinces given by sec. 93, and that in any case television communication by closed circuit landlines could not by any stretch of the imagination be encompassed by the phrase "radio broadcasting." The difficulties between the two orders of government had not been resolved by mid-1974. If the provinces seemed to have the best of the issue in legal terms (which other students might dispute), the case for centralized control over all broadcasting was bolstered by the upsurge of nationalism that swept English-speaking Canada during and between the general election campaigns of 1968 and 1972.

Racism is by far the most difficult of phenomena to analyze for its influence on concepts of federalism. Always there have been publicly and intellectually respectable grounds on which to urge simplification of the state structure, and many persons have done so on this basis. While some have been quite open about their preference for one culture or race over another, others have not been, and fair assessment is virtually impossible. Cultural considerations played an open and determining role in inspiring many French Canadians to defend the independence of their geo-political bastion, the province of Quebec, and that forms the subject matter of parts of later chapters. On the other side, the racist feelings of some English-speakers has been an important inspiration for the continuing strength of the centralist concept. Some there have been, from D'Alton McCarthy to the present writers of myriad letters to newspapers, who believe in the essential rightness of Durham's analysis and prescription for the necessary assimilation of the French-speaking. The vigour of these feelings in the past gave rise to André Siegfried's influential book, *The Race Question in Canada,* and in the near-present they provided the major backdrop against which the Royal Commission on Bilingualism and Biculturalism held its hearings and reported its findings during the sixties. Even where job security was not at issue, the racism of English-speakers contributed mightily to the massive resistance to implementation of the official bilingualism policies of recent Liberal governments. English-speakers who feel their racist inclinations strongly enough are, naturally, centralists but, it is unfortunately necessary to point out, not all centralists are racists who wish the disappearance of the French-Canadian culture.

Socialists, economists, and some other groups in Canada often espouse centralist ideologies because they believe federal structures too obstructive to the attainment of goals such as the reduction of social inequality, the control of capitalist enterprises, or the proper management of a diverse and vulnerable economy. Besides these "functional" or "instrumental" centralists, support for the concept is frequently found in two other groups, among those identified by Professor John Meisel as the British Canadians and the pluralists. He described the first group in this way:

> Some Canadians have a strongly British conception of Canada, not only in the sense that they themselves value the British connections and its heritage but, much more important, in that they believe the whole country must share these values. . . . To many (but certainly not all) of those holding this view, the presence of French-speaking Canadians is the result of their conquest by the British. . . . Most Canadians belonging to this school of thought see nothing wrong in, and often welcome, the anglicization of French Canadians. And while they deplore the loss of British elements in Canadian life, they do not lament the possible or actual decline of French Canadian culture.[119]

The pluralists have a different view of Canada, one of it as a community comprising many ethnic and cultural groups. The French and the English were but the first and second of many waves of immigrants who built what is essentially an English-speaking culture. This conception of the country is seen to be incompatible with the idea of according special privileges or official recognition to any minority— such as the French Canadians. As Professor Meisel says, there are many Scandinavians, Ukrainians, Italians, Germans, and others "whose families have lost their language and cultural traditions, [and] who do not see why French Canadians should accept this kind of metamorphosis any less willingly than they did themselves, as the price of leading a safe and reasonably prosperous North American existence."

SUMMARY

Proponents of the centralist concept seek to reduce the provinces' independence of political action in order to increase the federal government's effectiveness in shaping and executing national policies. A century ago, control over social welfare, the economy, and education could safely be left exclusively to local jurisdiction. But today, according to this viewpoint, this is no longer possible. The wishes of the voting public and the exigencies of modern statehood combine to demand the intervention of the central administration in a much wider range of issues than was once the case. The working constitution must be modified to facilitate this intervention.

The centralists argue that the Fathers of Confederation, working out from the quasi-federalism resulting from the Act of Union, really designed a highly-centralized federation. This is evident from the debates in the founding conferences and in the Parliament of United Canada, as well as from the provisions of the British North America Act of 1867. This act assigned to the central authority all the important duties of government and unlimited financial powers. This contrasts with the minor obligations imposed on the provinces and their dependence for funds on the central government. That the provinces were clearly intended to be subordinate is shown by the legislative provision of centralized controls over the local governments. These devices included the appointment of a federal supervisor for the provinces (the lieutenant-governor), the disallowance and reservation of provincial statutes, the over-riding character of federal laws in concurrent fields, and the assignment of all residual powers to the central régime. These statutory provisions were freely and deliberately used by both Sir John A. Macdonald and Alexander Mackenzie— both prominent figures in the preconfederation negotiations. That the country today has a different federal system is due, according to this viewpoint, to the rulings of the Judicial Committee of the Privy Council, which either misunderstood the constitution, or attempted to frustrate its provisions.

The centralist concept found its greatest expression during the two world wars when—by reason either of the Crown's prerogatives in defence or emergency powers implied in the B.N.A. Act—the country became a highly-centralized state in which provincial governments acted primarily as agents of the federal cabinet.

Support for the centralist concept revived, after a lapse of some decades, during the economic depression of the nineteen-thirties. This period found the provinces unable to cope with the social crisis and the federal government constitutionally unable, or politically unwilling, to effect a redistribution of legislative jurisdictions. While some lawyers and socialists claimed the central government had sole authority to amend the constitution, the federal cabinet tried to circumvent the question through legislation that relied on the treaty and residual powers. This legislation was declared to be *ultra vires*.

During the nineteen-forties, the central government entered the social welfare field in a decisive manner and attempted to perpetuate the wartime régime of a centralized fiscal system in order to devise effective state controls over the economy, educational standards, and national welfare. During the decade following the Second World War, the centralist viewpoint was bolstered by the newly-aroused desires of the English-speaking population to protect its culture against the threat of subordination by that of the United States. Strong support for the concept is found among socialists, macro-economists, cultural nationalists, "British-Canadians," and those descended from other than French- or English-speaking immigrants.

The centralist concept may now be assessed in light of the criteria adopted for this inquiry. Inherent in the centralist concept is the notion of federalism as a transitional form, one which contemplates the evolution of a confederal alliance into a unitary state. Consolidation of the various subpolities is thus the chief objective. In striving for this end, economic methods play a critical role; the major fiscal powers should be concentrated, according to this viewpoint, and the centre should be able to allocate all state finances without hindrance by subordinate bodies. Political methods available to further the objective lie in the exercise by Ottawa of its legal powers of superintending the provinces to integrate their political life and in the transference of initiative for important policies to the federal capital. The cultural methods are probably of secondary importance to the centralist concept. In this area, however, the concept looks to the designation of civil liberties as a federal responsibility, the determination of language rights by the central régime, and the establishment of national educational and welfare standards. As an ideal, the centralist advocates extension of Parliament's right to amend the constitution on its own authority, but as a practical objective, the centralist proposed adoption of a procedure which would permit amendments with the approval of a simple majority of the provinces.

CHAPTER

$$3$$

Administrative Federalism

"It must not be thought," said Lord Atkin in a famous passage, "that Canada is incompetent to legislate in performance of treaty obligations. In totality of legislative powers, Dominion and Provincial together, she is fully equipped." But, he said, where matters are to be dealt with that concern provincial as well as federal jurisdictional areas, they must "be dealt with by the totality of powers, in other words by co-operation between the Dominion and the Provinces."[1] Lord Atkin recognized that "the ship of state now sails on larger ventures" than had been anticipated in 1867, but said that this vessel must still retain "the watertight compartments which are an essential feature of her original structure." Given this interpretation of the constitution, how can the "totality of powers" be mobilized for use in the larger ventures which engage the state today? Lord Atkin did not explore the question, and it fell to the master and mates of the ship of state to find a course. The answers were derived, pragmatically, through the methods of administrative federalism, sometimes known as cooperative or functional federalism.

This concept of federalism seeks to solve problems arising from the federal distribution of powers by utilizing the combined authority of two or more jurisdictions, each of which by itself is impotent to resolve the difficulty. These problems may be settled by: (1) harmonizing the laws or regulations of the various governments; (2) establishing boards or committees authorized by the interested administrations to act in some way on its behalf; (3) conferring authority reciprocally on each other so that one government performs some task on the other's behalf; and (4) lending or training personnel for the other's use.[2] Such combination of authority is nearly always the product of intergovernmental negotiations conducted by appointed officials, sometimes formally, perhaps under the wing of a national, functionally-oriented association, but more often conducted through the highly informal channels of personal acquaintance networks. The essence of this approach is, as Professor J. R. Mallory says, that "while the central and regional legislatures nominally retain their separate jurisdictions over different aspects of the same subject, there is close contact and discussion between ministers and civil servants of both levels of government so that even changes in legislation are the result of joint decisions."[3] Its most characteristic manifestation is the shared grant program in which the federal government has purchased policy influence in an area of provincial jurisdiction by making grants to the participating governments on certain conditions.

"Cooperative federalism" is the term most popularized in Canada to refer to the ever-increasing network of intergovernmental arrangements. Its connotations, however, are too many and ambiguous to be helpful in analytic discussion far removed from the campaign platform. The New Democratic Party took up the term and used it widely during the 1962 general election campaign to suggest notions of inter-racial collaboration to facilitate achieving social reforms from the centre. After the 1963 change in government, Prime Minister Lester Pearson took over the catchphrase and applied it generally to his heterogeneous mosaic of federalist policies. Yet another variant is found in a widely quoted article on "Cooperative Federalism," by Jean-Luc Pépin, a political scientist and member of several Liberal cabinets.[4] A distinguishing feature of his usage was the explicit recognition of the "two nations" in combination with great respect for the sovereignty of the individual provinces, but while such considerations were of course known, even to mention them in the negotiation and operation of the intergovernmental programs would be thought most ungentlemanly. Whatever might be the rhetorical value of "cooperative federalism" it is more than outweighed in utility by the greater specificity of administrative federalism.

The approach is highly developed in the United States. An authoritative statement of the attitudes underlying its growth may be found in the words of the Meyer Kestnbaum inquiry of 1955, which urged that "the National Government and the States should be regarded not as competitors for authority but as two levels of government cooperating with or complementing each other in meeting the growing demands on both."[5] A plethora of formal interstate compacts has arisen in the United States[6] and only part of the reason for this growth is found in the specific constitutional provision for them. More important has been the professionalism of civil servants. Functional cooperation has grown on a large scale almost totally unhampered by the "more niggling reservations of the politicians," as Professor J. A. Corry put it. He pointed out that, because state governors very often cannot exercise effective control over their administrations, "federal and state officials, many of whom have a professional devotion to their tasks, are relatively free to develop satisfactory arangements" crossing state lines.[7] Speaking of Canada, Professor D. V. Smiley described the phenomenon in this way: "Under functional federalism the major responsibilities for federal-provincial collaboration are given to officials of the two levels concerned with relatively specialized public activities. These activities are carried on with a relatively high degree of independence from control . . . and tend to be regulated in accord with the perceptions, procedures and standards prevailing among specialists in these fields."[8] But, of course, the cabinet system in the provinces has always given the political masters of the public service professionals the means (quite often matched by the will) seriously to control or even to prohibit such activities. While administrative federalism continues to thrive in the U.S., it began to decline in importance in Canada during the early sixties as the provincial cabinets developed greater self-confidence and more comprehensive views of their place and rights within the federation.

Constitutional Background

Administrative federalism may be manifested by intergovernmental cooperation taking place along two distinct but complementary axes: interprovincial and federal-provincial. Neither type is barred by the constitution. While the British North America Act makes no mention of coordinating mechanisms, it does not prohibit intergovernmental cooperation, and, in some places, the statute rather obviously contemplates joint action. Section 94, for example, envisions joint agreement to codify the common law in the English-speaking provinces, while sections 91 and 92 provide that the provinces shall administer the single system of courts which the central authorities are charged to establish and maintain. Provincial officials are responsible for enforcing all laws within the province, whether federal, provincial, or municipal in origin; the attorney-general of a province, for example, acts for the Crown in prosecuting those accused under the federal criminal code.[9]

Federal-provincial collaboration (which some see as *vertical* collaboration) similar to that in the legal field might have been fostered by the detailed provisions in the B.N.A. Act respecting the lieutenant-governors who had been visualized as provincial superintendents in 1864. But what the statute permitted, the course of events discouraged. Federal-provincial collaboration was gravely impaired by the atrophy of the supervisory aspect of the lieutenant-governorship, and by two other factors: the provincial revolt of the eighteen-eighties with its consequences, and the frequent occurrence of situations in which the federal opposition party controlled the provincial cabinets. Interprovincial or *horizontal* collaboration remained minimal. Significant steps in this direction might have been initiated by the 1887 premiers' conference, but the provinces were too isolated from each other to encourage interprovincial cooperation; the main lines of communication ran through Ottawa. For a few years prior to the First World War, the Maritime provinces pressed joint complaints about their representation in the House of Commons, but for all important purposes intergovernmental action was virtually restricted to the federal-provincial axis until the nineteen-thirties.

FEDERAL-PROVINCIAL ACTIVITIES

Despite the rigidity characterizing the federation's legal structure, many of the country's internal stresses and strains have been eased to the point where they are tolerable. Perhaps the most important factor in this process has been the extra-constitutional resolution of some of the financial problems which beset most modern federations. The most useful classification of these problems is that proposed some years ago by Professor W. A. Mackintosh:[10] 1. The allocation or sharing of revenue and tax fields; 2. Financial implications of the distribution of legislative responsibilities; 3. The equalization of standards across the country; 4. The coordination of governmental fiscal policies to facilitate management of the economy; 5. The unified control of borrowings by different governments. During the 1945-46 reconstruction conferences, the central government sought powers which would enable it to deal with all these problems by itself. While in those terms, the conference was a failure, the country was not overwhelmed by these problems of financial coordination. The first two types of difficulties were essentially hammered out through the political process of hard intergovernmental bargaining. The third was tackled by the central government through conditional grant programs on a piecemeal basis. It was not until the late sixties and early seventies that the last two types of problems began to command significant attention from people other than academic economists, perhaps because it was not until then that the relatively great and growing impact of provincial fiscal activities became obvious to all.

Tax Harmonization

For some students, one of the most remarkable achievements of administrative federalism has been the harmonization of the various governments' taxation bases and structures together with the development of the centralized tax collection agreement. Had it not been for these arrangements and the unconditional grant device, the country's federal aspects must certainly have been debilitated by crises resulting from the chronic imbalance of constitutional obligations and the provinces' financial resources. While the unconditional grant device promotes rather than reduces interprovincial distinctiveness, the tax rental and tax collection devices did much to promote intergovernmental correlation on the fiscal side. During the 1867-1939 period, the continuous adjustments of unconditional subsidies helped to make the provinces financially able to fulfil their constitutional responsibilities generally and in large enough measure to keep the federal system viable. The tax rental device was initiated during the Second World War and, with some modification, it was employed for another seventeen years after the war. A number of different formulas was employed, each variation designed to tempt individual provinces, or groups of provinces, into signing agreements that would guarantee them revenue appreciably greater than those they could reasonably expect without the agreements. But before this development is examined, a brief review of the financial-fiscal relations that prevailed up to the Second World War is merited.

The British North America Act gave the central government authority for "the raising of Money by any Mode or System of Taxation." Judicial interpretations have prohibited the central régime from trespassing on the provinces' licensing powers, but this is only a minor limitation; the federal cabinet has virtually unrestricted fiscal competence. The provincial governments were given various subsidies and restricted to fees from licences in matters within provincial jurisdiction, income resulting from exploitation of natural resources, and direct taxes. It was assumed that the central administration would receive most of its revenue from the indirect taxes, customs and excises, and that the direct taxes would be left to the provincial treasuries. This was the situation that obtained until the First World War, although even the provinces had not exploited the direct levies with any vigour.[11] The central government entered the corporation and personal income tax fields during the First World War, and from this time on the overlapping of provincial and central taxes continued to grow. In some respects it is this vulnerability to double taxation that is the most salient feature of the dual citizenship conferred by the federalist constitution. Not only can both the central and regional governments impose whatever taxes they like on the same income but they can do it on the basis of widely different definitions of income, and divergent calculations of exemptions to be claimed, expenses allowed or denied, and credits to be given or taken away. "At the start of World War II," says one student of federal finance, "Corporation taxes showed perplexing diversities as between the provinces."[12] Such were the differences between governmental systems that "tax jungle" was the class of adjective most commonly applied to the situation by commentators.

A completely unified system was imposed during the Second World War. The federal finance minister, J. L. Ilsley, told the provinces they could either discuss the tax transfer recommendations made by the Royal Commission on Dominion-Provincial Relations, or else they could suffer the consequences of being frozen out of the revenue sources by the heavy federal taxation for war purposes.* This ultimatum led to temporary wartime agreements which were translated into the tax rental and tax collection agreements of the postwar period.

The rationale for a peace-time agreement was given by the federal finance minister in a speech to the House of Commons in 1946. He pointed to the "tax scrambles" that had obtained in the immediate prewar period, and to the impending expiry of the wartime agreements. Every government has suffered from the prewar chaos in fiscal policies, he said, and business had suffered most of all. "If the prewar situation was unsatisfactory," he continued, "the post-war position will, in the absence of new agreements, become intolerable."[13] Without some settlement of the problem, no government could be sure of meeting its increased commitments; and, without some harmonizing of policies, he said, Canada might be gravely handicapped in its efforts to avert the ill-effects of the postwar depression that was generally expected.

The agreements which were finally concluded involved the central government and seven provinces at first, but by the end of a decade all governments except that of Quebec had agreed to the new fiscal arrangements. A number of options obtained in these agreements and only the general pattern need be indicated.[14] An agreeing province would undertake for a five year period to refrain from levying taxes on personal and corporation incomes; it might also refrain from levying estate duties or remain active in this field with an appropriate

*Canada, *Minutes of the Dominion-Provincial Conference, Plenary Session 1941,* (Ottawa, 1941), 75. The royal commission had proposed that the provinces give up the various subsidies they received from the central treasury and that they agree to assign exclusive rights in the corporations and personal income tax fields to the central government. In return, the federal government was to assume all provincial debts, take on responsibility for relief of the employable unemployed, and pay to the provinces large unconditional grants based on fiscal need. Canada, *Report of the Royal Commission on Dominion-Provincial Relations* (3 vols.; Ottawa, 1940). 2: 269-276. The question of priority of governments to the revenue produced by a single tax field to which both orders of government have constitutional rights had not been settled in the courts. Authoritative opinion is, however, that the right of the federal government would likely prevail, in such a test, in accordance with the "paramountcy" doctrine. See Bora Laskin, *Canadian Constitutional Law* (2nd ed.; Toronto, 1960), pp. 96-97, 106, 210, 658.

adjustment being made in the agreement. The provincial government would, however, remain in the corporations tax field to the extent of imposing special taxes on companies engaged in natural resource exploitation.[15] In compensation for not exercising their taxation rights in these fields, the provinces would receive a large "rental" payment from the federal treasury. The "rental" arrangement would guarantee that a province would receive a substantial and determinate income greater than that which it could expect by its own activities in the shared tax fields.

Three subsidiary programs accompanied the different tax agreements. The most important was a system of equalization payments, based largely on fiscal need. By the second and third programs, the central government agreed to share the revenue it received from taxation of certain public utilities, and to grant tax credits up to a certain maximum (roughly equal to what that province would have received under a rental plan) to citizens in provinces that refused to accord sole occupancy of a field to the central government.

The two major political parties held dissimilar views on the tax rentals system. The Liberals, under W. L. Mackenzie King and Louis St. Laurent, initiated and extended the system with agreements signed in 1947, 1953, and 1957. In June, 1957, the Progressive Conservatives won a general election and formed a new government. The Conservatives continued administering the tax rental agreements for a time,[16] but with some reluctance. In 1960, three federal-provincial conferences were held, and the premiers pressed hard for substantial upward revisions of the "rentals." After some delay, the prime minister announced that the federal cabinet would not renew the agreements after their normal expiry in 1962. Despite the criticism of those on the opposition benches and the evident unhappiness of some provincial cabinets, the era of the tax rentals came to an end in 1962. The editors of the *Canadian Tax Journal* said of the announcement in 1961: "Thus ends, in part, the bold postwar experiment to centralize major tax collections."[17]

In 1962 the Federal-Provincial Fiscal Arrangements Act inaugurated a completely new régime of fiscal cooperation. Under it, the federal government reduced its own levels of taxation and encouraged the provincial governments to legislate and levy their own taxes on the three major sources involved (personal income, corporations income, and estates). The prime minister and his minister of finance asserted that healthy government at the provincial capitals required application of the principle that he who spends the money should exact it from the taxpayers. The Ottawa authorities were, however, prepared to give the provinces some assistance. To make more room in the tax fields which the federal authorities had occupied by themselves for some years, the finance minister announced in his 1961 budget speech[18] that the national corporations levy would be reduced by nine percentage points, and that the national personal income tax would be reduced by twenty percent over a five year period. Equalization payments would also be continued, but under a system that would be more equitable than the one devised by the Liberal government, according to the finance minister.

More important, in terms of federal-provincial cooperation, was a tax collection service offered to the provinces. The Ottawa government announced its willingness, and later had permissive legislation enacted, to sign agreements providing for the centralized collection of provincial income taxes and for their transmission to the appropriate treasuries. The provincial taxes could be set at any rate so long as their general plan corresponded to the federal model if they were to be collected by the Ottawa officials. The provincial treasuries were also given the option of continuing to levy their own estates duties—as some had been doing—or, to refrain from doing so and receive half the federal revenues from estates duties in the province. Despite the complaints and objections with which some premiers greeted first word of the federal proposals, nine provinces accepted the collection offer. The autumn and early winter of 1961 saw a spate of provincial statutes which harmonized the various provincial taxing schemes, or else brought in new levies to take up the opening offered by a reduction of the federal tax. While the new agreement differed in theory from the earlier ones, they did not appear to be that different administratively, for Ottawa still acted as the tax collector and equalization continued at comparable levels.

This system of tax collections displaced a scheme of tax rentals which had greatly improved the central government's ability to ease the ups and downs of the business and growth cycles. The tax rentals had removed differences in tax levels as a factor in regional economic development; the provinces had gained an assured income of considerable magnitude without the political and administrative trouble of raising that income; and, perhaps just as important, the "tax jungles" of the nineteen-thirties had been wiped out.[19] All this had been achieved without an amendment to the British North America Act—through the medium of voluntary agreements which the parties could not enforce in a court of law. While the Diefenbaker government at Ottawa had attacked the tax rentals plans for a variety of reasons, the tax collections scheme would probably have been nearly impossible to inaugurate had the tax rentals not previously been in effect. In the space of 25 years the federation moved from a tangle of wildly conflicting, confusing, and competitive multi-government levies, through a highly unified wartime system, and gradually into one in which individual citizens made but one complete tax accounting (save in Quebec) but where each "sovereign" government decided its own taxes and had to assume electoral responsibility for them. The situation was somewhat more complicated for Quebeckers and for corporations in some provinces, but even for them the structures had been largely harmonized and made relatively comprehensible.

Conditional Grant Programs

In areas other than tax rentals and tax harmonization, the collaboration between federal and provincial administrations follows many of the same patterns evident in other federations. These commonly include the development of national standards in certain areas, the loan and training of personnel, collaboration in law enforcement, model legislative acts, cross-authorization of personnel or agencies to act for cooperating governments, and centre-regional functional boards and operating agencies. The most striking feature of all is the federal grant-in-aid. While examples of nearly all the types of collaboration cited may be found in Canada, here, as in the United States, "the most characteristic device of functional federalism is the conditional grant arrangement," as Professor Smiley puts it.[20]

For our purposes, a conditional grant is a money subsidy paid by the federal treasury to provincial governments to stimulate provision of a public service conforming to federal standards. The conditions on which the central government pays the money varies from program to program but most such arrangements in Canada exhibit these characteristics:

1. The program falls within provincial rather than federal legislative jurisdiction.
2. The province pays a proportion of the program costs.
3. The service meets certain minimum standards which are usually the same in every participating province.
4. The province provides certain facilities and administers the program although it may be carried out by a joint board.
5. While physical inspection of the program may be carried out by federal personnel, auditing program expenditures is usually (in Canada) left to the provincial administration.

The subsidy arrangements are not uniform. As James H. Lynn has explained, "a wide variety of arrangements are possible, as the central government share might be a lump sum, matching or a fixed proportion of total expenditures, or a per capita or per unit of services."[21] Not all shared cost programs involve conditional grants. There are a few cases, such as the Maritime Marshland Rehabilitation program, where the federal government assumes financial and administrative responsibility for one aspect of a carefully coordinated project and the provincial government another. While there are technical differences in the two types of programs, the political consequences for the federation would not seem to be substantially different.

Although shared cost arrangements have not been used in Canada to the extent that some students of federal finance think appropriate, their history extends over more than half a century. Even before the First World War, shared cost arangements were in effect in the fields of agriculture, technical education and transport. Immediately after that war, the federal government began a trans-Canada highway building project which took nearly sixty years to complete. Grants-in-aid were also made for technical education and old age pensions which Professor Smiley distinguishes as the first permanent conditional grant commitment of the central government. Despite fierce Liberal criticism of Conservative government grant-aided projects during the worst years of the great depression, W. L. Mackenzie King's accession to power in 1935 led not to a diminution but to an expansion of shared cost programs. Their purposes ranged from technical and agricultural education (as before), to fur conservation, distress relief (welfare), public health, and employment services.

The most visible of the conditional grant programs, the Trans-Canada Highway, typifies administrative federalism in both its problems and strengths. Its construction, which stretched over half a century, was marked by major intergovernmental conflicts over route selection, construction standards, contract procedures, and financing methods. The provinces enjoyed sole legislative responsibility for highway building and they had priorities and interests which were different and often diametrically opposed to those of the federal government, but if they wanted Ottawa's money they had to accept Ottawa's terms. During the interwar period, those federal conditions are said to have brought about the expansion and radical reorganization of all the provincial highways departments together with ancillary results which were popular with anti-patronage reformers but not with close government supporters. Ottawa's administrators imposed their standards in the name of honest and technical efficiency and seldom were willing to acknowledge the differing values of "traditional" political régimes. In Quebec, for instance, the government had long sought to spread employment opportunities widely among the rural poor by using a day labour system for public construction works. The federal administration, seeing only and deploring the partisan possibilities of the practice, insisted on the "more efficient" system of public tendering and project contracts. The provincial cabinet objected but had to submit to federal wishes or do without federal funds.

Throughout the building of the Highway, future-oriented federal engineers sought to weld provincial road systems into a design for national development, while the provinces sought to meet the local traffic demands of their electors and taxpayers. Where roads and rights-of-way were torturous and narrow, federal engineers put priority on remedying these deficiencies while provincial governments, which not only shared in the construction costs but bore the full cost of right-of-way acquisition, thought the money should be otherwise spent. This was the case particularly in Quebec and sometimes in the Maritimes, but their protests were seldom effective until the last decade of the project. While examples might be drawn from British Columbia or other provinces, the Ontario case illustrates very well the opposition of federal and provincial interests. Some 80-90 percent of Ontario's taxpaying and motoring population lives far to the south of the 49th parallel, yet federal objectives meant that the Ontario government had to be persuaded that it had a substantial stake in building a long, expensive highway across her isolated north country in order to connect the West efficiently with Ottawa and Eastern Canada. Eventually the Trans-Canada Highway was completed but not without the working out of a great many compromises between the legitimate interests of provincial cabinets and those of federal engineers. Successful completion of the project would probably have been impossible without close collaboration between Ottawa's transport specialists and the highway engineers of the provinces; the latter's commitment to professional colleagues and standards was critical to the integration of extra-provincial objectives into the programs of provincial politicians devoted to local works as a major object and instrument of elective politics. It may be, as some assert, that the Trans-Canada Highway is a triumph of civil engineering, but there can be no doubt that it ranks as one of the major triumphs of administrative federalism in Canada.

Joint programs like the Trans-Canada Highway proliferated after the Second World War and became one of Ottawa's major policy instruments. The bulk of the funds went into health and welfare which, together with the highway project, accounted for more than 90 percent of the federal share of all joint programs in 1959, a proportion that remained representative of the nineteen-sixties as well.[22] Frustrated as it was in securing implementation of its comprehensive post-war Reconstruction proposals (discussed earlier in chapter 2), the federal government was able to achieve most of its social policy aims in a piecemeal fashion through its conditional grant projects of the late forties and early fifties. The most important single program of all those established in the fifties was one apparently not contemplated in the Reconstruction proposals, that established by the Hospital Insurance and Diagnostic Services Act of 1957. Under this legislation Ottawa paid roughly half the cost of specified hospital and diagnostic services provided under provincially-administered hospital plans. A multitude of specific conditional grant programs grew up in

Table 1 — **Conditional Grant and Share Cost Programs at October 1971** (table abridged from Canada Year Book 1972)

Department and Project	Year Established	Provinces Participating	Provincial Share	Federal Contribution 1969-70
			p.c.	$'000
Agriculture —				
Freight assistance on livestock to Royal Winter Fair	1946	9(Ont.)	25	67
4-H Club activities	1900	9(N.S.)	50	268
Crop insurance	1961	8(Nfld., N.B.)	0.50 of admin. costs	4,678
Compensation — rabies control	1959	8(Nfld., P.E.I.)	60	60
Barberry eradication	1964	Que., Ont.	50	8
Grants to special fairs	1957	Nfld., N.B.	5	36
Central Mortgage and Housing Corporation —				
Urban renewal	1944	10	50	23,971
Public housing	1949	10	25 or 50	5,451
Urban redevelopment	1954	10	50	2,191
Sewage treatment projects	1960	10	75	6,192
Emergency Measures	1952	10	25-50	2,983
Energy, Mines Resources —				
Water conservation	1938	Ont.	37½-62½	32
Greater Winnipeg floodway, etc.	1962	Man.	25-62½	314
Roads to resources	1958	Nfld., N.B., Sask.	50	346
Flood control	ad hoc	Ont., B.C.	50	566
Environment —				
Construction subsidy — fishing vessels	1942	Atlantic, Que.	—	565

	Year	Jurisdiction	Rate	Amount
Industrial development	1959	6(Man., Sask., Alta., B.C.)	50	920
Relocation — fishing families	1967	Nfld.	—	140,0
Spruce Budworm eradication	1953	N.B.	33½	—
Finance —				
Canada student loans — service fees	1965	9(Que.)	6	368
Indian Affairs and Northern Development —				
Non-reserve schools for Indians —				
Capital contribution	ad hoc	various school districts	ratio white to Indian children	—
Instructional contribution	1948		—	34,391
Welfare services to Indians	1960	Nfld., Ont., Man., Sask., Alta	0.50	247
Industry, Trade and Commerce —				
Vital statistics	1909	9(P.E.I.)		74
Manpower and Immigration —				
Agricultural manpower	1941	9(Nfld.)	50	159
Vocational rehabilitation of disabled persons	1953	9(Que.)	50	5,013
Technical and vocational training —				
Technical and vocational training research projects	1937-66	10	varies 25 to $480 per capita	−1,338
Capital contribution	1945	10	+50 to $320 per capita	88,359
Municipal winter works	1958	10		378
National Health and Welfare —				
National health grants —				
Hospital construction	1948	10	50	12,896
Professional training	1948	10		1,604

Table 1—*(continued)*

National health grants *(continued)*

Department and Project	Year Established	Provinces Participating	Provincial Shares	Federal Contribution 1969-70
Mental health.	1948	10		4,523
Tuberculosis control.	1948	10		973
Public health research.	1948	10		3,942
Cancer control.	1948	9 (Man.)	50	798
General public health.	1948	10		9,977
Child and maternal health.	1953	10		645
Medical rehabilitation and crippled children.	1943-48	10	50	808
Health resources fund.	1966	10	50	34,383
Hospital insurance.	1958			
Medicare.	1968	Sask., B.C.		180,955
Old age assistance.	1952	10	50	1,517
Blind persons' allowances.	1937	10	25	3,309
Disabled persons' allowances.	1954	10	50	11,879
Unemployment assistance.	1955	P.E.I., N.S. Que., Ont. Alta.	50	14,343
Canada assistance plan.	1966	10	50	449,052
Fitness and amateur sport.	1962	9 (Que.)	40	1,126
National welfare grants —				
Welfare services.	1962	10	50	208
Demonstration projects.	—			
Hospitalization and welfare of indigent immigrants.	1947	N.S., Que. Ont,	50	114

National Research Council —				
Technical information services	1952	7(Nfld. P.E.I., Que.)		375
Public Works —				
Trans-Canada Highway	1950	10	10-50	26,772
Matana-Gaspé North Highway	1965	Que.		1,104
Portage du Fort Bridge	1966	Ont., Que.	50	—
Okanagan flood control	1950	B.C.	50	46
Regional Economic Expansion —				
Agricultural and rural development	1962	10	50	24,050
Fund for rural economic development	1966	N.B., Que.	0-40	22,186
Shellmouth Dam	1962	Man.	50	493
Coal subvention — electric power	1965	N.B., N.S.	—	6,156
Secretary of State —				
Immigrants, language —				
Instruction	1951	9(Que.)	50	372
Text books	1963	9(Que.)	—	68
Transport —				
Railway grade crossing fund	1909	10	12½-15	4,386
Railway abandonment — highway improvement	1965	N.B.		—
Trunk highways	1965	Atlantic	25-50	8,123
Municipal airports —				
Operational subsidy	1927	10	—	807
Capital	1927	10	50	1,081

the health and welfare fields for purposes such as old age assistance, allowances for the blind and disabled, health care for needy persons, and general social assistance to the impoverished. Many of these were gathered up and rationalized to a degree in the Canada Assistance Plan of 1966. This was an "umbrella" arrangement providing for province-by-province agreements under which the provincial government help the needy on the basis of individual requirements and a review of income and resources. Federal grants to the provinces under the C.A.P. amounted to $293.5 million in 1969-70.

Conditional Grants: Scale and Impact

The variety and ubiquitousness of shared cost programs in Canada is best indicated by Table 1 which shows not only the programs operating in the period prior to the 1973 federal-provincial conference agreements but the year of their origin, the provinces participating, the apportioning of costs between governments, and the federal contribution to each program. Examination of these data confirms the longstanding tendency of these programs to be concentrated overwhelmingly in the areas of welfare and health services.

Payments to the provinces grew in the course of one decade from a total of almost $145 millions in 1958 to more than $1,340 millions in 1968. (During the same period the gross national product grew from $34 billions to $71 billions in current dollars.) For a number of provinces, the federal conditional grants provided one of the major components of the revenue budget. At one extreme, Prince Edward Island's net general revenue in 1968 was $33 millions to which were added federal conditional grants of $11.6 millions. At the other extreme in the same year was Quebec with net general revenues of $2,288 millions and federal conditional grants of only $129 millions. (In both cases federal payments based on post-secondary education expenditures have been treated as unconditional rather than conditional grants.) The significance of the difference is, perhaps, more easily appreciated if percentage representations are used. In 1968 federal grants made to Prince Edward Island on certain conditions added 35 percent, and those to Quebec only 6 percent, to the net general revenue of each province. In terms of all the provinces, federal conditional grants added 15 percent to the total net general revenues. Variations in the size of these grants brought variations in the scale and type of impact that they had on provincial policy-making.

Federal policy intervention—in the form of unilateral inauguration or discontinuance of joint programs—was particularly disruptive and unwelcome for those provinces making some attempt at planning the future whether in the short or the medium run. Saskatchewan was the first to voice complaints which originated in federal disruption of provincial planning, and it was ironic that the objections came from a government formed by the C.C.F. party, the most centralist-minded of all the parties. At the federal provincial conference in 1950, Saskatchewan's premier, T. C. Douglas, complained of the federal government that:

> Without consultation with the provinces, it is vacating the field of rental control, after permitting substantial rent increases, and thus thrusting upon the provinces the responsibility of meeting a social crisis.
>
> Without consultation with the provinces, it has announced a comprehensive irrigation scheme, which we now learn must be supported by substantial provincial contributions.
>
> Without consultation with the provinces, it has announced the construction of a Trans-Canada highway, and it is later found that the Provinces will not only have to stand fifty per cent of the cost of construction but also the entire cost of the right-of-way.
>
> Without consultation with the provinces, it has decided upon a housing program for which every province must contribute twenty-five per cent of the cost, without regard to its ability to pay.
>
> By these unilateral decisions, the federal government has embarrassed the provinces in respect of their capital programs and has virtually dictated policies to which their consent has not been obtained.[23]

During the heyday of Ottawa's power and of the conditional grant—the nineteen-fifties—few provincial governments other than Saskatchewan's formulated their budgets with adequate concern for the longer run or for making hard choices allocating different priorities to different services. During the early sixties, that situation was transformed and, indeed, it was the Progressive-Conservative premier of Manitoba, Duff Roblin, who was most publicly associated with criticisms of federal interventionism based on disruption of provincial priority systems. The much enlarged responsibilities which the provincial governments assumed for matters like regional economic development together with the vast increases in social services costs made such planning unavoidable and external intervention intolerable.

In general, all provincial cabinets have expressed dislike for shared grant programs which were said to compromise provincial independence to an intolerable degree. A new federal program was welcome only when it effectively meant that the federal government would help to pay for a program or service which the province was already financing by itself or when it was about to embark on a new venture of the same specific type. Some provincial leaders refused to join grant-aided programs on the ground that they tended to concentrate authority at Ottawa that properly belonged to the provincial governments. Supporters of shared-cost projects argued that they were not centralizing in nature because they could always be turned down by provincial ministries, but it was questionable whether Ottawa's well-advertised financial inducements combined with regional partisan pressures and propaganda did not frequently take the choice out of the hands of the provincial cabinets. The medical care project of the late sixties was a prime example of this phenomenon. Comments from two provincial premiers will serve to illustrate the attitude. At the 1960 federal-provincial conference, Premier W. Shaw of Prince Edward Island said: "It is true that no province is obliged to participate in the shared-cost programs. However, experience has demonstrated that it is most difficult to refuse to join in such a program regardless of the budgetary difficulties . . . provincial governments can never be sure when the federal government may decide to embark on a new conditional grant program or expand an existing one." And in the report of the federal-provincial Tax Structure Committee on the September meeting in 1966, Premier Manning of Alberta is quoted thus: "The right to reject such shared-cost programs is theoretical rather than real, in that rejection . . . means only that the people of the dissenting province receive no benefits from the program but, as federal taxpayers are forced to help bear the federal share of the cost in those provinces which do participate."

Quebec and some other provinces objected, as well, to the uniform standards established for the aided programs. Too often, it was contended, these standards were fixed unilaterally by federal officials or by a bare majority of provinces. Quebec suggested that the federal system was designed to give minorities some protection from the imposition of simple majority rule, particularly from any majority views that threatened the minority's character or individuality. Even where the provinces had been consulted and the uniform standards unanimously agreed upon, they were enforced by centrally-appointed inspectors who were sometimes partisans of the Ottawa régime and foes of the provincial cabinet; in any event Ottawa's inspectors were centrally-oriented and seldom sympathetic to particularistic methods of doing business.

Despite radical tax system changes and other political developments, the nineteen-sixties saw not the death but a marked transformation in the nature of administrative federalism.[24] While elected leaders had always sought to milk maximum political advantage from conditional grant arrangements, much of the impetus for their institution had come from program specialists within the federal bureaucracy who successfully exploited their professional and other connections with provincial specialists to produce a great range of joint programs. Important agreements were initiated during the sixties but they appear to have been much more the product of inter*government,* rather than inter*specialist* negotiation. All were affected with a high political content, political in that elected politicians had made campaign promises about them and then perceived a much greater electoral stake in them than had previously been the case. Where the Canada Assistance Plan was, in one sense, simply a rationalization and tidying up of previous programs, it did provide, and largely on provincial terms, large sums of federal money for expanding and redesigning welfare systems attuned primarily to each province's appreciation of its particular needs rather than to Canada-wide priorities dictated by Ottawa.

Biggest and most important of the conditional grant projects of the sixties was that for medical care, but grants were also made for agricultural land rehabilitation, municipal winter works, land assembly and housebuilding, university student loans, and centennial year capital buildings. Medicare, although subject to fewer conditions of detail than any previous program, was also the most controversial. In the federal capital, the argument revolved around economic matters of timing and impact, while in the provincial capitals there was distress and dispute on grounds of both expedience and principle. Particular objections was taken to federal financing of Ottawa's share of the cost through an income tax surcharge, the proceeds of which were not shareable with the provinces. While provinces badly wanted the additional money, they chose not to incur whatever electoral risks were involved in imposing surcharges of their own—an open but unattractive route which federal politicians kept pointing out to unhappy provincial finance ministers and premiers. Other provincial complaints were better based on differences of principle. New Brunswick, and others, saw that their share of medicare would be very expensive and would cause postponement of programs to which they attached higher priority. The governments of the wealthy provinces objected vehemently to Ottawa's requirements of universal and compulsory coverage and to the federal prohibition of any private company participation (which provided the bulk of such care in pre-existing plans in Ontario, Alberta, and British Columbia). Despite their strong disinclination toward the federal medicare project, so great did the political costs and financial penalties for non-participation appear to be that within four years all ten provincial governments had swallowed both their principles and idiosyncratic priorities and surrendered to Ottawa's terms.

A Quantitative Approach

If conditional grants did not significantly affect the independence of a provincial cabinet in at least some of its policy choices, the grant program would have failed its basic rationale. The whole point of a conditional grant is to persuade recipient governments to take decisions they would not adopt in the absence of the grant program. Where central governments employ conditional grants, the effective political freedom of the regional governments depends crudely on their relative revenue independence of the centre; in short, whether they are rich or poor. It is possible to conceive of situations in which a regional government enjoys apparently absolute legislative and legal independence from the centre with respect to its constitutionally assigned areas of power, but where all its decisions and all its legislation are effectively determined by the wishes of the central government expressed through the conditional grant programs offered. The belief that "money talks" in getting one's way is as popular in discussion of conditional grants as elsewhere. Theoretically the numerical characteristics of public finance should make it fairly easy to give an objective indication of the relative influence which conditional grants exert on provincial policy freedom. In practice, different valuations of the conditional grant device make it difficult to construct a generally acceptable index of policy limitation.

An index of provincial policy limitation under conditional grant systems may be constructed in a number of ways. A fairly common way of talking about the problem in Canada implies calculations showing conditional grants as a proportion of all provincial revenues. For purposes of comparison, we can represent this approach in this way:

(1) Policy Limitation Index =
$$\frac{\text{Conditional Grants}}{\text{Net General Revenue} + \text{Conditional Grants}}$$

For convenience:
$$PLI_1 = \frac{CG}{NGR + CG} \times 100$$

This approach (PLI_1) produces low absolute figures and is subject to the valid objection that it ignores a critical aspect of the entire system; conditional grants require "matching funds" from the provinces in almost all cases in Canada. Far from being "windfalls" to provincial governments, shared cost programs of this sort impose heavy financial obligations on provincial budgets thereby reducing the money available for all other programs. While somewhat different proportions have been used, the matching grant required has usually been 50 percent. If, in the judgement of the federal government, the conditional grant is necessary to get the desired programs launched, then without the federal program provinces would spend their part of the cost on other programs, some of which they are no longer able to adopt. Then, the funds available for their own freely-chosen programs will be the residue of the net general revenue after the matching grant has been deducted. If, as seems reasonable from Canadian practice, we assume the matching funds (MF) to be roughly equal to the federal grant, we can represent this approach thus:

(2) Policy Limitation Index:

$$\text{PLI}_2 = \frac{\text{CG} + \text{MF}}{\text{NGR}} \times 100 = \frac{2\ \text{CG}}{\text{NGR}} \times 100$$

This formula yields a policy limitation index of 100 whenever the province is required to allocate fully half of its own revenues to match the federal conditional grant programs in being. The 50 percent of revenues remaining to a province would not admit of any meaningful discretion in provincial policy choice, given the effective irreducibility of many of the continuing budget responsibilities of a modern government. Many alternative formulas are equally possible in logic, and the utility of this one (PLI_2), which has been adopted for Table 2 lies entirely in the comparability between years and provinces which it permits; the assumptions built into the formula guarantee that the index figures have no other connection with the real world.

Table 2 **Policy Limitation Index** *
(Constraint on provincial independence in policy-making; comparison of impact of conditional grant system across provinces and over time)

Year	Nfld.	P.E.I.	N.S.	N.B.	Que.	Ont.	Man.	Sask.	Alta.	B.C.	All
1958	30	43	25	31	10	12	23	13	10	20	14
1960	60	58	45	50	15	36	45	36	22	35	31
1962	63	48	50	54	45	40	53	39	30	42	43
1964	91	78	55	63	51	48	63	37	41	42	49
1966	94	62	53	69	26	39	53	34	34	36	37
1968	74	70	69	58	11	33	52	41	39	32	30

*The lower the index figure the greater is the freedom of policy choice enjoyed by a provincial cabinet. The higher the figure, the more the provincial government's freedom is constrained by the wishes and programs of the central government. For full explanation, see text.

Table 2 probably represents the maximum case that could be made in statistical terms for the proposition that federal conditional grant programs significantly reduce the policy-making freedom of provincial governments. As absolute figures, the index numbers would gain in credibility if precise figures could be supplied for the provincial matching funds instead of the 50-50 approximations which have been used. Because some conditional programs have equalization features built into them, the index figures are perhaps more accurate indicators of the relative impact of federal policy wishes than of the relative freedom or lack of freedom of the provinces to legislate as they wish. ("Equalization features" mean that the wealthier provinces pay relatively more from their net general revenues for a grant-aided service than do poorer provinces. On the other hand, because they are wealthy these provinces have more disposable income after meeting all basic service costs than have the poorer provinces. These two considerations have been treated as though they were cancelling, on average.)

The most striking feature of the table is the markedly different impact of the central government in determining the kind of services provided in a province such as Newfoundland than in provinces such as Quebec or Alberta. The fluctuations over the decade are also striking with federal impact rising to its zenith in 1964 and tapering off thereafter although in different degrees, depending on the relative wealth of the province. (It should be noted that some students of conditional grants, such as George E. Carter, do not interpret the statistics in the same way. He, for example, treats educational grants as conditional, and, for this and other reasons, sees conditional grants generally rising quite steadily.)

Provincial criticisms of federal shared cost activities mounted during the nineteen-sixties. In 1969 a federal government white paper entitled *Federal-Provincial Grants and the Spending Power of Parliament* pointed out the legal authorities sustaining the virtually unfettered spending power of Parliament, and then observed:

> The governments of the provinces have advanced three criticisms of Parliament for its use of the spending power to establish new federal-provincial programs:
> (1) That the Government and the Parliament of Canada are deciding, without the formal participation of the provinces in such decisions, as to when federal-provincial programs ought to be started.
> (2) That shared cost programs forced upon provincial governments changes in their priorities.
> (3) That "taxation without benefit" occurs when the citizens of a province whose provincial government has refused to participate in a shared-cost program are required to pay the federal taxes which finance the federal share of the program.

After this rather truncated summary of provincial criticisms, the paper attempted responses to each of the three points. The first was dismissed by the argument that it was only political pressure to which the provinces were objecting and that they remained free in constitutional law to refuse participation if they so wished. The second response abandoned constitutional law for justification and, in effect, asserted the higher value of Canada-wide priorities over provincial priorities (regardless of constitutional jurisdictions). To the third argument it was said only that parliamentary representatives from each province (i.e. M.P.s) participated in the decisions made at Ottawa. Whatever might have been the adequacy of those responses, neither mention of, nor response to, two other major criticisms was made:

(4) That federal conditions specified for shared cost programs effectively amounted to central government legislation in areas legally denied to it by the British North America Act.

(5) That no reasons existed, other than federal government presumption or arrogance, to explain Ottawa's failure or refusal to consult and develop the programs jointly with the provinces before public announcements about matters which were constitutionally assigned to the provinces.

Despite these shortcomings, the document as a whole appeared to be basically sympathetic to provincial government complaints. Through it the federal government advanced a basic proposition about shared cost programs which might be considered for inclusion in a revised Canadian constitutional document:

The power of Parliament to make general conditional grants in respect of federal-provincial programs which are acknowledged to be within exclusive provincial jurisdiction should be based upon two requirements: first, a broad national consensus in favour of any existing program should be demonstrated to exist before Parliament exercised its power; and secondly the decision of a provincial legislature to exercise its constitutional right not to participate in any program, even given a national consensus, should not result in a fiscal penalty being imposed upon the people of that province.

The proposal outlined above would not apply to regional programs, that is to say shared-cost programs which involved some or all of the provinces of one or two Senate divisions. Such programs would continue to be negotiated directly between the Government of Canada and the Governments of the provinces concerned.

This proposal[25] would have made federal conditional grant programs dependent on prior provincial government approval and, thus, far better examples than ever they had been of "cooperative federalism." Eventually, however, the larger scheme of constitutional revision to which it had been closely tied collapsed and little more came of the idea of constitutionally restricting Ottawa's power to spend funds for purposes outside its legislative jurisdictions.

INTERPROVINCIAL EQUALIZATION

That some provinces are rich and some poor has been a commonplace of politics and public finance for a century. The reasons are varied and much debated: the chance distribution and exploitation of natural resources, the unequal impact of world trading patterns and changes, weather, the skills and dispositions in the labouring and entrepreneurial groups, and most contentious, the unequal sharing of the benefits and costs of participating in the federal arrangement. The disputes go on and the differences remain. In the process of building a Canadian state an ethic of Canadianism has developed that requires continuing efforts to minimize some of the disadvantages which citizens suffer from the accident of being born in a poor rather than a rich province. "This concept, which is a particular expression of egalitarianism, has facilitated satisfaction of some of the poorer provinces' claims, whether stimulated by a sense of historical injustice or simple envy."[26] Whatever their professed view of the economic causes, political leaders have been unwilling to accept the consequences of provincial poverty in terms of visibly inferior public services. Professor Alan C. Cairns has put it in this way:

> The interaction of inequalities in provincial revenue capacities with the widening frames of reference within which people judge their lot resulted in pressures for federal action to redress the perceived inequities. Funds were transferred from the wealthy to the less fortunate provinces with the federal administration performing the redistribution. Such recent attempts to reduce regional differences in public services, and consequently to minimize the price Canadians pay for their federal way of politics, are but modern manifestations of conventions and understandings which have been fashioned during the past century for promoting the welfare of the various provincial communities. That regional grievances are satisfied, at least partially, through the transfer of funds from the centre outward rather than by the consolidation of functions at Ottawa reveals the persistent resistance to centralization.[27]

Where the conditional grant was the major instrument of service equalization during the late forties and fifties, "national adjustment" or "equalization" grants became the major such instrument during the sixties and early seventies. First proposed by the Sirois Commission in 1941, revived in principle in a proposal by an Ontario premier,

George Drew, soon after the war, equalization grants first achieved substantial form in the Atlantic Provinces Adjustment Grants which the Diefenbaker Government introduced in 1958. The system was elaborated and modified during the sixties as sophisticated efforts were made to ensure that the basis on which the equalization grants were paid was itself equitable. Under the system begun in 1967 and continued for the post-1972 period, federal officials calculated a national average provincial revenue figure which took account of all major and most minor provincial revenue sources; equalization payments were then made to all but the richest provinces in terms related to the national average revenue figure. It should, perhaps, be stressed that these funds were transferred to the provinces entirely without conditions and that the only pressures on the allocation of these funds were those arising from the provincial political system. Their scale is indicated in the section following.

Intergovernmental Dependence

As conditional grants have been the sina qua non of administrative federalism, so unconditional grants have perhaps been the most reliable indicator of the political strength of the provinces within the federation. But what might be more important than the terms on which the funds are transferred might simply be the overall extent to which one government depends financially on another government. Taken together, conditional and unconditional grants to the provinces comprise a major portion of the federal revenue budget: $2.4 billion or about 24 percent of the total in 1969. From the other point of view, federal transfer payments play a markedly different role in the finances of some provinces than they do in others, and these are differences which have persisted, even through periods of great changes in other federal-provincial relationships.

The relative importance of transfer payments can be represented fairly simply in statistical terms as the proportion of the total provincial budget coming from Ottawa for all purposes. For convenience this proportion has been expressed in percentage terms and labelled the "Finance Dependence Index." An index figure of 50 would indicate that fully half of the province's revenues came from Ottawa by way of transfer payments. Over the dozen years or more covered by Table 3, the extremes of dependence on federal finance ranged from a high of 70.7 (Newfoundland 1960) to a low of 13.4 (Quebec 1958). During the period, the four Atlantic provinces never raised more than 55 percent of their revenues from their own sources and almost invariably more than half came by way of transfer payments (through Ottawa) from the more prosperous parts of Canada.

The contrast with the two central provinces is quite marked. Never during this period did the financial dependence index exceed 30 for

Table 3 **Finance Dependence Index**
Figures represent all federal fund transfers as a proportion of total provincial revenues.

Year	Nfld.	P.E.I.	N.S.	N.B.	Que.	Ont.	Man.	Sask.	Alta.	B.C.	All
1958	56	60	51	46	13	18	52	30	23	28	24
1960	71	65	56	57	18	27	52	40	29	34	32
1962	65	55	53	54	26	28	49	39	33	36	33
1964	61	58	46	48	27	24	34	26	21	18	25
1966	59	56	48	52	19	20	30	24	17	16	22
1968	63	61	58	49	24	19	36	29	23	16	25

either. Comparably low indices were noted for Alberta and British Columbia during the last half of the period, although those for the first half are no better than the Canadian averages, despite public images to the contrary promoted by premiers of those provinces. Manitoba's financial dependence on transfer funds gives it a statistical location more like that of the Atlantic provinces than of the western —an observation frequently found in interprovincial comparisons.

A common theme running through public and semi-public discussions during the nineteen-sixties concerned the transfers from English-speaking Canada to Quebec which were seen as "massive" and, by implication, as inequitable. While the sums involved were large ($593.7 millions in 1968 for example), the index figures suggest that in terms of total revenues Quebec was no more and no less dependent on funds transferred from Ottawa than was Ontario. While there are year-to-year variations, the Quebec indices are also comparable to those for Alberta and British Columbia. If not in "tax effort," "fair shares," or other proportionate measures, justification for the anti-Quebec complaints about fund transfers must be sought, where necessary, in terms either of the absolute sums involved or in non-statistical factors. As a whole, the fund transfers were equivalent to at least 20 percent of federal government revenues in any one year and to about 25 percent of the revenues of the provinces collectively.

However attractive indices of policy limitations and financial dependence may appear, their utility for the political analyst is very limited. For, as Professor Richard Bird has commented, "in addition to the ambiguity of any measurement of the degree of centralization and the inability of such measure to capture the power relationship which is at the heart of this discussion, the great diversity of Canada makes simple answers impossible."[28]

Traditional wisdom dictates that the federal politicians should get some return on their money from the provincial authorities—presumably in terms of policy acquiescence and that in some reasonable proportion to the degree of financial dependence. If this were the case Newfoundland and New Brunswick should be far more politically subservient to Ottawa than are Alberta and Saskatchewan. While reading reports of federal provincial conferences over the past twenty years suggests that this has sometimes been the case, the evidence is entirely impressionistic and quite unsatisfactory. Intergovernmental dominance and deference is difficult to specify conceptually and has not been assessed quantitatively, presumably because it has so far escaped the interest and/or skills of students of Canadian federalism. The idea that political subservience derives from substantial financial dependence assumes that the central authorities have considerable discretion to vary the size of the fund transfers. The assumption is questionable. The poor provinces proclaim what amounts to a constitutional right to such subsidies; the right is asserted on the ground that past actions such as the national tariff enriched the central provinces at the direct cost of the impoverishment of others. The moral entitlement of all Canadians to a certain minimum level of public services is also cited as another justification for the constitutional right to fund transfers. If a claim is a broadly constitutional one, and it often seems to have been tacitly accepted as such, the central authority's role in fund transfers comes close to that of a facilitative trustee and not much more. Considerations such as these impose significant limits on the federal government's apparently unfettered discretion with respect to the fund transfers and make it more appropriate to view them as good examples of "cooperative federalism."

TECHNICAL COMMITTEE COLLABORATION

Not until after the Second World War had begun in 1939 did the governments of Canada initiate significant measures of fiscal cooperation. Perhaps only the exigencies of a major war could have brought this about, for the seventy years following confederation were almost barren of instances of cooperation, even in technical matters. Events of the nineteen-thirties had revealed the paucity of intergovernmental understanding, and even of goodwill at times. Added to this problem was what appeared to some observers as seventy years of ceaseless quarrelling about the proper interpretation of the British North America Act; one hundred and sixty cases had been sent to the Judicial Committee of the Privy Council for final decision.[29] The prospects that governmental leaders might be persuaded to correlate their policies and administrations to some significant degree appeared slight to some of the social scientists making special studies for the Royal Commission on Dominion-Provincial Relations. Two of them, L. M. Gouin and Brooke Claxton, concluded in 1939 that "the failure of the Dominion and the provinces to co-operate to deal with such matters as insurance and company legislation, having little or no political implications, shows how unlikely it would be for the Dominion and provinces to co-operate to deal with any important and controversial question."[30]

The need for coordination of the provinces was recognized early; Sir John A. Macdonald's first ministry included a secretary of state for the provinces, but the office was abolished six years later and never revived.[31] While the two orders of government did not, of course, operate within separate and wholly self-contained areas, the problems that did arise were usually dealt with by the provincial government and the appropriate office at Ottawa. Formal acknowledgement of the need for a broad, continuing collaboration was made at the dominion-provincial conference of 1935. The prime minister, W. L. Mackenzie King, told the assembled premiers that cooperation between the central and the provincial authorities was too vital a matter to be left entirely to intermittent conferences and correspondence beween governments. "At the present conference," he said, "we can examine the basic principles underlying the [current] questions, and provide machinery for their continued study and treatment. In this manner, their final, satisfactory disposition can be ensured at subsequent conferences."[32] The premiers agreed with King's proposals and a committee was organized to make more permanent arrangements. Nothing permanent came of its discussions of the need for a secretariat to coordinate intergovernmental cooperation. Five years later, in 1940, the Royal Commission on Dominion-Provincial Relations told the federal government: "[i]t is imperative that means be found for . . . promoting co-operation between the provinces and between the Dominion and the provinces which is so essential to efficiency and economy in administration under modern conditions."[33] The commissioners proposed the establishment of a permanent secretariat for federal-provincial conferences and the exchange of information between governments.

Six years of wartime conditions showed Canadians that federal and provincial governments could work in harmony on a sustained basis. The possibilities for joint action by governments were discussed by those concerned about the postwar reconstruction. One such person was Prof. Maxwell A. Cohen who, in a tract looking toward the reconstruction conference that year, said that federalism could survive neither total centralization nor total decentralization; to revitalize federalism new methods were needed. Among the possibilities he proposed was "administrative collaboration." He defined it this way:

This is the device that would accept the present general constitutional position and would not try to attack it by the politically difficult process of amendment. Rather the method seeks to work out comprehensive schemes for such matters as health, welfare, educational standards, labour laws, with the Dominion and provinces collaborating on the details and agreeing to the basic legislation but with the actual legislation and administration left to the provinces under very strong technical and policy leadership by the Dominion.[34]

He envisioned agreements that would increase technical uniformity, preserve local authority, and promote "an authentic sense of provincial participation in the fashioning of important national policies."

The extent of federal-provincial collaboration was suggested in 1945 with the publication of *Dominion-Provincial Co-operative Arrangements*,[35] one of the many reference books which the federal government produced for the Dominion-Provincial Conference on Reconstruction. Many boards, councils, and committees were listed by the book, but their relative importance for promoting cooperation cannot be gauged with any exactitude. Some were insignificant advisory committees to which federal and provincial governments nominated members; others were actually policy-making boards executing functions at the behest of two or more governments. Some of these groups may be discussed briefly.

The National Advisory Committee on Agricultural Services co-ordinated government policies in agriculture. It comprised the deputy-ministers of agriculture, heads of certain colleges and research institutes, and railway representatives. While the committee possessed only advisory powers, its personnel exercised enough influence to eliminate much of the duplication of work within the federal and provincial agricultural departments. While agriculture is still a field of concurrent legislative jurisdiction, administrative aspects of the field have been functionally divided between federal and provincial departments. As a result of this committee's work, federal government personnel are now responsible for nearly all the pure agricultural research carried on under government auspices, while provincial agriculturalists are responsible for applied research and extension services. (Besides the National Advisory Committee on Agricultural Services, a number of other committees work in specialized, or functional areas.)

Committees also existed to coordinate the administration of old age pensions, to make inspections and investigations in the fisheries industry for both orders of government, and to further cooperation in conservation and mining. Three provinces used federal insurance department personnel to improve on the supervision of insurance companies. The administration of justice was apparently greatly facilitated by the activities of the Conference of Commissioners on Uniformity of Legislation in Canada, whose permanent officers and

regular meetings were jointly financed. Substantial measures of collaboration were reported in labour matters: inspection services, vocational education, legislative uniformity (except for industrial relation), and employment estimates and bureaus. Agreements were in
force in 1945 by which the Royal Canadian Mounted Police was
responsible for policing all the rural districts, and some cities and
towns, in six of the nine provinces.[36] Similar examples of cooperation
were evidenced in other areas of concern to both provincial and federal governments.[37]

The 1945-1946 dominion-provincial meetings on reconstruction
were notable for the refusal of the premiers to agree to greatly aug-
mented powers for the Ottawa government;[38] consensus was reached,
however, on the desirability of continued functional collaboration.
The premiers of Ontario and Quebec also endorsed the idea of a permanent federal-provincial conference secretariat. A permanent secretariat was not set up, but a preparatory committee of officials from
all governments was organized for the 1955 dominion-provincial
conference. As a result of the work of this *ad hoc* body, there was
established the Federal-Provincial Continuing Committee on Fiscal
and Economic Matters which met for the first time in 1956.[39] The
committee comprised senior treasury and economic officials. The
nature of their work has been outlined by R. M. Burns, then director
of the central government's federal-provincial relations branch:
"Matters of administrative co-operation have had the attention of the
group and views have been exchanged on various economic matters
in which a joint interest is shared, such as the condition of the money
market, revenue trends in various tax fields, and problems of financial
administration."[40]

Collaboration along functional lines grew in a great many areas
during the postwar decade. Among the most significant institutions for
promoting technical and administration cooperation was the Institute
of Public Administration of Canada, which held its first annual conference at Toronto in 1949. The I.P.A.C. membership came to include nearly all the senior civil servants of federal and provincial
governments, as well as many other persons concerned with administrative problems. While this organization is entirely unofficial and its
contribution is difficult to assess, public servants of the Ontario provincial government, to give one example, seem to believe it has been
a most significant influence in harmonizing administrative practices of
the provincial governments.

This influence is largely exercised, it would appear, through the
participation of public officials in the annual conference presentation
and discussion of problem papers. At the 1949 conference of the
I.P.A.C., to take one instance, questions arising in dominion-
provincial administration were discussed by several senior officials

engaged in functional, joint enterprises.[41] Vigorous debate followed each paper. In one of the papers, D. M. Stephens, of the Manitoba government, illustrated a situation giving rise to functional collaboration in his sketch of the joint fur rehabilitation program of the Manitoba and federal governments. Officials had discovered that, in The Pas, Manitoba, there were "two separate offices, one Dominion and one Provincial, each attempting to duplicate and emulate the other and both attempting to do almost identical jobs, one for treaty and the other for non-treaty trappers, people who, in the degree of their dependence upon the fur industry were hardly distinguishable, one from the other."[42] Mutual appreciation of the anomalies of the situation led to the establishment of a joint advisory board and the consolidation of the two projects under one administrative head. Another significant example of cooperation was sketched by J. M. Wardle of the Eastern Rockies Forest Conservation Board.[43] This board was established as an independent organization by the Alberta and federal governments to effect the conservation and efficient use of the waters and forests of a large area of the eastern slopes of the Rockies. The national interest had been involved because of the intimate concern of the other prairie provinces with mountain water run-off. The board supervises a wide range of conservation activities on the mountain slopes and advises the federal and Alberta governments on a large number of applications they refer to the board. The board's advice on these applications apparently has the effect of authoritative decisions.

The decade of the nineteen-fifties saw the proliferation of joint committees dedicated to harmonizing policy and administrative details. In 1957, Dr. K. W. Taylor, the federal deputy-minister of finance, set out to list all the federal-provincial committees that were more or less formally constituted and had extended terms of reference.[44] He listed sixty-four groups. Fourteen of these committees had generalized terms of reference and acted in the fields of agriculture, health, finance, civil defence, insurance, uniformity of legislation, mines, water resources, and scientific research. The remaining fifty committees had fairly precise terms of reference, ranging from the Vocational Training Advisory Council to the Coordinating Agency on Diseases of the Beaver.

Subsequently intergovernmental cooperative arrangements grew in such profusion and complexity that even the participating governments felt the need for clarification. This commission was carried out in 1968 by R. M. Burns in his *Report: Intergovernmental Liaison on Fiscal and Economic Matters*. The author, the director of the Institute of Intergovernmental Relations, Queen's University, listed more than 190 apparently regularly meeting committees, groups, joint boards, and other bodies engaged in the work of coordinating the activities and plans of the various Canadian governments. These groups he classified broadly into those dealing with General Government, Financial and Economic Matters, Financial Institutions Regulation, Agriculture, Rural Development, Education, Manpower, Labour, Mines, Water (Energy), Forestry, Fisheries, Health, Welfare, Industry and Trade, Public Works, Highways, Housing, Statistics, Civil Service, Emergency Services, Indian Affairs, Revenue, Transport, and many miscellaneous categories. As in the earlier survey, the *Report* listed committees composed of many different levels of governmental officials, all the way from heads of government to field officers. Before the Report itself could be published, an addendum was necessary to cope with the burgeoning of even more intergovernmental groups.

Perhaps the most important of all these groups to engage our attention are those formed to deal with the problems of fiscal coordination. After a beginning in 1956 with the Continuing Committee on Fiscal and Economic Matters, which was mostly concerned with tax rental negotiations, a more important start was made in 1964 with the Tax Structure Committee consisting of the financial ministers and concerned with equalization, tax harmonization, tax-sharing, and fiscal consultations in advance of the budget process each year. This committee acted in a purely consultative fashion and, given the nature of parliamentary government, it could probably never have achieved executive coordinating power but it did appear to act to reduce some potential fiscal policy clashes. For a time during the late sixties there existed another potentially very important set of intergovernmental institutions, a series of committees and a secretariat concerned with constitutional amendment. After apparently accomplishing a great deal in the mounting of negotiations and the correlation of viewpoints on many details, these particular institutions atrophied and died with the collapse of the Victoria Conference project in 1971.

THE FEDERAL-PROVINCIAL CONFERENCE

The most obvious point of contact between the regional and the central governments—the formal federal-provincial conference—has no precise counterpart in the American federation, perhaps because few American political leaders can speak with authority equivalent to that of the prime minister and the premiers. The conferences began almost seventy years ago and, in theory, they could have led to many significant measures of intergovernmental cooperation; the conferences were usually attended both by the political heads and by their senior administrators. In practice, however, the conferences prior to the Second World War did not lead to much cooperation between governments. The conference principals almost invariably had their attention fixed on one of two topics: the unconditional subsidies and the problem of devising a new procedure for constitutional amendment.[45] Effective cooperation in non-political matters may also have been hampered by the poor staff work that attended the conferences.

The federal-provincial conferences became a more vital factor in the years following the Second World War. The reason for this development was allied to the initiation of the tax rental device, and to the general growth in size and complexity of all governmental activities, which required a high degree of coordination to keep the federal system viable. The postwar evolution of the federal-provincial meetings helped to bring about the needed collaboration. The conference of 1955, in particular, illustrates how these conferences served as clearing houses for some of the thorny issues of federal politics. While the chief topic was fiscal relations, many other matters were discussed, among them the following: agricultural marketing, farm credit, educational assistance, the nature of confederation, measures to provide employment, development of highways and natural resources, and standards in the provision of health and welfare services.[46] Consensus was not reached on all these matters at the conference, but opinions were sounded and negotiable limits indicated by the governments' most important leaders. These discussions set authoritative frameworks within which functional and technical agreements could be reached by senior administrative officials, or by subsequent conferences of more limited scope. In the eyes of Professor Corry, a legal scholar as well as political scientist, the federal-provincial conference came, to a limited degree, to fill the same role in Canada that the United States Supreme Court played in adjusting the American constitution to social change. And, in his opinion, it was just as well because of the reluctance of the Canadian court during the fifties to move very far from "classical federalism." It might even be fair, Professor Corry observed, to say that "the adjustment of federal relations is now too delicate, too complex, as well as too serious, a matter to be entrusted in any extensive way to judges, because of the inflexibility of the techniques they apply."[47] The comment was made in 1959 and there has been some change in legal thinking since. Nonetheless, the seventies do not appear to have brought changes in judicial approaches different enough to warrant alteration of this judgement about the basic unsuitability of judicial technique for the "adjustment of federal relations" in important respects. That task necessarily fell to the political leaders for whom the natural medium increasingly became the heads of government meeting.

The transformation in intergovernmental relations during the early sixties was marked by changes in federal-provincial conferences.

Where earlier conferences were chiefly inspired by the bureaucrats and oriented toward their concerns, today the emphasis has altered. While hundreds of officials' meetings still go on every year, one type of meeting has assumed predominating importance, that of the heads of government, and they are concerned with issues much more political in nature than administrative. While the plethora of mass media attention to the heads of government gathering could be misleading, one cannot disagree with the judgement of Professor Smiley that the "Federal-Provincial Conference of Prime Ministers and Premiers has come to be one of the most crucial institutions of Canadian federalism." He comments further: "Prior to the beginning of constitutional review in 1968 such Conferences dealt almost exclusively with fiscal and economic matters and, from time to time, with attempts to agree on a formula for constitutional amendment. However, this range of discussions has come to be more extensive and such meetings are held with increasing frequency, at least twice a year."

The Federal-Provincial Conference very much needs detailed study. It is inaccurate to suggest, as some have done, that it has become the third level of government in Canada. Such an assertion ignores the important difference between the actual and potential powers of this emergent institution. In terms of potentiality, the Conference could prevail over even the constitution because the constitution could and would be amended in any direction on which the federal and all the provincial governments could agree. In fact, the capacity to reach agreement is very much circumscribed by the divergent policy and partisan-political interests of its members.[48] One of the most valuable of all recent studies of Canadian federalism was that by Professor R. E. B. Simeon, *Federal-Provincial Diplomacy: The Making of Recent Policy in Canada.*[49] The title aptly characterized the changed nature of intergovernmental relationships, a change which may also be seen as a transformation in practice from administrative to coordinate federalism.

Joint Programs

Two further intergovernmental programs deserve brief attention at this point: the federal pension plan and the educational finance scheme instituted during the late sixties. While neither involves conditional grants nor is an expression of administrative federalism as earlier defined, both are frequently claimed by federal politicians to be examples of "cooperative federalism" and may be conveniently touched on here.

The public pensions field is a complex one. The federal government sought to stimulate provincial plans with conditional grants during the twenties, and by the nineteen-fifties it was well launched into limited but wholly federal pensions of its own. An amendment to the

British North America Act in 1954 (sec. 94A) explicitly stated a right of the federal government to legislate in the pensions field but subjected that right to an over-riding power of the provincial governments. When the L. B. Pearson government sought during the sixties to enact a major, comprehensive Canada Pensions Plan it required the acquiescence of the provinces; without it, any federal plan could have been upset without notice in the future by overlapping or contradictory provincial pensions legislation. As the course of the negotiations has been admirably set forth and analyzed by Professor Simeon, we need note only a few points. Here for the first time was a reversal of the usual power positions in federal-provincial relations: the provinces now had the ability to frustrate Ottawa's objectives completely. This they did not do but they did force the federal government to: 1. Abandon its drive for one Canada-wide plan and recognize that Quebec would run its own plan, without tax-loss penalty. 2. Abandon its own proposal in substance and adopt one based on the Quebec model which the other provinces also preferred; 3. Give the provincial governments the major access (through loan funds) to the vast investment funds generated by the Canada Pensions Plan. In the end, the federal government gained its social objective (significant pensions coverage for all Canadians) and the provinces gained very important capital resources.

Education beyond the secondary level is financed by both the federal and provincial governments, although sec. 93 of the B.N.A. Act gives the provinces exclusive legislative rights. (How broadly the word education is construed in that section is a matter of dispute.) During the fifties, federal involvement was restricted to vocational and technical training—which it justified as part of its employment responsibility—and to university grants, the justification for which was much more disputed. University grants for both capital and operating expenditures were distributed on the basis of provincial populations and student enrolments. The operating grants began at a level of 50 cents per capita in 1951-52 and rose in four unequal steps in the years 1956, '58, '62, and '67 to about five dollars. After some years of refusing the grants on principle, Quebec negotiated an agreement with Ottawa under which the province increased grants to its universities and raised the corporations income tax to suit, while Ottawa made a proportionate reduction in the tax it levied on Quebec corporations. (This, the first "opting out" arrangement, was concluded with the approval of the prime minister, the Rt. Hon. J. G. Diefenbaker, who later fiercely attacked his successor's extension of the same principle which, he said, tended to divide Quebec from the rest of Canada and to promote the "two nations" fallacy. These aspects are further discussed in later chapters.)

Following proposals it put to the federal-provincial conference of

October 1966, the federal government embarked on a remarkable support scheme for university education, one which committed it to a high level of rapidly-escalating expenditure which it could not control. Under the arrangements, Ottawa terminated both the capital and operating grants which had been made directly to the universities. In compensation, the federal government increased its support for individual university research projects and, most significantly, made directly to the provincial governments an unconditional grant calculated on the most generous of the two alternative formulas: either a flat 15 dollars per capita or an amount equal to 50 percent of the total expenditures made within a province through formal institutions of post-secondary education. Although the amount depended on actual expenditures made and the grants are treated in some federal statistics as conditional transfers, these funds were paid over to the provincial treasuries completely without conditions for their expenditure. Federal ministers of finance grew increasingly unhappy about the open-ended nature of this commitment and by the early seventies Ottawa was seeking some method of extricating itself from this expensive involvement in university education. The central government had to content itself in 1972 with an agreement that the sums payable would not be increased from year to year by more than 15 percent. The 1966 "package" also involved termination of intergovernmental programs relating to technical and vocational education and their replacement by the Adult Occupational Training Act of 1967 under which Ottawa began spending greatly enlarged resources on retraining adult members of the labour force. Under this scheme, the federal government purchased education and training services directly from the provinces on behalf of participants in its program.

A change in the emphasis in administrative federalism from inter-specialist to intergovernmental arrangements did not mean the diminution of joint programs. If anything, their numbers continued to grow. In January 1974, the Privy Council Office of the federal government published a *Descriptive Inventory of Federal-Provincial Programs and Activities* which, in more than 427 pages, classified and described 215 such programs. The total value of payments and tax offsets made to provinces and municipalities were there estimated at more than five billion dollars or roughly one-quarter of the federal budget for 1973-74. (See Table 4.)

HORIZONTAL COLLABORATION

The federal structure provides a central apparatus formally charged with furthering the political interests common to all the provinces and

Table 4 **Major Federal Expenditure Estimates for 1973-74
under Joint Programs**

Department	Purpose	Amounts
Finance:	Prov. Revenue Equalization (net)	$1,218,300,000
	Contracting Out (Tax Abatement)	(636,100,000)
	(Cash Payment)	183,400,000
	Grants in Lieu of Taxes	65,321,000
	Statutory Subsidies	33,772,000
	Public Utilities Income Tax	
	Transfer	28,180,000
Manpower:	Manpower Training Program	175,500,000
Health &	Hospital Insurance &	
Welfare:	Diagnostic Services	1,061,500,000
	Canada Assistance Plan	942,900,000
	Medical Care	677,700,000
	Health Resources Fund	36,988,000
Reg. Econ. Exp.:	Special Areas	70,573,000
	Fund for Rural Economic	
	Development	64,068,000
	Special Highways	30,955,000
	Agricultural and Rural	
	Development Act	25,500,000
	Prairie Farm Rehabilitation Act	18,203,000
Sec'y of State:	Post-Secondary Education	466,907,000
	Bilingualism in Education	70,482,000
Transport:	Railway Grade Crossing Fund	16,636,000
		($5,822,985,000)
		5,186,885,000

*Slightly condensed from tables in Canada, Privy Council Office,
Descriptive Inventory of Federal-Provincial Programs and Activities
(Ottawa 1974).

informally charged with promoting a certain unity of feeling within
the state. A fairly elaborate set of institutions was established to deal
with the common political interests, but no institutions were provided
in the constitution to assist the growth of understanding and sentiment
between the sections. This understanding and sentiment were left to
germinate and mature as an incidental result of the developing vertical
relationships between the provinces and the federal capital; and, in
fact, this kind of unity may be all that could be tolerated in a new
federation embracing half a continent and disparate political and cultural communities. Logically, however, there is no necessity of neglecting the potentialities of intersectional relationships. Proper
exploitation of this horizontal aspect of intergovernmental relations
might serve the common interest just as well as does attention
paid to the vertical, or federal-provincial, axis. The greater the understanding between provinces, the easier is the task of furthering those

common interests that brought the regions into the federation. While the dissolution of many private partnerships is ample indication that better understanding does not always come about through joint enterprise, it may be suggested that the possibilities for interprovincial cooperation are greater if the provinces are in communication with each other, rather than isolated, aloof, and making contact only through the federal capital. But interprovincial cooperation has not been the norm for relations between governments in Canada.

"On a comparative basis," it has been observed, "it would seem that neither interprovincial relations nor interprovincial cooperation in Canada have been developed to anything like the degree interstate relations have in the United States."[50] Despite the example provided by the "compact clause" of the American constitution, the draftsmen of the British North America Act do not seem to have foreseen the possibility of interprovincial agreements, for the act makes no provision for such compacts. Nevertheless, the provincial governments do coordinate policies and administrative arrangements to a considerable degree. This developing cooperation between provinces has been so overshadowed by the topic of dominion-provincial relations that it has been generally ignored, although it is beginning to attract a little scholarly attention. Interprovincial collaboration takes the form of uniformities in legislation, adoption of joint standards (often drafted by the professional associations to which civil servants belong), reciprocal legislation to set up joint ventures, and conferral of power on extraprovincial authorities (such as by giving local effect to educational examinations taken elsewhere). Cooperation may be effected by parallel legislative enactment, by order-in-council or ministerial regulation, or by informal administrative understandings.

Both the general and the functional conferences bring together senior civil servants. While the conference focus is national, two or more of these officials will often confer privately to discuss, settle, or arrange for the settlement of, various administrative difficulties. Sessions during the Dominion Council of Health, to cite one example, resulted in "the acceptance by all the provinces of uniform regulations for control and reporting of communicable diseases and the uniform plan for the administration of the Salk poliomyelitis vaccine used by every province with outstanding success in 1956."[51]

The Dominion Council of Health was only one of a number of associations of senior public and private officials influential in promoting interprovincial cooperation. A partial list may be abstracted from a study by Professor Richard Leach: The Queen's Printers Association of Canada, Provincial Governments' Trade and Industries Council, Canadian Association of Administrators of Labour Legislation, the Conference of Commissioners on Uniformity of Legislation in Canada, the Association of the Provincial Superintendents of Insurance, and the Canadian Education Association.[52] Professor Leach has also suggested that a great deal of cooperative effort may result from the membership of public servants in a large number of other national associations. While this cooperation may be extensive, it is like the cooperation resulting from personal correspondence, full of potentialities for cooperation but impossible to assess. This type of collaboration must not be deprecated because of its *ad hoc* character; the informal methods could possibly be so successful that they make the development of extensive formal arrangements unnecessary.

The formal arrangements appear to have been restricted to the inter-governmental boards and organizations for conservation and similar purposes, to reciprocal legislation, and to a very few legal commitments. These measures have been supplemented by a number of understandings to provide for cost-sharing or charge-backs for the care of indigents and certain social welfare and hospitalization cases, for technical education of out-of-province residents in some fields, and for the training of fire protection personnel and similar types of public servants.

Political Conferences

Not until 1960 did there exist a Canadian equivalent of the American conference of state governors. Provincial leaders met frequently in the past[53]—1887, 1902, 1910, 1913, and 1926—but their concern was almost exclusively with concerting their complaints against the central government, and not with harmonizing their individual sets of administrative practices. Quebec's *Report of the Royal Commission of Inquiry on Constitutional Problems*,[54] of 1956, urged the desirability of frequent, close consultation by the provinces without the participation of federal government officials. "That is the only means of working out a provincial policy, suited to each province but still Canadian in nature." The commission said that creation of a permanent Council of the Provinces, or some similar organization, was necessary for the preservation of federalism. If the provinces did not agree to assist each other, the commission warned, then "the country's own interest will finally require the federal government to take over the supreme command."[55] While the Quebec government did not call for the creation of such a council, a premier of Quebec, Jean Lesage, issued the invitations that initiated the annual conferences of all provincial premiers.[56]

The premiers met at Quebec City in December, 1960, and agreed to confer annually thereafter. A second meeting was held at Charlottetown in 1961, and others have been held in the different capitals in the years since. During the first two meetings, the premiers discussed the model offered by the American state governors' conference, but apparently decided that the machinery developed during the previous fifteen years of federal-provincial talks made somewhat different arrangements desirable. The premiers held council informally and privately without phalanxes of advisers. Views were exchanged and memos prepared to guide the growing series of meetings of provincial ministers. It is understood, for example, that the premiers in 1961 discussed issues involved in "portable" pensions and national educational standards, and drafted guidelines in these matters for their senior provincial officials. A recurring note in the premiers' press statements about the conferences is that they are highly informal and that no attempts are made to "gang up against Ottawa" on particular issues. An even more recent development has been regular meetings of the premiers of the prairie provinces and, during the early seventies, of the maritime provinces. Exchanges of information and opinion rather than formal agreement seem to be the hallmarks of the regional premiers' meetings as well.

Frequent conferences are held by provincial ministers concerned with specific functional areas. The ministers of highways, to give one example, usually hold several private sessions during the annual convention of the Canadian Good Roads Association, which brings together political leaders, senior civil servants, and representatives of the construction industries. Gatherings of the ministers of mines, of health, and of education take place at frequent but irregular intervals. Sometimes these sessions are called during the course of various national conventions; at other times, the ministers meet alone, at the suggestion of any one of their number, to debate particular problems. The most highly developed of the interprovincial associations would appear to be the Canadian Council of Resource and Environment Ministers which has an energetic director and a burgeoning staff concerned with coordinating the work of all governments in the resource area. Intergovernmental cooperation on the pollution problems with trans-boundary effects are a particular concern and, lately, federal officials have also been involved in the Council's work.

The general situation does not appear during the seventies to be much different from that of the nineteen-sixties when Professor Burns made the following assessment:

> Interprovincial, as distinct from federal provincial conferences have not, at least so far, assumed great significance in Canadian affairs although they have had some influence in certain technical areas. . . . The state of uncertainty that prevails with respect to interprovincial activity is exemplified by the fact that some regard it as a move to compensate for a lack of federal leadership, others look upon it as a means of protecting provincial interests against federal domination while still others find it a device of influence properly applied only in matters of purely regional or local interest.[57]

INTERDELEGATION OF POWERS

Possibly one of the most effective methods of further intergovernmental collaboration would be by the delegation of legislative powers between Parliament and legislatures, so that effective legal powers could be combined to deal with almost any jurisdictional problem. The British North America Act says nothing about delegation, but the case of *Hodge* v. *The Queen* made it clear that the maxim *delegatus non protest delegare* "has no constitutional significance relative to the delegation of legislative power by Dominion Parliament or provincial legislature to some other subordinate agency."[58] The real question, however, is whether there could be delegation between Parliament and a provincial legislature, or vice versa, for this would have the effect of making one the subordinate of the other for certain purposes. Lord Atkin's "watertight compartments" view of the distribution of legislative powers illustrated the Judicial Committee's firmly negative answer to this question. Since then, the Supreme Court of Canada seems to have supported the Judicial Committee's stand with its advisory opinion in 1951 that delegation from Parliament to a legislature, and vice versa, was unconstitutional.[59]

The court's finding in this *Nova Scotia Delegation* case did not, however, prohibit a legislative body from incorporating into its own statutes valid legislation enacted in the past or future by some other legislative body, a device that had found wide application even before the Second World War.[60] What Professor (now Chief Justice) Laskin called an "escape from the doctrine" of the *Nova Scotia Delegation* case was discovered in 1952 when the Supreme Court upheld the right of both Parliament and a provincial legislature to delegate administrative authority to a subordinate board of the other legislature.[61] In his concurring judgement in the *Willis (P.E.I. Potato Marketing Board)* case, Mr. Justice Estey observed that "the scheme here created is, throughout, a cooperative effort on the part of the respective governing bodies in which each maintains its own respective legislative fields." Mr. Justice Rand observed that in some fields intergovernmental cooperation might be the only effective means of regulating trade. "Both legislatures have recognized the value of a single body to carry out one joint, though limited, administration of trade," he said of the *Willis* case, adding that the delegation was effective because "at any time the Province could withdraw the whole or any part of its authority." In 1954 Parliament used this power in the Motor Vehicle Transport Act which vested its authority over interprovincial traffic in provincially-appointed boards. This specific delegation was later approved in *Coughlin* v. *Ontario Highway Transport Board* (1968 SCR 659) where a challenge that the board's action was *ultra vires* was turned back and the delegation sanctioned.

EXPOSITION AND EXAMINATION

One of the most articulate pleas for greater cooperation between governments was made in a study published in 1954 by a French-speaking economics professor, Maurice Lamontagne.[62] His book, *Le fédéralisme canadien: évolution et problèmes,* must surely be one of the most maligned books ever written on federalism, for it was widely and bitterly attacked by French-speaking academics and supporters of the Union Nationale government of Premier Maurice Duplessis.[63] Mr. Lamontagne asserted that it was time for French Canadians to effect a "lucid reintegration" of Quebec into confederation. His critics claimed that this reintegration obviously meant that Quebec should give up the historic struggle of *la survivance* and assist in the complete centralization of the country. But what the author really proposed was an acceptance of the "new federalism" which, he felt, had arrived in Canada to stay. He insisted that Quebeckers must begin collaborating in joint efforts to solve the problems of modern government; if the province's leaders refused to do so, then, said the writer, the problems would be solved by English Canada alone and in its own way.

Mr. Lamontagne proposed extending the constitutional areas of concurrent jurisdiction and reassigning responsibilities for day-to-day administration. He urged the provinces to cooperate in permitting the central management of the national economy to whatever degree was necessary to ease the worst shocks of economic fluctuations. Government policies should be harmonized, he said, with the assistance of a permanent secretariat of federal-provincial relations. While, under his plan, both orders of government would assume a few new obligations (and lose others), the chief emphasis was that of joint action by government to resolve mutual difficulties. He concluded of federalism, generally, that "en définitive, les relations intergouvernementales sont la pierre d'achoppement de cette forme d'unité politique."[64]

Partisan Expression

This brand of "new federalism" found political expression on November 6, 1961 when the national Liberal party leader, Lester B. Pearson, set forth his party's attitude toward federalism. He stated these views at the Quebec East Liberal party convention which chose Maurice Lamontagne as its candidate for the 1962 federal election. The federal leader said that his party, if elected, would reinstate an equitable system of equalization of provincial revenues which would become "un instrument important de decentralisation." Further,

> Nous croyons en effet que le gouvernement fédéral devrait sortir du domaine des programmes conjoints qui ont un caractère permanent, une fois que ces programmes sont bien établis à travers le

pays. Cette proposition s'applique surtout au domaine de la secu-
rité sociale. En cessant de participer financièrement à ces programmes, le gouvernement fédéral devrait compenser les provinces
en leur cédant plus de place dans le champ de la taxation directe
et en y ajoutant la peréquation, de facon à ne pas augmenter leurs
charges financières.[65]

The federal leader said several such programs could be abandoned
immediately, others would be developed with the objective of turning them over to the provinces, and new projects which were undertaken would not last more than five years before being turned over to
the provinces. Flexibility and full provincial cooperation was to be
sought for such programs. Mr. Lamontagne made basically the same
points in a speech to a luncheon club in Montreal on January 17,
1962. Implementation of these cooperative ideas would contribute, he
said, "à accroître la flexibilité de notre fédéralisme tout en garantis-
sant son équilibre et son dynamisme."[66]

Belief that Canadian federalism required more structural flexibility
and greater intergovernmental cooperation was evident in several of
the essays edited in 1961 by Professor Michael Oliver for his *Social
Purpose for Canada*. Pierre-Elliott Trudeau, for example, pointed
out that under the British North America Act close coopcration by
governments was not only possible but "constitutionally indispens-
able." There might be swings of the pendulum—between centralizing
and decentralizing trends—but coordination of government policies
and activities was always a necessity. "And since the future of Canadian federalism lies clearly in the direction of co-operation," he said,
"the wise socialist will turn his thoughts in that direction, keeping in
mind the importance of establishing buffer zones of joint sovereignty
and co-operative zones of joint administration between the two levels
of government."[67] A similar respect for the necessities and possibilities for intergovernmental cooperation could be noted in an essay by
Professor Frank R. Scott. The thorough-going centralist attitudes that
had once characterized his thought had plainly been tempered by the
course of time and the experience of the years of postwar collaboration between administrations.

Theoretical Considerations

Little evidence exists of much theoretical inquiry into the implications
of administrative federalism; the foregoing discussion of the concept
had to be drawn from pragmatic applications of the approach to
disparate problems of the federal system. This lack of speculation
may be partially explained by the unobtrusiveness of the phenomena.
Had there been constitutional provisions suggesting and facilitating
joint activities by governments, cooperative efforts might well have

begun earlier in the state's history and thereby provided a range of phenomena for reflection. As it happens, intergovernmental coopera- tion is relatively new to the country; its debut seems to have awaited the conjunction of three developments.

The first of these developments was the economic and social inte- gration of the federation's various regions. For many years, the various provinces lived in virtual isolation from each other, more dependent on overseas markets and the international community than they were on each other. The second development was really the revelation of a significant disjuncture in the federal system: at a critical time, the final interpreter of the British North America Act refused to construe that statute as a constitution capable of conforming with changing sociological circumstances. At this point, the umpiring of the federal system started to pass from the courts to the political arena where de- cisions were negotiated on the basis of policy rather than settled on the basis of law.* The third development conducive to the growth of administrative federalism was the involvement of all governments in a vast range of public activities. As the various governments increased their spheres of operation, they began to interpenetrate and become aware of each other. Different administrations came to occupy the same or similar fields, and demands were made for services that no single government could meet because of constitutional or financial limitations. Collaboration, which had been a luxury, became a neces- sity of life for the federal system. Until the Second World War, a limited degree of federal-provincial cooperation sufficed for most purposes. After the Second World War, the increasing complexities of state activities demanded the maturation of interprovincial forms of cooperation, and it has been only recently that nearly all the major interstices in the network of federal jurisdictions have been fully occupied. The result of this increase in government cooperation has been described by Professor Corry in these words: "Under the heat and pressure generated by social and economic change in the twen- tieth century, the distinct strata of the older federalism have begun to melt and flow into one another."[68]

Criticism and Assessment

Administrative federalism is not a complete theory of federal govern- ment; it says only that problems arising from the federal distribution of authority should be approached pragmatically and settled by co- operative action between governments. In this pragmatism, the con- cept is naturally subject to the fundamental objection of those who

*Professor Corry suggests that the change in umpires has come about partially because of the growing centralization of the economic system and the reluctance of provincial governments and business interests to challenge Parliament's authority through the courts. *Evolving Federalism,* p. 122.

favour solving social problems according to some preconceived master plan of government. Both the idealist and the rationalist are correct in asserting that administrative problem-solving approaches to federalism lack any long-term goals and that it is difficult to tell whether a state could achieve its objectives by this method. As criticism of this state is essentially a restatement of the classic dispute between the pragmatic conservatives on the one hand, and the liberal idealists on the other, little more can be said with profit on this topic within the compass of the present inquiry.

The substance of the criticism of Lamontagne's *Le fédéralisme canadien* was that the "new federalism" leads irretrievably to a centralized state, and must therefore be considered a frontal attack on *la survivance*. As the manifestations of administrative cooperation did not abate during the years that followed so French-Canadian criticisms did not abate either. The tenor of this was indicated by J. M. Leger in an article entitled "Le 'fédéralisme coopératif' ou le nouveau visage de la centralisation" and published in the influential newspaper *Le Devoir*.[69] In discussing one of the federal-provincial conferences of 1963, he argued that "despite the various modifications and adjustments, despite the alternative choice offered to Quebec in particular, no one can deny that this is another advance toward centralization and another violation of both the spirit and the letter of the B.N.A.A." He characterized the approach as a clever ploy designed to persuade the provincial governments to "lay down their powers one by one and on their own, and under the guise of cooperation and by means of general and in depth consultation, to link them with the federal government's insidious and patient efforts to achieve centralization."

A sturdy defence of what he called "cooperative federalism" was mounted in the early sixties by M. Jean-Luc Pépin, an articulate French-Canadian academic who later became a member of the cabinets of Lester B. Pearson and Pierre-Elliott Trudeau. Speaking of the necessity for pragmatism rather than legalism, Mr. Pépin preached the virtues of intergovernmental cooperation and of ethnic binationalism and supported moves toward tax and program decentralization. Essentially the statement[70] was represented as an idealized version of the constitutional attitudes and policies of the central government of the day, a program which owed its components to at least three different concepts of federalism as they have been defined in this study. Here, as in so many other cases, the term cooperative federalism was appropriated more for its favourable value connotations than for any descriptive precision it might convey.

Most commentaries in English have been directed at questions relating to improved realization of the idea in practice rather than at the basic concept of administrative federalism. Both in his official report, *Intergovernmental Liaison on Fiscal and Economic Matters,* and in his other writing, Professor R. M. Burns has been critical of the inadequacy of consultation between governments and especially of federal negligence in this respect. This negligence (and at times it appeared deliberate) was the continuing target for provincial government criticism for many years as Ottawa authorities publicly announced fresh sorties into provincial jurisdictions, and which were to be jointly financed, without first having engaged in "meaningful consultations" with the provinces. While Professor Burns seemed persuaded that this difficulty could be significantly avoided by establishment of a full-scale intergovernmental bureaucratic apparatus or secretariat, Ottawa's practice over a twenty year period suggests the problem may be inherent in the nature of intergovernmental cooperation organized and inspired by functional specialists. While also noting deficiencies in the theory and practice of federal consultation with the provinces, Professors Smiley and Carter have made numerous criticisms of conditional grant programs in terms of design, finance-sharing, audit procedures, continuity, and other administrative specifics. Nonetheless, "conditional grants have made a valuable contribution to the social and economic development of Canada," according to Professor Carter, while Professor Smiley concluded that "with all their defects, conditional grants have brought an invaluable element of adaptability to a federal structure which has proved remarkably resistant to change through constitutional amendments or evolving patterns of judicial review."[71] Writing during an earlier period, Professor R. MacGregor Dawson was doubtful that the provinces benefited financially from the programs. "They received more and better services, but they paid out more of their income in the process, and the majority of them could not afford assistance on those terms."[72] The dislike of conditional grants by the Royal Commission on Dominion-Provincial Relations as a corrosive of meaningful democracy at the provincial level was fundamental to the whole scheme of reforms which was proposed. Even Professor James Maxwell, the American student of Canadian public finance who favoured extending the shared grant programs, warned that "the government which controls the purse strings can use its power to get control of the activity. Some extension of federal authority is desirable but this might easily go too far."[73] That point was reached, he thought, when the central authority was tempted to embark on joint programs which ignored the basic federal features of the country.

Much of the controversy over certain aspects of administrative federalism and conditional grants was rooted in a provincial struggle for greater financial independence. Legally, the provinces could levy almost whatever level or type of taxation they needed to underwrite soaring social and local government expenditures but they perceived what they saw as prohibitive public attitudes. The intergovernmental fiscal disputes of the sixties have been characterized by D. G. Hartle, an economist, as an attempt by the provinces, and through them the municipalities as well, to obtain greater financial resources without being obliged to pay the political price of levying the necessary taxes themselves. His analysis continued:

> Having said all of this I think it must be recognized that the present system has not worked well in adjusting to a new allocation of revenues among the three levels of government. While I cannot prove it, I expect that, in the past, the federal government has proceeded with projects that, had there been a national referendum, would have been given lower priority by the majority than some of the projects that the municipalities shelved rather than finance through higher taxes. The majority would have been better off had the federal government transferred the funds to the municipalities (directly or indirectly) and allowed the project to proceed with an unchanged tax burden at the municipal level.[74]

While few have made much of it, federal-provincial financial transfers, whether conditional or unconditional, represent a theoretically massive violation of the traditional doctrine of public finance that the government imposing taxes should be capable of being held accountable for expenditure of the revenue.

Administrative federalism may also be criticized as inadequate because not enough has been achieved through its processes; jurisdictional lacunae are still evident. Most frequently deplored is the lack of effective authority in five areas: (1) environmental pollution control; (2) foreign economic investment; (3) regulation and pricing of agricultural products; (3) formal constitutional protection for the citizen's fundamental liberties; and (5) legislative ability to implement international treaties. That all these matters could be effectively dealt with through intergovernmental collaboration seems clear. That they have not been does not reflect on the efficiency or otherwise of administrative or cooperative federalism. What the situation does reflect is the absence of generalized political agreement on the primacy of these objectives as social goals. The extent to which federal arrangements should be structured to bring about particular political outputs is, of course, one of the basic debates about values inherent in every state.

A major question requiring attention is whether the manifestations of administrative and cooperative federalism can be kept under close public scrutiny. No unusual problem is raised under the parliamentary system so long as intergovernmental cooperation is restricted to matters under the exclusive control of one cabinet. An electorate that becomes incensed, for example, by the adoption of labour union statutes similar to those in another jurisdiction has electoral means for bringing its government to heel. But the ramifications of state activities today make accountability a difficult problem under the best of conditions. Accountability may become a near-impossibility (or at least an improbability) when bureaucrats extend their activities into a shadowy no-man's-land existing between two distinct jurisdictions and two sets of political masters. There can be little immediate harm in public servants negotiating with each other in terms of the common good and, as Professor Simeon says of the process, "there is little evidence that it has frustrated widespread public demands in recent years."[75] The danger is that such collaboration will so diffuse responsibility that political leaders cannot be brought to answer for the full range of their governments' activities. Increasingly that seems to be the situation engendered by the ever-multiplying series of intergovernmental arrangements. (The heads of government conferences are a little different. In these cases, virtual diplomatic negotiations are conducted in private and agreements are concluded having the status of international treaties not to be altered by, and usually not even submitted to, representative assemblies which in most cases are under the cabinets' firm control.) As in so many aspects of the complex modern society, the benefits of administrative federalism have in large part been purchased in disregard of the true value of the coin of the realm stamped "public accountability."

SUMMARY

The strict segregation of two sets of legislative competences in a federal state gives rise to difficulties which administrative federalism seeks to overcome by encouraging various governments to combine their authority or to harmonize their policies. The British North America Act made little provision for cooperation between provincial governments. Neither Parliament nor a legislature may delegate legislative competence to the other, although any legislative body may delegate regulatory authority to any governmental executive agent. The most obtrusive forms of administrative federalism are conditional grant programs, federal-provincial conferences, and the agreements respecting tax-rentals and tax-collection. In the absence of judicial interpretation adjusting the constitution to sociological change, some of the critical points of stress in the federal system were eased by the development of three devices: equalization grants, the tax rental agreements, and the dominion-provincial conference.

While federal-provincial cooperation takes place across a wide range of activities, most of it is concentrated in the fields of agriculture, health, welfare, labour, and natural resources. A few jointly-supported enterprises have been set up, but the largest amount of cooperation is effected by intergovernmental committees working informally in specified functional areas. Interprovincial cooperation, inhibited for a long time by the virtual isolation of the provinces, has not developed to the degree that interstate relations have in the American federation. Recently, the premiers have begun to meet annually, chiefly to exchange views informally and to prepare instructions for the frequent consultations of provincial ministers. Correlation of the administrative practices of all governments may take place to a significant but immeasurable degree as a result of the membership of senior public servants in national professional organizations.

Apart from one or two scholars, Canadians have devoted relatively little attention to the theoretical implications or critical examination of administrative federalism. Maurice Lamontagne proposed in his book, *Le fédéralisme canadien,* that the province of Quebec integrate itself into the "new federalism," but his plea was dismissed as another demand for a centralized state. Supporters of the Liberal and the New Democratic parties found much to commend in "cooperative federalism" but seldom defined it very precisely. The most serious criticism to be made of the concept is its inherent tendency to diffuse political responsibility.

Consideration of the Criteria

Administrative federalism seeks the strengthening of both orders of government to permit them to do through joint agreement or action that which neither one could achieve by itself. While the approach now numbers among its supporters some persons and groups previously identified with centralist attitudes, centralization is not necessarily the logical or practical outcome of this type of federalism. Greater cooperation between governments may well produce some further uniformities across the country, and, what appears to be most likely in the Canadian setting, such cooperation will lead to formulation of few government policies that are incompatible with those of other governments. Greater harmony between a federation's political leaders is not the same thing as centralization of political decision.

Because administrative federalism is the most pragmatic of all concepts of federalism, it is not easily measured against the theoretical criteria suggested earlier for this study. Where these criteria deal with problems which have not been dealt with in some definite fashion, little can be said about them. Administrative federalists seem sympathetic to bringing about the financial independence of each government by guaranteeing distribution of revenues levied through centralized tax collections. Some oversight of an "independent" government's policies is exercised through harmonizing the methods of executing those policies. This coordination may be effected through an office within the federal department, through an intergovernmental organization, or, more informally, through some national association tangentially concerned with the policy area.

The civil obligations and liberties of citizens in nine provinces could be rendered uniform by the joint agreement of their governments. Sec. 94 of the B.N.A. Act, providing for the codification of the common law, stands as one of the few constitutional encouragements to administrative federalism. It has had little effect and is probably a political dead letter. The ranks of the most active practitioners of cooperation between government have included the attorney-general, the minister of justice, and the legal scholars of their departments, but they declined to seek joint action in the civil liberties area. Their lack of action constitutes a decision in favour of the status quo, and differentiates them from proponents of the centralist concept. Administrative federalism does seek to bring about some general administrative standards in education, but it has avoided trying to suggest standards of quality and content. Its educational policy would also put this concept of federalism closer to the coordinate and compact theories than it does to the centralist concept. Most senior bureaucratic advocates of administrative federalism seem to have favoured joint government efforts to foster bilingualism; in this they are akin to proponents of the two nations concept, and are lacking sympathy with adherents of a strict compact conception of confederation.

The cooperative approach to federal problems was manifested in the proposed system of constitutional amendment which would require varying degrees of government collaboration for altering different groups of legislative competence. This "mixed list" proposal might well have been discussed as an aspect of administrative federalism but the subject is more appropriate to the next chapter in which is concentrated the discussions of federalism as a unified system of legally coordinate governments. The administrative concept is differentiated from the centralist theory chiefly by its acceptance of federalism as *une chose donnée* in Canadian life; it differs from the coordinate theory chiefly in its attempts to breach the legal bulkheads dividing the two compartments of jurisdiction.

CHAPTER

$$4$$

The Coordinate Concept

Federalism, according to the Diceyan tradition, means weak government, political conservatism, and, above all, a litigious polity. As A. V. Dicey put it, "federalism . . . means legalism—the predominance of the judiciary in the constitution—the prevalence of the spirit of legality among the people."[1] Judicial argument serves English Canadians as political thought, for precious little philosophy either preceded or attended the birth of confederation, and the evolution of the union inspired very little more speculation about the theories of government. "The closest we get to theory," said a leading social historian, "is the theory which comes out of the courts; extremely acute judicial reasoning, logic fine spun enough to delight any scholastic philosopher, and semimetaphysical distinctions of enormous subtlety."[2] It this be so, much of this type of political theory has been bequeathed to Canadians by Lords Watson, Haldane, Sankey, and Atkin, of the Judicial Committee of the Privy Council. Certainly it was chiefly to the law lords of Her Britannic Majesty that citizens of her North American Kingdom owed the concept of coordinate federalism.

Coordinate federalism corresponds closely to the classical form of federal government,[3] typified by Professor K. C. Wheare's definition: "a system of government [embodying] a division of powers between general and regional authorities, each of which, in its own sphere, is co-ordinate with the others and independent of them."[4] The concept is primarily legal in its inspiration. It accepts the idea that sovereign authority exists within a state, and that it can be divided between, and exercised by, national and regional governments. A fundamental premise holds that these governments are of the same order, equal in rank with each other, and similar in legal status within their constitutionally-determined orbits.

While constitutional usage grants coordinate rank to the governments of Canada, the British North America Act very clearly does not.[5] Not only were the provincial governments made inferior to the central regime, but the different provinces were given slightly varying spheres within which to exercise their authority. Despite these statutory provisions, the coordinate concept of federalism took root and came to be the doctrine of those who viewed the constitution in essentially legal terms. Thus, a leading constitutional history of the interwar period took as its base "the generally-accepted theory that Canada is a federation in which sovereign power is divided among co-ordinate governments, none of which are delegations and among which the provincial governments are not new creations but retain 'their independence and autonomy.' "[6]

Three manifestations of the coordinate concept will be examined in this chapter; the political, juristic, and constitutive. Illustrations of the concept will largely be drawn from the *Report of the Royal Commission on Dominion-Provincial Relations,*[7] from the work of the postwar constitutional conferences,[8] and from judicial decisions bearing on the distribution of legislative powers and the status of the various governments; the "opting out" arrangement of the sixties will also be examined. Denominating the juristic viewpoint a Canadian concept might be challenged on the ground that it arises almost exclusively from the decisions of the Judicial Committee of the Privy Council of the United Kingdom. Little doubt exists, however, that domestic arguments did influence these decisions, and that they were incorporated into the reasoning of Canadian courts.[9] An attempt to gauge the extent of this incorporation might be made through assessment of the recent decisions of the Supreme Court of Canada, which lost its "captive court" status in 1949 and became the final interpreter of the British North America Act and other constitutional statutes. Unfortunately, no clear picture emerges from the court's decisions since 1949; the evidence so far suggests that while the Canadian court is slowly moving away from some of the rigid attitudes associated with most of the Privy Council judgements, too few decisions have been made on questions of jurisdiction to give us much confidence about such observations.

THE SIROIS COMMISSION

Confederation underwent its greatest constitutional and economic strains during the nineteen-thirties, a decade in which the separate existence of whole provinces was called into question. These strains resulted from a world-wide economic depression that hit hardest at areas dependent on raw material exports, from the federal distribution of legislative responsibilities and taxing capacities, from the centralized aspects of the economy, and from the central government's reluctance or inability to use its monetary and tariff powers to soften the impact of the depression. So critical was the financial condition of some provinces, and so great were the regional economic disparities, that the federal government found it "expedient to provide for a re-examination of the economic and financial basis of Confederation and the distribution of legislative powers in the light of the economic and social developments of the last seventy years."[10]

Five commissioners were appointed to inquire into federal-provincial relations: N. W. Rowell, chief justice of Ontario; Thibaudeau Rinfret, justice of the Supreme Court of Canada; John W. Dafoe, Winnipeg newspaper editor; R. A. MacKay, Dalhousie University political scientist, and H. F. Angus, a political economist from the University of British Columbia. Both Chief Justice Rowell, who began the commission's inquiries as chairman, and Mr. Justice Rinfret were forced to resign from the commission by illness; Joseph Sirois, a constitutional law professor from Laval University, became chairman in succession to Chief Justice Rowell. The commissioners were men of unusual ability and independence of judgement. According to Professor J. R. Mallory, "the reason for this lay in the fact that, although royal commissions are usually appointed either to delay action indefinitely or to provide an acceptable innocuous solution for partisan ends, the problem faced by this particular Commission was one which the government was anxious to solve on a lasting basis."[11]

The commissioners were given a wide range of matters to investigate. They were instructed to make recommendations which, "subject to the retention of the distribution of legislative powers essential to a proper carrying out of the federal system in harmony with national needs and the promotion of national unity," would bring about a healthy balance between the financial resources and obligations of the various governments, and which would also "conduce to a more efficient, independent and economical discharge of governmental responsibilities in Canada."[12] The commission began work in 1937, conducted hearings in every governmental capital, digested ten thousand pages of evidence, instigated a wide range of socio-economic and political studies, and presented a three volume report in May 1940.

The commission reported that confederation had been conceived as a solution to pressing political and economic problems. "Politically, it was designed to establish a new nation to meet the changed conditions of British policies and brace the scattered provinces against possible American aggression." Union through a federal structure offered a way of achieving this external strength as well as a "plan whereby, through mutual concession, cultural and local loyalties could be preserved and reconciled with the political strength and solidarity of the whole."[13] Economically, according to the commission, confederation was expected to foster a diversified national economy which would leave the country less susceptible to the effects of American and British tariff changes. The financial arrangements were designed to give the central government enough strength to achieve the union's original economic and political objectives.

But since 1867, the commission observed, "there have been sweeping economic and social changes and no less important changes in opinion as to the appropriate functions of government."[14] These changes had produced serious imbalances within the federal system which required redressing. The commissioners set out to discover a solution that would be in harmony with the original pattern of Canadian federalism.[15] This original pattern was conceived to have within it large elements of provincial autonomy, which the commission was concerned to see protected and extended. The *Report* asserted that national unity and provincial autonomy should not be viewed as competitors for the citizen's allegiance. In Canada, "they are but two facets of the same thing—a sane federal system." Consequently, the commission sought to frame recommendations that would permit both national unity and provincial autonomy to flourish and to reinforce each other.[16]

The investigators did not feel free to inquire into such pressing problems as the cultural conflict, the plight of the municipalities, or aid to education. The commission's position, in short, was "that it was limited by its instructions to dealings with financial readjustments and to the functional rearrangements they would necessitate."[17]

Two possible methods of harmonizing financial resources and constitutional obligations were considered and dismissed by the *Report*. The first method involved the reallocation of functions between the two orders of government to match their taxing resources. This solution, the commission felt, would result in more centralism than either the commissioners wished or the public would accept. The second possible method, the reallocation of fiscal powers to put more money into provincial treasuries, could not be achieved on an equitable basis because of the great economic disparities between regions. The solution recommended by the investigators involved some slight rearrangement of functions, but its major feature was the centralization of tax levies in the federal government and the establishment of a scheme of guaranteed income for the provinces. The commission felt that such a solution would enable provincial governments to resolve most of their difficulties in their own separate ways.

The *Sirois Report* recommended that the federal government relieve the provinces of the entire weight of relief for the employable unemployed and their families, and assume the whole of the provincial debt. The provinces were to contribute funds equivalent to the revenue produced by the self-liquidating part of the debt, but the central régime would bear the whole cost of deadweight debt. Under the Sirois plan, the provinces were to withdraw from three major tax fields: corporations income, personal income, and estates. The provinces would also surrender all existing subsidies. Future provincial and municipal borrowing was to be either on the sole credit of the province, or on the credit of Canada subject to the prior approval of the finance commission which was proposed.

In lieu of these uncertain revenue sources which the provinces were to turn over to the central government, the provinces were to be assured that the Ottawa authorities "would recognize an obligation to respect the remaining revenue sources of the provinces." The federal government would also pay each province ten percent of the net income derived from mining, smelting, and refining of ores and oils within the province. Those provinces in need would be paid a National Adjustment Grant which would enable each province and its municipalities "to provide normal Canadian services with no more than normal Canadian taxation." The need of a province would be calculated by an independent finance commission according to a formula suggested by the Sirois commission. The original adjustment grants would be irreducible for five-year periods, at the end of which they would be reassessed. Provision would also be made for one-year grants recommended by the finance commission, to tide a province over temporary difficulty.[18] The royal commission felt that its financial proposals were, "in terms of the economic life of 1939, very similar to what the provisions of the British North America Act were in terms of the economic life of 1867."[19]

Fundamental to the commission's analysis was a belief that provincial independence was necessary to protect regional particularism, and that the local provision of health, education, and welfare services was more important to this autonomy than the regulatory aspects of government. The commission proposed a rule that provincial obligations be recognized as primary in health, education, and welfare matters; "Dominion functions should be deemed exceptions to the general rule of provincial responsibility."[20] Welfare responsibilities were to be given over to the federal government only in relation to unemployment and contributory old age pensions. In both cases, the *Sirois Report* made a point of illustrating the substantial disabilities of leaving these services as provincial obligations. The commission felt federal involvement in health matters should be strictly defined and limited to research, statistics, and leadership in the cooperative establishment of national standards in clearly technical areas. While the commission did approve central government grants for the universities, it insisted that education must remain a primary responsibility—and privilege—of the provincial administrations. "A free hand in something so important to the social and cultural life of the people seems to us to be vital to any provincial autonomy worthy of the name."[21]

Under a subheading, "Freedom of Provinces," the *Sirois Report* pointed out that no national control over provincial expenditure was contemplated in any area. Every province was to be quite free to improve its services by specially heavy taxation, or to neglect its services to obtain a lighter burden of taxation, or to develop some services above the Canadian average at the expense of others which would remain below that average. While the Sirois commission was persuaded of the need for "a generous provision for the education of the children of the nation," that provision must depend, "not on any arbitrary constitutional provision but on the persistent conviction of the mass of the people that they must be ready to deny themselves some of the good things of life in order to deal fairly by their children."[22] A similar attitude was struck with respect to the provision of health and welfare services. The commission felt its plan would put every provincial government in a position where it could discharge its obligations, but it was up to the provincial electorate to see that it did so. "No Provincial government," it pointed out, "will be free from the pressure of the opinion of its own people and if, when it applies for an increased adjustment on the basis of need, it has to produce figures which indicate that although it might, without specially heavy taxation, have provided better education but did not do so, it has, of course, to justify this to its own voters."[23]

While independent provincial governments were central to the commission's idea of confederation, those administrations must not be isolated from each other. "Co-operation between the autonomous governments of the federal system has today become imperative," the *Report* said.[24] To foster this cooperation and to permit future adjustment of the constitution to meet changing circumstances, new elements of flexibility should be introduced into the federal structure. The commissioners recommended the institution of an annual federal-provincial conference assisted by a permanent secretariat, regular conventions of labour legislation administrators and policy-makers, and the creation of a transport planning commission to deal with the competition between road and rail transportation and the divided authority over transport.[25] The commission also proposed that constitutional provision be made for a general power of delegation between the federal and provincial governments. The commission felt that any delegation should require the consent of all parties involved, that it could be for either a temporary or a permanent period, and that—depending upon the area involved—delegation could take place between the federal government and any one or more provinces.[26] The *Sirois Report* suggested that a scheme of delegated powers might be used, for example, to resolve the difficulties of regulating the marketing of natural products.[27]

The royal commission did not favour the method of "buying" intergovernmental cooperation through conditional grants-in-aid. The *Report* emphasized past dissatisfaction with the operation of such grants in Canada and expressed pessimism as to the likelihood of conditional grants ever becoming of general utility. The grants might be useful, and were recommended, for a very limited range of technically-definable subjects. But in general, "the experience with conditional grants leads us to doubt whether joint administration of activities by the Dominion and a province is ever a practical way of surmounting constitutional difficulties." Where legislative authority over a particular subject area was divided, the commissioners felt it desirable that these powers be pooled under the control of single government.[28]

The Royal Commission on Dominion-Provincial Relations exhibited a conservative attitude about the redistribution of service functions. Its approach was typified by the Report's comment about the burden of governmental health activities: "Mere importance of a service does not justify its assumption by the Dominion."[29] It is this last judgement, according to Professor D. V. Smiley, "which most sharply distinguishes the underlying philosophy of the commission from much of the more recent thinking about Canadian federalism and the directions that the Canadian federal system has taken."[30] In summing up its work, the Sirois commission said it did not consider "that its proposals are either centralizing or decentralizing in their combined effect but believes that they will conduce to the same balance between these two tendencies which is the essence of a genuine federal system."[31]

THE LEGAL VIEW OF FEDERALISM

The real intentions of the Fathers of Confederation may be forever in dispute, but little quarrel is possible about the legal intent of the British North America Act, 1867. Guidelines for the interpretation of that statute were laid down by the Judicial Committee of the Privy Council by a series of decisions during the last two decades of the nineteenth century. Three judgements in particular stand out.

In two decisions made in 1882, the *Mercer* case,[32] and *Hodge* v. *The Queen*,[33] the committee began to enunciate the doctrine that the provincial governments, when acting within their constitutional orbits, are fully as sovereign[34] as is the federal government when acting within its constitutional orbit. This doctrine was made explicit in 1892 in the *Maritime Bank* case,[35] which hinged on the right of New Brunswick's government to exercise an aspect of the royal prerogative. Counsel for the federal government argued that the provinces were subservient to the central régime and that they were not entitled to use the sovereign prerogative at all. The Judicial Committee's judgement rejected this argument. The B.N.A. Act had not severed the connection between the Crown and the provinces; "the relation between them is the same as that which subsists between the Crown and the Dominion in respect of the powers executive and legislative, public property and revenues, as are vested in them respectively."[36] During the decision, Lord Watson declared "The object of the Act was neither to weld the provinces into one, nor to subordinate provincial governments to a central authority, but to create a federal government in which they should all be represented, entrusted with the exclusive administration of affairs in which they had a common interest, each province retaining its independence and autonomy."[37]

From these judgements, and those following them, there developed the juristic view of confederation as a system of coordinate governments; neither Parliament nor the provincial legislature could be regarded as delegations of the imperial Parliament or of each other.[38] Each legislative body was to be considered supreme within its legal orbit. While for many years, the imperial tie effectively limited the sovereignty of the federal Parliament, the provincial legislature had a measure of constituent authority that was denied to Parliament. Under sec. 92.1 of the B.N.A. Act, the legislative assemblies were empowered to amend their provincial constitutions in any or all respects save only the office of the lieutenant-governor.

Executive and Judicial Aspects

The state's federal character extends to the executive power but not to the judicial branch of government to any appreciable extent. The B.N.A. Act carried over the executive authority existing in the colonies before 1867 and divided it between the federal and provincial governments in measure according to their legislative competence. To this existing statutory executive power, there were added certain prerogative powers for each order of government.[39] While the statutory provisions establishing the office of the lieutenant-governor makes him a federal officer for certain purposes, the Judicial Committee has ruled that "a Lieutenant-Governor, when appointed, is as much the representative of Her Majesty for all purposes of provincial government as the Governor-General himself is for all purposes of Dominion government."[40]

Traditionally it has been said that Canada has only a single system of courts with both the federal and provincial governments being involved in their organization and maintenance. A typical view, that expressed by W. J. Wagner, has held that "the whole judicial system of the Dominion is one integrated body of courts which appears still stronger in relief because of the fact that all judicial appointments, with the exception of some inferior courts, are made by the Chief Executive of Canada."[41] Such statements have depended too much on the fact of the Supreme Court of Canada as the country's ultimate appeal court and on the competence of all major courts (except for the new Federal Court, formerly the Exchequer Court) to interpret both provincial and federal legislation. The unifying effects of the appellate jurisdiction have been much overrated by non-legal observers and central appointment of judges means little in terms of central control over subsequent judicial behaviour and interpretation—especially in the light of the Canadian habit of appointing judges from the bar of the province in which they will sit. Far more significant for the federal situation than the judge's enjoyment of the traditional type of independence from the executive is his almost complete reliance on provincially-directed officers both for prosecution of cases in his court and execution of his judgements. In his recent study, "The Courts and the Governmental Process in Canada," Professor G. Campbell Sharman has pointed out that "Even though criminal law is a national responsibility in terms of legislative inputs, this is moderated by the fact that enforcement depends not only on the discretion of local police but also on the overall policy directives of the provincial attorney-general who has a considerable discretion over the rigour with which sections of the Criminal Code are enforced."[42] The variations in procedure are considerable, as Professor Sharman's study has demonstrated, and there is even the anomalous situation that in certain circumstances the federal attorney-general may take responsibility for some prosecutions in provincial courts (for example, in narcotics cases) but that in other prosecutions he may himself be subject to the overriding policy of the provincial attorney-general. The general consequence has been that executive inputs reflecting the diverse policy preferences of provincial and regional institutions permeate the handling of a large majority of public law cases.

Legislative inputs into the court systems may be even more diversified and significant than the executive factors. Provincial legislative authority over matters like highway traffic and alcoholic consumption has led to the definition of a whole series of provincial offences (and penalties) difficult if not impossible for the layman to differentiate from federal criminal law. Municipal councils also have considerable legislative authority in important areas of civil behaviour. At least ten divergent combinations of legislative inputs are fed into Canada's various courts such that the sum total of "law" interpreted and applied in any one province is markedly different from that in another. The fate of the offender (or even the definition of him as an offender) very much depends on what province he finds himself in. So intimate is the interweaving of the judicial with other aspects of government that the Canadian courts have been almost as fully exposed to federalizing influences as have the other institutions of government. While important, the consequences have not been much explored or understood outside the legal profession.

The Supreme Court of Canada was authorized to render advisory opinions as to the constitutionality or interpretation of the statutes and powers of the provincial governments as well as of the federal government.[43] It was contended in 1912 that the governor in council was not empowered to seek a reference on a provincial matter without the consent of the provinces, but the Judicial Committee ruled that such action was not barred by the B.N.A. Act, and drew on British practice to validate the legislation.[44] Provincial statutes make similar provision for putting references to the provincial courts.

The reference procedure promotes quick settlement of legal aspects of important constitutional disputes and is more efficient than the cumbrous American procedure of inventing test cases. While recognizing the theoretical hazards of "politicizing" the courts, most writers such as Professor G. Rubin[45] approve of the reference device. While it would be inappropriate here to question the disturbance of executive-judicial relationships which the procedure involves, we should note its consequences for intergovernmental relations and federalism generally. This power permits governments to require judges long trained in adjudicating the precise application of particular law to specific, detailed circumstances to abandon those practices and to consider whole series of hypothetical questions of constitutional law and philosophy. The government totally controls access to the courts on the general questions put and necessarily receives general answers in response. The result, as Professor Sharman put it, is the "destruction of the traditional pattern of constitutional clarification whereby a series of specific decisions outlines a general constitutional principle."[46] Where real cases find judges applying established principles of scepticism and parsimony to governments' claims to authority (with healthy consequences for boundary maintenance in a federal system), reference cases have permitted none of this because of their necessary generality. The authority which reference decisions have been accorded in Canada has also strengthened governments' preference for a device which may well be responsible for the Canadian paucity of individual challenges to government on constitutional grounds. Two recent references, the *Offshore Minerals* case and the *Chicken and*

Egg,[47] are examples of the courts being manipulated by the executive to effect settlement of major political disputes between governments.

Distribution of Legislative Powers

As important as are the judicial and executive aspects, the central problem of federal government would appear to be the distribution of legislative competences. John A. Macdonald had declared in 1865 that in the distribution of powers proposed by the Quebec Resolutions, "we have avoided all conflict of jurisdiction and authority,"[48] but since 1867 judges have spent many hours seeking the appropriate interpretation of the B.N.A. Act. The jurists were, however, spared one problem with the act; no legislative powers were reserved to the people as in the United States. As Earl Loreburn observed in the *Reference* case, "under this organic instrument the powers distributed between the Dominion on the one hand and the provinces on the other hand cover the whole area of self-government within the whole area of Canada."[49]

In the main, the distribution of legislative powers was accomplished by secs. 91-95 of the B.N.A. Act. The three concurrent powers need little discussion. Section 94A provides that provincial legislation in respect of old age pensions shall prevail over any similar but conflicting federal statutes. Section 95 provides for joint authority over agriculture and immigration and gives supremacy in these fields to the federal legislation. Subject to provision for some minority rights, exclusive jurisdiction over education is assigned to the provincial legislature by sec. 93. Section 109 gives to the provinces the ownership and management of natural resources within their borders, and sec. 132 empowers the federal government to make laws necessary for the execution of Canada's international obligations incurred under British Empire treaties.

The federal government is empowered, by sec. 91, "to make Laws for the Peace, Order and good Government of Canada, in relation to all Matters not coming within the Classes of Subjects by this Act assigned exclusively to the Legislatures of the Provinces; and for greater Certainty," says the act, "but not so as to restrict the Generality of the foregoing Terms of this Section, it is hereby declared that (notwithstanding anything in this Act) the exclusive Legislative Authority of the Parliament of Canada extends to all Matters coming within the Classes of Subjects next herein-after enumerated." A list of thirty-one subjects follows. Section 91 concludes by establishing a superior position for these enumerated subjects over the sixteen subjects which sec. 92 assigns exclusively to the provincial legislatures. Among these exclusive provincial powers is the right to regulate property and civil rights within the province.

The courts have discovered an inherent conflict between the provincial property and civil rights clause and the federal government's general grant of power to make laws for the peace, order, and good government of the country. In 1882, the Judicial Committee settled a case involving the validity of a federal prohibition law in favour of Parliament's authority. The committee observed during its judgement[50] that "few, if any, laws could be made by Parliament for the peace, order, and good government of Canada which did not in some incidental way affect property and civil rights." It decided that the B.N.A. Act did not exclude Parliament from exercising its general power just because provincial powers might be incidentally infringed. What should be decisive, the board said, was the chief character of the legislation and not its incidental effects. This method of interpretation was effectively repudiated by a series of decisions which enlarged the provincial jurisdiction at the expense of the national; among the leading cases are the *Local Prohibition* decision of 1896, and the *Snider* case of 1925.[51]

The cases enlarging provincial jurisdiction resulted in the adoption of an agreed set of principles for the interpretation of the distribution of powers by the B.N.A. Act. These principles divided the federal area of jurisdiction into two sections, the general grant of power and the enumerated subjects. The enumerated federal powers were generally held to prevail over the provincial subjects enumerated in sec. 92. But to give meaning to the *exclusive* grant of powers to the provinces, matters falling under sec. 92 were held to prevail over the general federal power. The general grant of power—the peace, order, and good government clause—had been thought to be the residuary clause of the constitution. It has, however, been reduced to virtual impotence except in time of war, pestilence, or famine, although some observers detect some interest in revivifying the clause as a result of some recent Supreme Court decisions.[52]

The reduction of the general residuary clause was accomplished as a result of attempts by the Privy Council to give meaning to the *exclusive* grant of authority to the provinces under sec. 92. The exclusive grant of authority included property and civil rights within the province, a subject that received a very general interpretation at the hands of Lord Watson in the leading cases of the eighteen-nineties.[53] Coincidentally, the Judicial Committee also gave a very restrictive reading to the federal government's supposed authority to regulate trade and commerce. The outcome was, as Professor R. MacG. Dawson put it, that "residual power had thus slipped away from the Dominion and reappeared in a somewhat altered guise in Section 92; property and civil rights had become, indeed, the true residual clause."[54]

Trade and Taxes

A substantial portion of the judicial doctrine regarding trade and commerce regulation was developed, it would seem, as an incidental result of the Judicial Committee's interpretation of the distribution of legislative powers.[55] In a decision in 1916, the board ruled that companies with provincial charters were not prohibited from doing business in other provinces so long as they were able to secure local consent. This judgement[56] cleared the way for a number of national companies to avoid Parliament's jurisdiction by seeking provincial rather than federal charters.

The central government sought, in 1919, to regulate the postwar fluctuation of supplies and prices by conferring appropriate authority on a board of commerce. "It was in connection with this board that the courts, perhaps for the first time," says Professor Mallory, "were confronted with the problem of fitting the positive state into the federal categories of the Canadian constitution."[57] The statute was referred for an opinion to the Supreme Court of Canada in 1920. The court split 3-3 on the constitutionality of the act, and its opinion went to the Judicial Committee. Lord Haldane delivered the opinion of the board[58] that the statute was *ultra vires*. The reasons given ranged from the undesirability of the legislation, to the impossibility of subsuming it under either the trade and commerce or the general power, and to the likelihood that the legislation trenched illegally on provincial jurisdictions. In *Toronto General Electric Commissioners* v. *Snider*,[59] decided in 1925, Lord Haldane found that the Lemieux Act, which had been in force for eighteen years, was *ultra vires* the federal power. Parliament was thereby restricted to a very narrow range of control over labour disputes. In 1937, another opinion by the Judicial Committee upset Parliament's attempt to establish a scheme to regulate the marketing of natural products,[60] even though the federal act had been supported by all the provincial governments. A general rule deduced from this line of judgements is that the federal authority over trade and commerce does not include the regulation of any individual business (such as insurance or margarine) in which citizens could engage under provincial authority. "It would appear," says Dean Scott, "that the only particular forms of trade and commerce which Ottawa may directly control, regardless of their magnitude, are the ones that can be brought within specific federal powers, such as banks and inter-provincial communications."[61]

To what degree the present Supreme Court of Canada would support this division of legislative jurisdiction over trade and commerce is difficult to say. The court's decision in the *Nova Scotia Delegation* reference in 1951[62] seemed to support the Judicial Committee's view that to permit delegation between legislative bodies would be to imply the inferiority of one to the other. This decision was partially overcome by the *Willis* case which, in 1952, said that the various federal and provincial governments could delegate authority to executive creatures of each other.[63] More significant in terms of suggesting a rejection of the Judicial Committee's attitudes was the Supreme Court's ruling in the same year which held that a purely Canadian treaty regulating aeronautics in Canada fell within the peace, order, and good government power.[64] Quoting Viscount Dunedin in the *Radio* case, Chief Justice Rinfret observed that although the Convention might not be looked upon as a treaty under sec. 132 of the B.N.A. Act, "it comes to the same thing." He therefore found provincial legislation invading the field to be *ultra vires* the Manitoba legislature. The Supreme Court has since shown some signs of following the trend of American decisions in accepting the notion that trade within a province may enter into a current or flow of interprovincial trade. The Judicial Committee had been reluctant to find that Parliament possessed much authority over interprovincial trade, but recent Canadian judgements have shown more willingness to do so;[65] a good example is the 1971 *Chicken and Egg* case cited earlier.

The federal government has virtually unlimited authority to levy taxes of any kind under sec. 91.3 while the authority of the provinces is restricted both as to kind and area. Both orders of government may, however, levy direct taxes. The reconciliation of this grant of concurrent authority resulted in the withdrawal from the federal government of any authority to impose direct taxation within a province to raise revenue for a provincial purpose.[66] There is no constitutional objection to double taxation. "Both income taxes may co-exist and be enforced without clashing," said Lord Macmillan in 1937. "The Dominion reaps part of the field of the Manitoba citizen's income. The Province reaps another part of it."[67] Professor F. R. Scott has suggested that the 1932 decision, *In re Silver Bros.,*[68] establishes priority for federal claims if they conflict with provincial claims, but this decision rested on the federal government's exclusive authority over bankruptcy matters, which enabled it to oust the province in favour of the federal treasury. In his text, (then) Professor Laskin said that the question of priority had not yet been settled, but thought a decision would probably go in favour of the federal government in virtue of the paramountcy doctrine.[69]

It is clear, however, observes Professor Scott, "that the present constitution does not give Ottawa the legal power to implement a policy that controls provincial taxing powers, except with provincial consent."[70] It was also clear that the federal-provincial tax rental agreements were not enforceable in law.[71] A province could even pass valid legislation in derogation of the agreements and the hapless citizen caught by a provincial taxing statute which violated the intergovernmental agreement had no recourse but to pay the provincial levy.[72] Although the provincial governments are supposed to be barred from the exercise of indirect taxation,* they have levied a large number of what seems to the layman to be indirect taxes—gasoline, general sales, and tobacco taxes—which have been sustained by the highest courts.†

Education and Language

"The section of the British North America Act dealing with education has . . . achieved a certain clearness of meaning out of many judicial battles," according to Professor W. P. M. Kennedy.[73] Section 93 gives the provincial legislatures exclusive jurisdiction over education, subject to four provisions. One provision prohibits legislatures from doing anything prejudicial to the rights or privileges which any class of persons had in educational matters at confederation. Another provision grants the right of an appeal to the governor in council from any provincial action affecting the rights or privileges of a minority in relation to education. These are the chief provisions with which the courts have had occasion to deal.[74]

One of the most important decisions was made in 1892 in the case of *City of Winnipeg* v. *Barrett*.[75] Two years previously, Manitoba had established a system of nonsectarian schools supported by public funds; separate school supporters were compelled to contribute to the general school rate. The Judicial Committee held that the provincial act did not prejudicially affect the Roman Catholic privileges as they had existed at union—the denomination was still free to support and utilize its own church schools. Following this decision, the Roman Catholic minority appealed to the governor in council under the provisions of sec. 93. The right to appeal was challenged in *Brophy* v.

---

*Since the *Lambe* judgement in 1887, the courts have traditionally tried to apply the classic, but sometimes confusing, definitions given by John Stuart Mill: "Taxes are either direct or indirect. A direct tax is one which is demanded from the very persons who it is intended or desired should pay it. Indirect taxes are those which are demanded from one person in the expectation and intention that he shall indemnify himself at the expense of another; such are the excise or customs." Quoted by Laskin, *Constitutional Law*, p. 661.

†"Under [Mill's] definition, a sales tax or excise tax in its usual form as a levy imposed upon the vendor of commodities would be an indirect tax and thus invalid. By the early nineteen twenties, the provinces were urgently in need of revenues from this general field of taxation, and devised the expedient (first with gasoline taxes) or imposing the taxes technically upon the consumer, the vendor being made the agent of the province for purposes of collection." John F. Due, "The Cairns Decision," *Canadian Tax Journal*, 9 (1961): 364. The decisive cases involving the vendor-collecting agent device were *Attorney-General of British Columbia* v. *Kingcombe Navigation Co. Ltd.,* [1934] A.C. 45; *Atlantic Smoke Shops Ltd.* v. *Conlon*, [1943] A.C. 550; and *Cairns Construction Ltd.* v. *Government of Saskatchewan*, [1960] 24 D.L.R. 2d. 1.

Attorney-General for Manitoba,[76] chiefly on the ground that permitting such appeals impaired the legislative sovereignty of the government of Manitoba.[77] In its decision, rendered in 1895, the Judicial Committee upheld the right of appeal to the governor in council. The dispute then passed from the legal to the political realm under provision (4) of sec. 93. Under that provision, Parliament was authorized to enact remedial school legislation, if an appeal to the governor in council had been made, and if the governor in council had recommended action that the provincial government refused to execute. The Manitoba Roman Catholics appealed to the governor in council, the Manitoba legislature refused to acquiesce in the suggested change, and pressure was brought to bear on the federal cabinet to have Parliament override the provincial legislation. The Conservative cabinet temporized as long as it could but finally introduced a remedial bill; its enactment was frustrated by a Liberal filibuster. In the general election which followed, the Manitoba schools question was one of the major issues contributing to the Conservatives' defeat.

Concentration on the words of the statute and cases interpreting it could give the unwary a misleading impression; the provisions of sec. 93 have not precluded the federal government from extensive involvement in the field of education as the discussion of education financing demonstrated in an earlier chapter. As Professor Smiley puts it, constitutional flexibility "manifests itself in its most developed form in respect to educational activities in Canada."[78] The major instrument used has not been the law, but the virtually unfettered spending power of the central government in company with a series of fine distinctions between what has been called the formal, classroom education of children (which is still acknowledged to be exclusively provincial) on the one hand, and, on the other, culture, manpower retraining for people in the labour force, university research, linguistic training, and publication of knowledge. These distinctions have been protested at various times since the Second World War by the Quebec government but constitutional challenges have never been made in the courts in this area.

The language to be used in schools has been put to the legal test. While sec. 133 provides that either French or English may be used in the Parliament of Canada or in the Quebec legislature, that records are to be kept in both languages, and that either may be used in Quebec courts, it says nothing about schools. The question came up in some of the sec. 93 cases. Most important of these was *Trustees of the Roman Catholic Schools* v. *Mackell,*[79] which the Judicial Committee decided in 1917. The question turned on whether a regulation prohibiting the use of French as a language of school instruction offended against the first provision of sec. 93. It was decided that the separate school trustees were entitled to decide the "kind" of school, but that "kind" related to the grade or character of the school and not to the language of instruction. The Judicial Committee pointed out that sec. 133 contained the only reference in the B.N.A. Act to language and that it said nothing about education. Sec. 133 has never been fully tested by the courts. The most significant activity in this area involved the central government's *Official Languages Act* of 1968 which extended the use of the French language within federal administrative jurisdictions and sought to encourage provincial governments to act similarly. Western provinces asked Ottawa to submit the act to the Supreme Court for an opinion as to its constitutionality. The federal government refused to do so and a private individual, J. J. Thorson, a former judge of what was the Exchequer Court of Canada, sought to challenge the legislation. His effort failed, however, for lack of standing in the case, and the legal support for extensive use of both languages in Canada rests on a combination of sec. 133, the Official Languages Act, and the limited provisions of Ontario and New Brunswick statutes.

Civil Liberties

No high authority puts civil liberties, to any measurable degree, beyond the legal reach of Parliament and the provincial legislatures.[80] The constitutional issues in civil liberties legislation are largely restricted to the question of proper competence under the distribution of powers made by the B.N.A. Act. The question of which order of government has principal jurisdiction is complicated by two factors. The first source of confusion is sec. 92.13 which gives the legislatures exclusive jurisdiction over property and civil rights in the province. The second source of confusion lies in a Canadian penchant for making minority rights the primary connotation of civil rights. To avoid this latter type of confusion, Professor Scott employs "civil liberties" and "fundamental freedoms" when dealing with "the basic freedoms of religion, of speech, or the press, and so on."[81]

The Judicial Committee of the Privy Council was never faced with any issue directly related to the fundamental liberties, and there is little in its decisions to say what these liberties are, or to permit definite assignment of exclusive legislative jurisdiction in the matter. Some Canadian judgements could be interpreted as meaning that sec. 92.13 comprehends civil liberties, a view which would make the provinces the chief guardians of the traditional Anglo-Saxon freedoms. Some aspects of civil liberties undoubtedly do fall within the provinces' exclusive jurisdiction if one includes in the term matters such as defamation, voting rights in provincial elections, the status of married women, and so on. One view holds that the federal government and the common law must be considered the guardians of civil liberties, an opinion that may be supported by recent judgements of the Supreme Court of Canada.

Judicial resolution of the jurisdictional problem has been obstructed by the difficulty of defining what is covered by the provincial authority over property and civil rights. Conflict arises from the intermeshing of this exclusive provincial power under sec. 92.13 with Parliament's peace, order, and good government power and with federal regulation of all criminal matters. A postwar freedom of religion case illustrates the problem. In *Saumur* v. *City of Quebec,*[82] the Supreme Court of Canada reversed a Quebec judgement which limited the legal right of religious dissenters to distribute pamphlets defaming the Roman Catholic Church. The high court decision to allow the appeal by Saumur (*i.e.,* sanctioned his pamphlet distribution) was supported by a five to four majority. Three of the nine judges, including Chief Justice Thibaudeau Rinfret, urged that freedom of religion and speech fell within the provincial powers. Six judges decided that the provinces did not have *exclusive* jurisdiction. Of these six judges, two felt that the federal government had exclusive competence, two suggested that both Parliament and legislature might act in the field, and two others suggested that perhaps neither Parliament nor legislature had jurisdiction to restrict civil liberties. As Professor Laskin commented, "the *Saumur* case makes it impossible to give a definite answer to the question . . . whether civil liberties are matters within federal or provincial power."[83]

Two important judgements following the *Saumur* case turned on civil liberties and the interpretation of the B.N.A. Act, namely the *Birks* and the *Padlock Act* cases. The *Birks* case[84] concerned a Montreal city bylaw, passed under a provincial statute, which required storekeepers to close on six Roman Catholic holy days. A unanimous judgement of the Supreme Court of Canada in 1955 reversed the Quebec Supreme Court decision, held that religious observance was the pith and substance of the law, and laid down the rule that laws affecting religious observance fall under the federal government's exclusive competence as an aspect of criminal law. The *Padlock Act* case[85] turned on a notorious provincial statute passed in 1937 which gave the Quebec attorney-general virtual *carte blanche* to padlock and forbid the utilization of any premises which he suspected had been used to further the preaching or teaching of communist or bolshevik propaganda. The Supreme Court of Canada held in 1957 that these matters fells under the exclusive competence of the federal government which alone could give a criminal character to actions of the type prohibited by the Quebec statute.

Occasionally, the courts have sought to resist the doctrine of legislative supremacy by resort to arguments asserting a right of the citizens to judicial review of legislative acts. In 1949, for example,

Mr. Justice O'Halloran wrote in a decision that Parliament must respect judicial decisions if the courts were to have any meaning beyond that of an instrument to serve the wishes of a dominant political party. He said that the preamble to the B.N.A. Act had incorporated into the Canadian constitution certain written aspects of the British constitution such as Magna Carta, the Petition of Right, and the Bill of Rights. On this basis, he decided that a federal amendment to the criminal code was "contrary to the Canadian Constitution and beyond the competence of Parliament or any provincial Legislature to enact so long as our Constitution remains in its present form of a constitutional democracy."[86] Mr. Justice Abbott, in the *Padlock Act* case, invoked the necessity of free debate in political matters as a ground for holding the provincial legislation *ultra vires*. He went on to declare that "the Canadian constitution being declared to be similar in principle to that of the United Kingdom, I am also of the opinion that as our constitutional Act now stands, Parliament itself could not abrogate this right of discussion and debate."[87]

During the sixties, fierce debates were waged about the better protection of fundamental liberties. Both orders of government had enacted "bills of rights" (whose effects were, of course, limited to the jurisdictions of the respective legislatures), and virtually all participants began with the assumption that jurisdiction was effectively divided between the federal and provincial governments. Critics were persuaded that these measures were inadequate because they had not been "entrenched," *i.e.,* incorporated into the B.N.A. Act, and thus were theoretically vulnerable to future amendments. A more important cause for criticism was the perceived reluctance of judges to accord much substance to the federal protective statute. Defenders of such parliamentary approaches to the protection of liberty could point to the political unlikelihood of legislative amendments openly reducing such liberties, to the considerable effect being given to the anti-discrimination statutes of the provinces, and, to the prematurity of judgements being made about the federal bill, the latter faith perhaps being evenually vindicated by the *Drybones* decision of 1970.[88]

Prime Minister Pierre-Elliott Trudeau had long been one of those devoted to "entrenchment" of a bill of rights in a new constitution. He proposed such a bill as the Canadian Charter of Human Rights in 1968 and made it a major federal government agenda item in the constitutional discussions of that time. The Charter encountered difficulties from the beginning, among other reasons because it would have extended the language rights of French speakers and imposed them on some reluctant provinces. Eventually the proposals emerged in considerably weakened form as part of a "consensus on human rights" included in the Victoria Charter of 1971; the proposals sank without immediate trace when the Charter as a whole foundered.[89] The result was to leave the legal situation on human rights unchanged and still divided between the areas of provincial jurisdiction and those of the federal government. As much of the federal authority here seems to depend on the criminal law power, Ottawa's real ability to extend human rights protection beyond the present situation is probably seriously constricted by the provinces' influence over the judicial process as a whole.

Some Unsettled Questions

Neither the extent of governmental spending powers nor the extra-provincial activities of local government has received very much attention from the courts. While it cannot be doubted that neither Parliament nor a legislative assembly can invade another's field of exclusive legislative jurisdiction, the validity of spending for purposes beyond a government's legislative competence has not been determined. The only restriction that the courts have put on the spending power is that appropriating statutes must not involve regulatory legislation that is *ultra vires* in its pith and substance. Thus, the government of Quebec, during the late nineteenth century, was able to make a gift of 10,000 dollars to the University of Toronto,[90] and has continued since then to contribute to the upkeep of other educational institutions outside the province. The federal government has also participated heavily in financing activities which are clearly under the exclusive legislative authority of the provinces. Professor Corry has suggested that the courts have not been asked to appraise this spending power because it is in nobody's interest to do so (save the tax-payer?) and too many organizations and politicians would be seriously embarrassed by a "wrong" decision in the courts.[91]

DISALLOWANCE AND RESERVATION

Disallowance and reservation developed as devices of imperial control over distant, self-governing colonies whose eccentricities might occasionally bring them into conflict with imperial policy or cause them to commit manifest injustices. The control was exercised by the executive. The governor could, if his discretion or instructions so directed, refuse to assent to colonial legislative measures and send them home for the imperial authorities to enact into law or abandon to the dustbin. This was the power of reservation. If, on the other hand, the governor had assented to legislation that the imperial authorities thought unwise or contrary to public policy, the Queen in council could disallow the statute and thereby nullify it. These two devices had been in use in British North America prior to 1867, and they were continued in force after 1867 by the B.N.A. Act. So far as the national government is concerned, the imperial powers were used but once—in 1873—and they fell into disuse after 1878.[92]

The B.N.A. Act continued the disallowance and reservation powers in effect for the provincial legislatures, but substituted the federal authorities for the imperial authorities.[93] The power thus given to the central government is entirely negative in character; it conveys no right to Parliament to enact measures replacing those that have been vetoed. The Fathers of Confederation adopted the device deliberately to prevent the provincial governments from pursuing policies contrary to those of the federal cabinet, and to prevent injustices which might arise through the limitations of judicial review in parliamentary systems.[94]

The policy grounds on which provincial legislation was to be reserved or disallowed were laid down in 1869 by the minister of justice, Sir John A. Macdonald. Objectionable legislation were those acts or bills which were seen: "1. As being altogether illegal or unconstitutional; 2. As illegal or unconstitutional in part; 3. In cases of concurrent jurisdiction, as clashing with the legislation of the general parliament; 4. As affecting the interests of the Dominion generally."[95] By "illegal," Macdonald apparently meant *ultra vires* the legislature's legal authority, and by "unconstitutional," he meant contrary to British parliamentary practice in that it was unjust or violated natural right.[96] Professor Mallory suggests that "in the context of the time, that meant the kind of 'unsound' or 'unreasonable' legislation which affected the rights of contract or vested rights generally," and says that the uses to which disallowance was put supports this opinion.[97]

Since the earliest days of confederation, judicial interpreters of the B.N.A. Act have said of disallowance that "in point of law the authority is unrestricted even with respect to statutes over which the provincial legislatures have complete jurisdiction."[98] Any doubts which might have existed with respect either to disallowance or reservation were ended by the Supreme Court in 1938. In the *Reference re Disallowance and Reservation,* the court found that the legal basis for disallowance rested upon the application of sec. 90 to sec. 56 of the B.N.A. Act. Reading these sections of the B.N.A. Act together produced this statutory effect, according to the court:

Where the Lieutenant-Governor of the Province assents to a Bill in the Governor General's Name, he shall by the first convenient Opportunity send an authentic Copy of the Act to the Governor General, and if the Governor General in Council within One Year after Receipt thereof by the Governor General thinks fit to disallow the Act, such disallowance (with a Certificate of the Governor General of the Day on which the Act was received by him) being signified by the Lieutenant-Governor of the Province, by Speech or Message to the House, or, if more than one, to each of the Houses of the Legislature, or by Proclamation, shall annul the Act from and after the Day of such Signification.[99]

Reservation was similarly based upon the application of sec. 90 to sec. 57.

The disallowance reference was made after the Social Credit government of Alberta passed legislation purporting to affect currency, banking and financial, and other business matters within the province. The federal government disallowed the Alberta statutes, the provincial government asserted that the disallowance power did not exist, and the Supreme Court was asked to give an advisory opinion on both disallowance and reservation. The court was asked four questions: (1) whether the governor in council still had the power to disallow provincial statutes; (2) if so, was that power subject to limitations of any kind; (3) whether the lieutenant-governor still had the legal right to reserve the royal assent to provincial bills; and (4) if the right of reservation existed, was it subject to any kind of limitations. The court was to specify the type of limitations, if any existed.

The court agreed that both the powers of disallowance and reservation continued to exist. Disallowance was subject only to the limitation that an act must be vetoed within one year of receipt of the statute by the governor general. The chief justice, Sir Lyman Duff, observed that neither the imperial Parliament nor the federal Parliament had made the powers subject to any enactment, and they continued to subsist. "It is indisputable," said Chief Justice Duff, "that in point of law the authority is unrestricted."[100] Mr. Justice Kerwin wrote in his opinion on the disallowance reference that "the circumstances under which the powers referred to may be exercised are matters upon which this Court is not constitutionally empowered to express an opinion." Those circumstances were wholly matters for political determination by the governor general's advisors.[101]

Legally, the federal government's power to intervene directly in provincial affairs remains as strong and unimpaired as it ever was. Politically, however, the federal government has found it wise to let the power rest in abeyance.[102] In 1960, the prime minister was asked to disallow a Newfoundland statute outlawing a union local which was at odds with the provincial government. In refusing to veto the act, which was *intra vires* the legislature, Prime Minister Diefenbaker observed that "disallowance is an extraordinary, sweeping and even arbitrary power under which the Federal Government can set itself up as judge and jury on provincial legislation." He felt that it was no longer "a proper and reasonable attitude" for a central government to take.[103] During the constitutional negotiations of 1968-71, abolition of the central veto powers seemed to have been taken for granted by some delegates but no public undertaking was given on this point.[104]

In 1961, Prime Minister Diefenbaker was embarrassed to learn that one of his appointees, Lieutenant-Governor F. L. Bastedo of Saskatchewan, had reserved assent to an important measure passed by the Saskatchewan legislature. The reservation was made wholly on the lieutenant-governor's own initiative and quite without instruction from, or warning to, the governor in council. Upon the advice of cabinet, the governor general promptly gave the Saskatchewan bill the assent which the lieutenant-governor had withheld.[105]

A PROCEDURE FOR CONSTITUTIONAL AMENDMENT

Although the British North America Act has been the legal foundation of confederation for almost a century, the statute remains today without provision whereby Canadians may readjust their federal division of legislative responsibilities. Amendment of the constitutive statute did not trouble the Fathers of Confederation. The B.N.A. Act was enacted as a British bill and it could easily be amended by another British bill. This arrangement meant the federal constitution could be changed with the utmost simplicity of procedure, without being easily subject to the sudden passions of local democratic pressures. Any changes that were required in the act were made by the United Kingdom Parliament, acting, in effect, as the voluntary agent of the Canadian federal government. The arrangement has continued in force with respect to the legislative distribution up to the present day. Accounts of various Canadian attempts to work out a method of transferring the amending power to Canada has been set forth and the events analyzed in three excellent works, Paul Gérin-Lajoie's *Constitutional Amendment in Canada*,[106] W. S. Livingston's *Federalism and Constitutional Change*,[107] and R. E. B. Simeon's *Federal-Provincial Diplomacy*. Consequently, this study will present only a brief sketch of events leading up to the present, and then pass on to consider the most recent designs for transferring the amending power from Britain to Canada. Nearly all these designs have embodied the concept of coordinate federalism.

A special committee of the House of Commons was established in 1935 to consider ways of amending the B.N.A. Act in Canada. The committee took evidence from expert witnesses,[108] and soon exposed the basic difficulty that has delayed agreement on an amending procedure ever since 1935. The trouble arises from the desire to keep the amending procedure rigid enough to give adequate protection to minorities and regional particularisms, but flexible enough to permit adjusting the constitutional document to cope with basic social and economic changes. The parliamentary committee pointed out some of these difficulties and turned its task over to a federal-provincial conference which convened in 1935.

The federal-provincial conference heard numerous expressions of the sovereignty of the provinces, and set out to find some method to which the provincial governments would agree. The key was believed to lie in devising a multiple list system of amendment. The different sections of the B.N.A. Acts[109] would be grouped according to their degree of essentiality to minority rights and provincial independence, and a separate amendment process would be devised for each group. One of these groups, for example, would be susceptible of amendment by a simple act of Parliament, while another group would require favourable action by every legislative body in the country. Difficulty arose over the classification of the various sections and the scheme was dropped in 1936 because of the opposition of the province of New Brunswick.[110]

A number of amendments to the B.N.A. Act have been made since the nineteen-thirties—with varying degrees of provincial approval. One such amendment conferred on the federal government power to enact laws in relation to unemployment insurance. Before requesting the amendment from the United Kingdom parliament, the federal cabinet secured unanimous agreement from the provincial governments. Another amendment in 1949 brought Newfoundland into confederation, apparently without any formal consultation with the provinces. Acting on Ottawa's request, the British Parliament enacted three other amendments which were vigorously opposed by provincial governments. The first of these sanctioned the wartime postponement of redistribution, while the second amendment carried out a redistribution of seats in 1946. In 1949, Parliament sought and obtained an amendment to the B.N.A. Act[111] which gave the federal government sole power to amend the B.N.A. Act in respect of strictly federal matters, so long as strictly provincial concerns or minority rights were not affected. This amendment, which now stands as sec. 91.1, was passed despite the bitter protests of about half of the provincial governments.[112] Two later amendments, in 1951 and 1964, giving Parliament concurrent power in the areas of old age pensions and survivors' benefits, were passed with full provincial approval.

In 1950, a series of meetings was held by the various heads of government and their attorneys-general. The premiers of six provinces (Alberta, New Brunswick, Nova Scotia, Ontario, Quebec, and Saskatchewan) objected to the authority that the central government had obtained in 1949 to alter part of the constitution unilaterally. Proposals made by three other premiers (British Columbia, Manitoba, and Prince Edward Island) obviously envisioned reconsideration of the 1949 amendment. Prime Minister Louis St. Laurent agreed that, if concurrence could be reached on a general scheme, the central government would not let the existence of that amendment become an obstacle. The federal-provincial conferences of 1950 adopted a scheme by which the various sections of the B.N.A. Act could be classified into six groups. The first group comprised provisions which concerned only Parliament, and which Parliament alone would be able to amend. In the second group were provisions which concerned, and would be amendable by, the provincial legislatures. A third group put together sections concerning Parliament and one or more (but not all) of the provinces; these sections would be amendable by concurrent acts of Parliament and the concerned legislatures. A fourth group included sections of interest to all legislative bodies and which would be altered by acts of Parliament and acts of an undetermined number of legislatures. The fifth group concerned changes in the amending procedure and sections fundamental to minority rights and provincial independence. Any amendment of these sections would require acts of Parliament and all the legislative assemblies. The sixth category comprised provisions which were considered spent or atrophied and which should be repealed. Agreement was also reached on the desirability of considering the subject of the delegation of powers.

The 1950 conferences failed to agree on the assignment of sections to the various categories.[113] At the two extremes were the governments of Saskatchewan and Quebec. Saskatchewan refused to agree to the adoption of a rigid amending formula, and Quebec insisted that a flexible formula would endanger her special position in the federation. Despite later conferences of attorneys-general, the question was dropped until after changes in government in Ottawa (1957) and Quebec City (1960).

The Fulton-Favreau Attempt

The attorneys-general resumed discussions on the amending procedure in 1960. In September, 1961, the federal minister of justice, E. Davie Fulton, reported optimistically that agreement on all essentials was very near; all that remained were some technical points about the delegation power. These points were apparently resolved soon after Mr. Fulton's speech to the Commons. A bill (to be passed by the United Kingdom Parliament) was drafted in early November 1961, and circulated to the provincial governments for their final comments. The draft bill was entitled "An Act to provide for the amendment in Canada of the Constitution of Canada." While it did not consciously utilize a multicategory system of classifying the sections of the B.N.A. Act., the draft bill did incorporate different amending methods for different parts of the Canadian constitution which was partially defined in sec. 8.* The bill was divided into three parts. The first part outlined the procedure for amending the constitution, the second dealt with intergovernmental delegation of legislative authority, and the third part contained the citation and commencement of the act.

While the provinces were accorded a very large part in this proposed amending scheme, their subordinate rather than coordinate status was marked by the bill's first section. This section said that, subject to other limitations in the bill, "the Parliament of Canada may make laws repealing, amending or re-enacting any provision of the Constitution of Canada." Parliament thus was given a veto power over all amendments. The second section entrenched a number of provisions which included minimum provincial representation in the Commons (B.N.A. sec. 51A), all the present powers of the provinces under sec. 92, and the use of the two official languages (sec. 133). None of these matters could be altered unless changes were "concurred in by the legislatures of all the provinces." Section 3 of the bill said that constitutional changes affecting one or more, but not all, provinces, could not be made unless the provincial legislatures concerned agreed. Section 4 provided that every provincial legislature except for that of Newfoundland must agree to any constitutional changes relating to education. Subsection 2 of sec. 4 gave the Newfoundland legislature power to veto any changes affecting its educational system.

One of the least flexible parts of the amending plan was that in sec. 5. It provided that, except for matters dealt with by the earlier sections, all constitutional changes would require the concurrence of the legislatures of two-thirds of the provinces representing at least fifty percent of the population of Canada. The range of matters to which this special procedure applied was limited by sec. 6. It said

---

*See D. C. Rowat, "The 1949 Amendment and the Pigeon-Hole Method," and other readings reproduced in Paul Fox, ed., *Politics-Canada* (first ed., Toronto, 1962). A text of the draft bill is presented there along with explanation of Saskatchewan's objections.

Section 8 reads: "without limiting the meaning of the expression 'Constitution of Canada,' in this Part that expression includes the following enactments and any order, rule or regulation thereunder, namely,

(a) the British North America Acts, 1867 to 1960;

(b) the Manitoba Act, 1870;

(c) the Parliament of Canada Act, 1875;

(d) the Canadian Speaker (Appointment of Deputy) Act, 1895;

(e) the Alberta Act;

(f) the Saskatchewan Act;

(g) the Statute of Westminster, 1931, in so far as it is part of the law of Canada; and

(h) this Act."

The second edition of Fox (Toronto, 1966) reprints the amended formula.

that nothing in the first part "diminishes any power of the Parliament of Canada or of the legislature of a province, existing immediately before this Act came into force, to make laws in relation to any matters." This provision continued Parliament's general authority under sec. 91.1. Section 7 of the amending bill was a "cut-off" clause for the United Kingdom Parliament; no British bill was to apply to Canada thenceforward.

Part II of the draft bill provided several methods of intergovernmental delegation. The provincial legislatures were empowered to delegate a limited number of their powers, those relating to reformatories and prisons (sec. 92.6), local works and undertakings (92.10), property and civil rights in the province (92.13), and matters falling under the provincial residuary clause (92.16). To legislate on any of these matters, Parliament first would have to obtain the approval of four legislatures for a delegating statute, or else Parliament would have to declare that fewer than four provinces were concerned and obtain the consent of those that were involved. Parliament might, however, delegate any of its powers to the provincial legislatures, provided that at least four legislatures agreed to receive such authority. The draft bill made provision for the unilateral withdrawal by Parliament of any of its delegated powers; one province could also have ceased to exercise a delegated federal power without disrupting the delegation made to other provinces.

Uniquely among contemporary federations, the central government of Canada had been given important powers in 1949 (through an amendment to the B.N.A. Act) to amend the country's central institutions by majority votes in the Parliament without the necessity of provincial approval. This situation was left virtually intact by the new Fulton amending formula (so named after the federal justice minister); some entrenched provision was made, however, for dealing with related powers specifically withheld by the central Parliament by the 1949 arrangements. For a time adoption of this formula seemed agreed but eventually the scheme foundered amid the intricacies of Quebec provincial politics.

The task was taken up again early in Prime Minister Pearson's term of office and at the insistence of Quebec the basic proposal was modified in one important respect which altered the balance of the Fulton plan. Under an amendment by the Liberal Minister of Justice, Guy Favreau, an important part of the former unilateral powers of the central Parliament became entrenched. The effect was to require the central government to win provincial agreement before any amendment to the central institutions could be effected. Although the former Progressive Conservative prime minister, J. G. Diefenbaker, objected that the provision constituted an undesirable concession to Quebec and made the whole much too rigid, the Fulton-Favreau plan found favour with the provinces and another draft bill was prepared for enactment.

Adoption of an amending scheme such as the draft bill proposed would have elevated the legal status of the provinces. Constitutional customs and usages would have been translated into legal requirements and subjected to the review of the courts. Such a scheme would also have given the provincial legislatures, for the first time, the legal right to an important voice in determining the shape of the federal constitution, and deprived Parliament of its legal freedom to bring about virtually any amendment it wished through the agency of the United Kingdom Parliament. Introduction of a delegation device would have implied granting to the legislatures a status almost equal to that of Parliament in the exercise of their constitutionally-assigned powers. Particularly would this be true where the provincial legislatures were authorized to receive from Parliament and to exercise a much greater range of legislative powers than Parliament could assume from the provinces. The draft bill did, however, acknowledge Parliament's preeminence by permitting Parliament to terminate any delegation scheme unilaterally, an authorization which would have been denied to the provincial legislatures in most instances.

Despite favourable auguries not even the Favreau amendment to the Fulton formula proved adequate to safeguard its passage through the turbulent shoals of Quebec provincial politics during "la révolution tranquille" of the nineteen-sixties. The compartmental or "pigeon-hole" approach to constitutional amendment had been in the air constantly for more than a dozen years. Eventually it too foundered because it was too rigid, too flexible, and sometimes both, depending on the debater, the political battle, and perhaps even on the day of the week.

The Victoria Charter Plan

A new zest and new talents were brought to the developing Great Canadian Hunt for a domestic amending formula by the entry into the Liberal government at Ottawa of Pierre-Elliott Trudeau, first as minister of justice and then as prime minister. His concern for entrenchment of fundamental liberties in statutory form together with the enlargement of linguistic rights took Mr. Trudeau headlong into the general constitutional amendment problem as representatives for Quebec refused to discuss such matters without including questions of the redistribution of legislative power. The result of the negotiations from 1967 to 1971 was the Trudeau-Turner formula, the constitutional amendment section of the Victoria Charter. After inter-official discussions, this scheme had been agreed with the provincial governments by the federal Minister of Justice, John Turner; it constituted a new approach to the problem. Under Article 49, amendments to the constitution would have required: 1. A "resolution of consent at the federal level"; 2. Consent of the legislatures of two provinces east of Quebec; 3. Consent of the legislatures of Ontario and Quebec (each of which had 25 percent of Canada's population); 4. Consent of the legislatures of two or more western provinces containing 50 percent of the western population; 5. Consent of the legislature in any province that in the future had 25 percent of the Canadian population. Article 50 provided that amendments affecting one or more, but not all the provinces, could be made after approving resolutions from Parliament and the legislature of the affected provinces. Article 51 provided that the "parliament of Canada may exclusively make laws from time to time amending the Constitution of Canada, in relation to the executive Government of Canada and the Senate and House of Commons," while Article 54 continued the provinces' power to amend their own constitutions. The more elaborate procedures specified under Article 49 (enumerated above) were required, however, for amendments affecting the monarchy, the governor general, the lieutenant-general, the sittings and duration of the assemblies, powers of the Senate, provincial representation in the Parliament, and the amendment of the formula itself. (Articles 55 and 56.) Some slight reallocations were proposed by the Victoria Charter as well as provisions for linguistic and certain other rights but these, along with the new amendment formula, went the way of all previous attempts to secure a wholly Canadian procedure. Faced with the Trudeau government's refusal to relinquish its involvement in social welfare (an involvement built on years of conditional grant and other programs), the government of Quebec refused its necessary consent to adoption of the amending formula which had been of much less interest to it than was regaining exclusive occupancy of the social welfare field.[114] That refusal marked the end of yet another chapter in the struggle to devise a generally acceptable formula for amending the distribution of legislative powers wholly within Canada.

A MOVEMENT TOWARD COORDINATE FEDERALISM

After two decades of vigorous employment of conditional grant programs and other extensions of Ottawa's involvement in provincial areas of legislative concern, the government of the Rt. Hon. L. B. Pearson set out in 1962 to implement policies which would give Canadian federalism a "new direction." Taking that path proved to be unusually stormy in political terms, possibly because Mr. Pearson never enjoyed a parliamentary party majority, but more likely, because, with three major exceptions,[115] his policy represented a turn toward the coordinate concept of federalism and away from the centralism identified with his Liberal predecessors. The context of the sixties made his actions appear to many English-speakers to be the manifestations of a weak government forced to make concession after concession to the stronger politicians who headed the provinces, and especially Quebec. Her leaders, both Liberal and Union Nationale, never lost an opportunity to demand that province's rights both to service areas of exclusive jurisdiction (seen to be guaranteed to the minority by the B.N.A. Act) and to the financial resources to allow them to provide public services on the same extensive scale found in neighbouring but wealthier Ontario. While the emphasis on sometimes almost continuous federal-provincial conferences supported Mr. Pearson's description of his policy as "cooperative federalism," the negotiation between political heads of government on a basis of equality and the development of the "opting-out" procedure certainly looked much like a modern form of classical federalism.

Despite the torrents of debate which it engendered, "opting-out" is simply described. Under this procedure, any province so wishing could terminate its participation in a federal shared cost program without suffering financial loss. Provided that the province continued a comparable program for a specified period of two to five years, the central government would reduce its taxes enough to enable the introduction of compensating provincial taxes yielding enough revenue to finance the new, wholly-provincial program. The main features of the plan were embodied in the *Established Programmes (Interim Arrangements)* Act of 1965. The offer did not apply at all to the Trans-Canada Highway, winter work, capital projects, and a number of other programs which continued on the old basis.[116] Cash payments rather than tax abatements were offered in lieu of programs dealing with hospital construction, roads to resources, forestry agreements, and several other minor areas. In the event, the major offer interested only Quebec at first and that province contracted out of twenty-nine programs dealings with hospital insurance, old age assistance, blind and disabled allowances, the welfare portion of unemployment assistance, technical education, health and other areas. The new arrangements resulted in reductions in federal income tax for individuals resident in Quebec on the order of 20 points and the imposition of compensating higher levels of provincial tax. In 1966 the Ottawa government urged the remaining provinces to follow Quebec's example and the offer was revised for, and attention focussed on, three major social programs: hospital insurance, the Canada Assistance Plan, and the remaining part of the national health grants. The new formula included an inflation and growth-compensating factor but still none of the other provinces was interested in withdrawing from conditional grant plans on these terms. The central government withdrew the offer in 1969, giving as its reason the impending revisions of the tax system. The prime minister at this time was P.-E. Trudeau, a man who as a scholar had long espoused coordinate forms of federalism. As prime minister, he promised there would be no new policy initiatives in areas which were clearly those of the provinces exclusively. (The one conditional grant program Mr. Trudeau introduced up to 1973 dealt with the promotion of bilingualism, a project he justified as lying within federal competence.)[117] While Mr. Trudeau insisted on his government's right to make income supplements and other welfare payments directly to all individual Canadians, he was prepared to make new intergovernmental arrangements. After rebuffing an Ontario inquiry in 1972 about reopening the contracting-out offer, the central government put a new offer to the provinces in May 1973. These proposals sought to substitute unconditional grants for the shared cost plans in the health care and Canada Assistance Plan (welfare) areas; new finance was also suggested for higher education. Although the new unconditional grants were to be tied to a Gross National Product "escalator," the only proposals finding provincial agreement at that time were those for health care, where Ottawa had promised as well to limit new policy initiatives on its part to broad-gauge block grants.

The sixties and early seventies saw three major developments exemplifying coordinate federalism: 1. Tax collection arrangements which effectively freed the provinces from federal determination of their major tax revenues; 2. Tax abatements encouraging the provinces to assume and to carry on federally-initiated programs independently; 3. Substantial recognition and use of unconditional grants replacing conditional grants as the major means of mitigating interprovincial inequality. The clearest abstract statement of a coordinate view of federalism which has appeared in recent years came from one of the senior constitutional advisers in the federal bureaucracy, Dr. A. W. Johnston. After a review of the alternative routes he saw open to the country, he described one in which an attempt might be made "to marry the stronger regional governments and a strong central government—the role of government as a whole having increased—on the assumption that strong federal and strong provincial governments can somehow reconcile and harmonize their priorities, policies, and administrative practices."[118] He acknowledged that the result might appear untidy and needing periodic adjustment of responsibilities. In addition, this approach called for "a reversal of the cumulative influence the federal government has come to have, through shared cost programmes, over provincial government decisions." And, he went on to say in what some saw as a strong statement for an Ottawa bureaucrat, "it calls for a greater respect on the part of the federal government than it has often displayed in the past for those areas of provincial jurisdiction which are critical to the preservation and the promotion of cultural diversity, in particular education." He also noted that not only should the governments be enabled, possibly through some constitutional changes, to resist central invasion of their responsibilities, but that Parliament should be protected from invasion of its jurisdictions by the provinces. To these principles he added two more: increasing emphasis by the central government in adapting its policies to Canada's regional diversities and the vigorous promotion of bilingualism in all its forms. He saw certain problems with putting this approach into practice, chief among them being questions relating to the need, desirability, and hazards of constitutional amendments which might be needed, to the problems of harmonization of different level programs, and the potential political difficulties in effecting whatever changes were deemed necessary. Finally, he asked:

> Is pluralism a realistic goal in modern society, or must one reconcile oneself to the gradual centralization of government—in the Canadian context to the development of two relatively centralized states? If gradual centralization is inevitable, is it reasonable to expect that pluralism could be expected to persist in the North American context—that an English-Canadian society and a French-Canadian society could be expected to flourish in a U.S.-dominated North America—if this is an unreasonable expectation within the Canadian context?[119]

CONCLUSION

The coordinate concept, which underpins the constitutional status quo, is the most conspicuous concept of federalism in the country. As such, it suffers peculiarly from the attacks of crusading reformers and the relative neglect of serious students of government, most of whom content themselves with exposition rather than close analysis. The existence of concepts rivalling the coordinate idea comprises a large body of implicit criticism, for it is in their opposition to the status quo that these rival notions find their *raison d'être*. Most of the criticism of the judicial view of coordinate federalism was directed at the Judicial Committee's interpretations of the B.N.A. Act. Scholars have made little effort to scrutinize the merits of the federal scheme developed by the British law lords. Neither can one find logical analyses of coordinate federalism as expressed in the proposed designs for constitutional amendment. In consequence, the present inquiry into coordinate federalism has only a limited range of criticism with which to deal.

Although the Sirois commission's proposals were approved by the federal cabinet and a number of the provincial governments, the plan envisioned by the commission satisfied neither the centralists nor those favouring the greatest possible degree of provincial autonomy.[120] The centralists approved the recommendations for more interprovincial cooperation and the concentration of the major taxing powers at Ottawa, but attacked the large measure of provincial autonomy suggested in the provision of social services. National standards in health, welfare, labour, and education were part of the socialist-centralist credo at this time, and the *Sirois Report* had no place for standards other than national averages to be used in assessing fiscal need. Accordingly, the left wing opposed the Sirois scheme of coordinate federalism because it did not go far enough in creating a state structure which could minister efficiently to the people's material needs.[121]

At the other end of the federal spectrum stood those who discerned in the Sirois scheme nothing more than an attempt to turn the provincial governments into vassals of an all-powerful central government. This criticism of the *Report* can best be illustrated by a quotation from a French Canadian historian: "En vérité, les propositions Sirois, qui sont des propositions Dafoc, enlèvent aux provinces, moins des prérogatives déterminées que les resources financières indispensables à l'exercice de leurs prérogatives. Elles dépouillent les province[s] de l'initiative fiscale, pour les mettre, à brève ou à longue échéance, à la merci du pouvoir fédéral."[122] Variations of this argument were made by the premiers of Quebec, Ontario, New Brunswick, and Alberta at the 1941 federal-provincial conference, which discussed but failed to agree on measures to implement the Sirois recommendations.

While most academic reviews of the *Sirois Report* concentrated on its historical account and the appended special studies, the economic historian H. A. Innis went to the heart of the proposals.[123] He castigated the commission for political tactlessness and thought the suggested redesigning of confederation was naive in its contemplation of a "reversal of the trend in which the provinces assumed the lead in political change." Professor Innis charged that the federal recommendations showed signs of infatuation with national income growth and a complete neglect of the basic problems caused by the uneven incidence of the tariff structure. He claimed that the comparison made with 1867 in relation to debt assumption was fallacious; recommendations that the central regime assume highway development costs would have been more to the point. This critic felt that in framing its proposals the commission had overestimated the capacity of the central civil service and underestimated the efficiencies of the provincial services. Finally, in Professor Innis' view, the objective of "provincial equity may imply a rigid framework checking economic adjustments." The plan for turning the de jure equality of the provinces into a de facto equality might well exact a price higher than that suffered as a result of the existing inequities.

Professor Alexander Brady, a political scientist, focussed his analysis on the equilibrium which the commission had sought to strike for the federal system.[124] Noting the strong centralizing effect of the proposed tax transfers, he observed that "the power to tax is the basis of most other political power." On the other hand, the recommendations for the social services demonstrated the commission's "jealous concern for provincial autonomy." Professor Brady wondered "whether a balance which candidly rests on a premise of provincial equality will not prove to be too delicate and difficult to maintain, owing to the clash of centrifugal and centripetal forces." But, however precarious the balance sought, the proposals should be welcomed as a step toward a "better integrated state."

SUMMARY

Coordinate federalism is a system of government in which legislative and executive powers are divided between general and regional authorities, each of which is, within its constitutionally-assigned sphere, independent of the others and equal in legal status. Political expression of the concept is found in the work of the Sirois commission on federal-provincial relations, whose inquiries during the late nineteen-thirties were largely restricted to financial implications of the discrepancy between the constitutional obligations and financial resources of the various governments. The *Sirois Report* suggested the centralization of the major tax powers at the federal capital and a rationalized scheme of provincial subsidies based on need. The commission recommended that the central government assume provincial debts, and the cost of relief for the unemployed. The provinces were to be put into a financial position which would enable them to meet their responsibilities—to the extent and in the manner which they severally preferred. The royal commission felt that the practical independence of the provinces should be enhanced and that facilities to promote intergovernmental cooperation should be improved.

The coordinate idea of federalism was given legal sanction by the decisions of the Supreme Court of Canada and the Judicial Committee of the Privy Council. A series of judgements in the late nineteenth century established the rule that the British North America Act should be interpreted as a statute, rather than as an organic constitution. These judgements widened the effective orbit of the exclusive provincial powers by principles of construction which assigned them priority over the federal government's authority to legislate for peace, order, and good government. Primacy was accorded only to Parliament's enumerated powers, and one of them—the regulation of trade and commerce—was minimized greatly to the benefit of the exclusive provincial authority over property and civil rights. Provincial authority over education is limited by guarantees for certain minority group rights. Responsibility for fundamental liberties is, in the legal view, divided between the two orders of government; dispute exists as to which authority has the greater responsibility in the matter.

Executive power is divided federally. The lieutenant-governor is as much the representative of the monarch for purposes of provincial government as the governor general is for federal purposes. Nevertheless, the lieutenant-governor remains liable to service as an agent of the central government, should it wish to exercise its legal right to veto provincial legislation.

Both federal and provincial authorities can amend certain parts of the constitution, but they have been unable to agree on a procedure whereby the constitution might be changed in Canada in any or all respects. Consequently, only the United Kingdom Parliament has the legal right to amend the B.N.A. Act in all particulars. Canadian governments have made a number of recent attempts to design an all-Canadian amending procedure. These efforts involved classifying the various legislative jurisdictions into separate categories according to the relation of these powers to minority rights and provincial autonomy. The different categories were to be amended by procedures incorporating different degrees of flexibility. One project also made provision for the intergovernmental delegation of legislative authority. The Trudeau-Turner approach employed a regional concurrent majorities amending scheme but this project, like the others, failed of adoption, and the situation remains that only the United Kingdom Parliament has the legal power to alter Canada's federal distribution of powers.

Applying the Criteria

The coordinate concept emphasizes the equal status of the federal and provincial governments and urges the desirability of strengthening the two sets of government concurrently. Both federal and provincial authorities are entitled to raise general revenues through separate taxation schemes. Taxation agreements between governments are unenforceable in courts of law. The various governments are similarly independent of each other in the determination of how public finances should be managed. This stress on double sets of sovereign rights distinguishes coordinate federalism from the centralist and administrative concepts, but allies it to the compact and dualist ideas.

Fundamental to the coordinate concept is the right of each public authority to determine its political policies free from interference by other governments. The persistence of the disallowance and reservation powers, found in the judicial view of confederation, clashes with the notion of coordinate status. Assertion of the central veto powers coincides with the centralist, but not with the compact or dualist, conceptions of federalism.

Different aspects of civil rights or fundamental liberties fall within the keeping of the two types of government; neither provincial nor central authorities have exclusive jurisdiction over the entire field. In its view of liberties, the coordinate concept is thus at one with the administrative idea and differs from the centralist, dualist, and compact notions. The exclusive jurisdiction of the province to set educational standards is acknowledged by coordinate federalism, as it is by the dualist and compact concepts, subject, however, to the right of the central government to intervene on behalf of specified minority groups. The equal status of the French and English languages is guaranteed within a limited range by the courts, which are established by Parliament. Any extension in range of this equal status lies within the exclusive competence of the legislative assemblies. In thus limiting strictly the sphere within which equality of language status is asserted, the coordinate concept diverges from the centralist and dualist ideas which support a wider range of activity for the central government.

Coordinate federalism is implicit in the Fulton-Favreau and Trudeau-Turner types of constitutional amendment plans, which acknowledge the equal right of both federal and provincial governments to participate in certain changes. In this respect, the coordinate, administrative, and dualist concepts are in accord. By contrast, the centralist idea emphasizes the sole authority of the central government to amend the constitution, and the compact theory stresses the right of any one government to veto any proposed change.

CHAPTER

5

The Compact Theory

Confederation was a compromise that embraced not simply different geo-economic communities and separate political entities, but two distinctive cultures rooted in historic enmities, antagonistic religions, and different tongues. In threshing out this compromise, civil strife arose frequently but never did it burst into an inter-cultural war. Partial explanation why it did not may be found in the reluctant admission of the English that the French must be tolerated for they would not be absorbed, in the *Canadiens'* ready mastery of English institutions which they turned to their own advantage, and, after 1860, in the frightful example to the south of the results of open warfare based, in part, on divergent conceptions of the social ideal. The *modus vivendi* which the Canadians were compelled to find gave rise to the compact theory of confederation. Despite the juridical implications of the word "compact," this theory was more dependent on the notion of a morally-binding entente than it was on a developed legal system of thought. An historian suggests: "If we attempt to look upon this pact or entente as a legal contract, freely entered into by two parties and intended by them to be legally enforceable in a court of law, our vision will be so limited as to be distorted; for a pact or compact is not a contract in the legal sense. It is a gentleman's agreement, an understanding based on mutual consent, with a moral rather than a juridical sanction."[1]

Whatever the dangers of distortion might have been, scholars and politicians in Quebec have long taken a legalist view of the union as a solemn compact or treaty made by the British North American colonies. "The government at Ottawa, it is even said, is the creature of the provinces who brought about Confederation."[2] Adherence to this point of view has not been limited to Quebec although the theory has there found its most vigorous exposition and defence. *Québecois* relied heavily on the compact theory to justify their claims for recognition of the provinces' sovereignty within their constitutional sphere. Respect for provincial autonomy[3] is considered "condition essentielle à l'épanouissement de la province de Québec, à la survivance du peuple canadien-francais, et au bon fonctionnement même de la Confédération."[4]

The compact originated as a racial concept, but, as Professor G. F. G. Stanley has said, "once Canadians (as distinct from Maritimers) began to identify provinces with specific linguistic groups, the idea of a pact between races was transformed into the idea of a pact between provinces."[5] Seeing confederation as the result of an agreement between colonies permitted supporters of the compact theory to demand that no changes be made in the British North America Act without the consent of all the provinces, or, at the very least, without the consent of the original partners that were said to have created the federation.

Evidence that the union was based on a compact was drawn from a number of sources. One such source was John A. Macdonald, who is credited with uttering what was probably the first statement of the compact theory in English Canada: the union of 1840 was "a distinct bargain, a solemn contract,"[6] he said in 1861. Several years later, he called the same Act of Union "the treaty of 1840."[7] More substantial foundations for the theory were found in the agreement at Quebec City in 1864 that approval for the Quebec Resolutions would be sought from each provincial legislature, and in the subsequent debates on those resolutions when they were presented for approval to the Parliament of the Province of Canada. These debates supplied a wealth of material to suggest that the Fathers of Confederation thought that it was a treaty they were discussing.

The Quebec Resolutions were presented to the Parliament of Canada by John A. Macdonald, the Attorney-General West. In seeking approval for the federation plan which the resolutions embodied, he claimed that "the scheme was not one framed by the Government of Canada, or by the Government of Nova Scotia, but was in the nature of a treaty settled between the different colonies."[8] This treaty quality of the resolutions meant that, "if not adopted in their entirety, the proceedings would have to be commenced *de novo.*"[9] George Brown, the Toronto Grit, argued with L. H. Holton, of Chateauguay, about the authority of the conference delegates to negotiate treaties, a traditional prerogative of the imperial Crown.[10] The record of these debates is replete with references to the treaty aspect of the resolutions.[11] The issue was a critical one. Those on the opposition benches favoured a union of some type but, if the proposed federation truly

involved a treaty, they would be forced to support the plan as it stood
or be marked in the public eye as foes of the new "nation."

Supporters of the compact theory have noted that at all the Charlottetown, Quebec, and London meetings, the provinces voted as equal
units.[12] To critics, claiming that the British North America Act,
1867, was a far cry from the Quebec Resolutions, one supporter of
the theory rejoined: "A Charlottetown, on s'entendit sur les principes: à la conférence de Londres, des précisions importantes furent
apportées au projet mais c'est à Québec que les provinces aussi bien
que les deux races conclurent une entente qui contenait l'essentiel et
la plupart des détails de l'Acte de l'Amérique du Nord britannique."[13]
The classic "compact" view of Britain's role in 1867 was set forth in
1889 by a young lawyer who later became a justice of the Supreme
Court of Canada: the federal union resulted from a treaty between
provinces, the British North America Act of 1867 was only Britain's
legalization of that treaty, and the future of confederation depended
upon an exact observance of that pact.[14] Substantially the same conception illumined the defence of the compact theory made sixty years
later by Richard Arès who wrote: "La Confédération est à la fois un
pacte et une loi, une loi anglaise promulguée en Grand-Bretagne et un
pacte canadien fait d'abord au Canada, la première réproduisant
substantiellement le second, le sanctionnant et lui donnant effet."[15]

Such was "la doctrine traditionelle et exclusive de 1867 à 1925"
which the Judicial Committee decisions had embodied up to the
Aeronautics decision of 1932 and the social legislation cases of 1937.
There can be little real dispute that the compact theory represented
the accepted view prior to the economic depression of the nineteen-
thirties.[16] Criticism of the doctrine centred on its validity rather than
on its existence.

DEVELOPMENT OF THE THEORY

The legal aspects of the compact theory have been subjected to frequent and searching criticism. None of the critics, however, have
undertaken to answer the first well-reasoned exposition, that of T. J. J.
Loranger, a retired justice of the Quebec Supreme Court. In his
*Letters upon the Interpretation of the Federal Constitution known as
The British North America Act (1867)*,[17] Mr. Justice Loranger observed that constitutions have necessarily four interpreters—the legislatures, the executive, the judiciary, and the jurisconsults; he placed
himself in the role of a member of this fourth group. He wrote in a
sense of crisis. He saw that the newly-established Supreme Court
of Canada had been reversing the lower courts which "understood"

the provinces' coequal authority with that of Ottawa; the *Mercer* case particularly had revealed "the centralizing and absorbing tendencies of the Supreme Court." The Judicial Committee also "misconstrued" the law for it had ruled against Ontario in the now-famous case of *Russell* v. *The Queen.*

The *Letters* claimed that the central government was "essentially the creation of those states, as an ordinary partnership is the work of the partners." "At the outset of confederation," he contended, "no person had any idea of forming a political association; it was rather a commercial league of the nature of the Hanseatic League." He argued from the American, Swiss, and German precedents that "in the absence of contrary provisions, the particular governments are managed by the organic rules which constituted them before forming the confederation, and preserve all the powers which belonged to them, if they do not delegate a part to the central government." Noting the difficulty of interpreting the division of legislative powers in the provincial favour, he proposed rephrasing secs. 91 and 92 of the B.N.A. Act to obviate this difficulty. "To ascertain the nature of any power whatever, it is necessary then, first, to examine all classes of local subjects," and if it does not interest all the provinces, but only one or two, then it is obviously a local power. He felt the conclusion could then be drawn that the provinces had a right to priority in matters of direct taxation, and similarly, that provincial legislation should prevail over federal legislation in the (then) two concurrent fields.

Mr. Justice Loranger summarized his propositions thus:

1. The confederation of the British Provinces was the result of a compact entered into by the provinces and the Imperial Parliament, which, in enacting the British North America Act, simply ratified it.

2. The provinces entered into the federal Union, with their corporate identity, former constitutions, and all their legislative powers, part of which they ceded to the Federal Parliament, to exercise them in their common interest and for purposes of general utility, keeping the rest which they left to be exercised by their legislatures, acting in their provincial sphere, according to their former constitutions, under certain modifications of form, established by the federal compact.

3. Far from having been conferred upon them by the federal government, the powers of the provinces not ceded to that government are the residue of their old powers, and far from having been created by it, the federal government was the result of their association and of their compact, and was created by them.

4. The Parliament has no legislative powers beyond those which were conferred upon it by the provinces, and which are recognized by section 91 of the British North America Act, which conferred upon it, only the powers therein mentioned or those of a similar nature, *ejusdem generis.*

5. In addition to the powers conferred upon the legislatures by section 91 and section 92, their legislative jurisdiction extends to all matters of a local or private nature, and all omitted cases fall within provincial jurisdiction, if they touch the local or private interests of one or some of the provinces only; on the other hand, if they interest all the provinces, they belong to Parliament.

6. In case it be doubtful whether any special matter touches all, or one, or a few provinces only, that is to say, if it be of general or local interest, such doubt must be decided in favour of the provinces, which preserved all their powers not ascribed to Parliament.

7. In the reciprocal sphere of their authority thus recognized, there exists no superiority in favour of Parliament over the provinces, but, subject to Imperial sovereignty, these provinces are quasi-sovereign within their respective spheres, and there is absolute equality between them.

An eighth "summary" proposition itself requires condensation: The B.N.A. Act was not an imposed constitution but an imperial ratification of the provincial agreement; it must be interpreted as if the provinces had been sovereign bodies empowered to make the agreement, a fiction which Britain had reified through the statute which retroactively legalized their acts.

Loranger contested the decision in *Russell* v. *The Queen*, which had found that a federal liquor licensing law was *intra vires* the trade and commerce clause of sec. 91. Such an argument, he said, would force one to conclude that "Provincial Legislatures have no right to make police regulations for the protection of good moral and public order, when such protection may injure commerce." Indeed, if this principle of incidental effects were extended, nearly all federal laws would be *ultra vires* in their turn, for they encroached, or might be liable to encroach, either directly or indirectly, on property and civil rights. "Its application would be, in fact, the overthrow of the Constitution." Both common sense and the terms of the compact demanded judicial interpretations in favour of the provinces, according to this jurist.

Mr. Justice Loranger's work was almost a complete statement of the compact theory. It lacked only two elements; the right of the province to veto proposed constitutional amendments and the right of a province to fiscal autonomy. Loranger's *Letters* were published just as the provincial revolt was getting under way. The compact theory with the concomitant doctrine of the quasi-sovereignty of the provinces was asserted everywhere, but most of all in Quebec. At the opening of the legislative session of 1889, the deputy for Shefford, Tancrède de Grosbois, seconded the Reply to the Address from the Throne in these words: "Nous ne sommes ni une colonie, ni une dépendance de la Confédération. Nous en sommes une partie intégrante. La source des pouvoirs, on ne saurait trop le répéter, ne va pas du

Canada aux provinces, mais des provinces aux Canada. Elles sont constituantes; il est constitué."[18] The premier, Honoré Mercier, endorsed the member's phrases.

Conceptions of the compact theory underpinned provincial arguments against the federal power; the philosophy justified the remedies which the provinces sought for the difficulties in which they found themselves. It would, however, be inaccurate to claim that the compact theory led to the provincial revolt of the eighteen-eighties and eighteen-nineties. This revolt had other causes. As the Sirois commission put it:

> Indeed, there had never been any large transfer of loyalty from the older communities to the new Dominion created for urgent common purposes. The achievement of Confederation and the spectacular activity of the Federal Government in the early years had merely overshadowed or, at most, temporarily subordinated the separate interests of the distinct regions and communities. From the very date of the union, there had been a widespread and burning conviction in Nova Scotia that it had been manoeuvred into a bargain prejudicial to its vital interest.[19]

The new state had been plunged almost immediately into a depression from which it took decades to emerge. Maritime shipbuilding industries were imperilled by technological revolution, Ontario sought an economic panacea in commercial union with the United States, and in the West there burned a racial war that soon engulfed both Ontario and Quebec.

These sectional differences were articulated in complaints at the interprovincial conference of 1887. Five Liberal premiers attended the meeting but it was boycotted by Macdonald and the two Conservative premiers. Mercier, who had issued the invitations, and Oliver Mowat, who was chairman of the sessions, set the tone: the conference represented all the original parties to the compact of 1864, and the partners should now assess the state of their joint enterprise.

In suggesting an agenda, Mercier asserted that "the Constitution of 1867 was based upon a treatise published in 1858 by Dr. Taché." In default of any other textbook, he said, "this work may serve as a guide for interpreting the obscure or defective points in the Confederation Act."[20] Mercier then quoted from the book to bolster Quebec's demand for added sources of taxation, for the right of the provincial legislature to elect federal senators, and for the transfer from Ottawa to London of the right to disallow provincial statutes.

The resolutions adopted by the provincial premiers looked toward the implementation of the compact theorists' views. The modified federal system which the resolutions envisioned called for the exercise of disallowance by the imperial Parliament "upon the same principles as the same is exercised in the case of Federal Acts." In practice, this would have meant the virtual disappearance of political supervision over the provinces from above. The premiers wanted half of the senators to be nominated by each province, and the abolition of life terms for senators—the better to enable fulfilment of the Senate's leading purpose which, it was said, was "to protect the interests of the respective Provinces as such." Lieutenant-governors should be recognized as representatives of the monarch rather than of the governor general. The conference also called for the use of provincial voters' lists for federal elections and the reduction of federal powers over public works. Federal subsidies were to be increased under the proposed new terms of the compact, and the provinces would be given more advantageous taxing positions. Finally, the premiers decided that, while the federal government would be notified about the resolutions, the provinces themselves should take steps to have the imperial Parliament enact the necessary amendments to the British North America Act.[21]

The conference thus openly challenged Macdonald's view that confederation was designed to set up a highly-centralized state. The Sirois commission on intergovernmental relations commented in 1940 that "in its swing to the other extreme, emphasizing the primacy of the provinces," the conference of 1887 "was no doubt employing a theory of federalism similar to the doctrine of 'states' rights' in the United States."[22]

The chief detailed discussion of the compact theory which we have from a leading politician is that of G. Howard Ferguson, premier of Ontario. His remarks were inspired by the deliberations of a commission set up, after the imperial conference of 1926, to study the legal status of legislation in the dominions *vis à vis* British statutes. When the commission's report appeared in Canada, R. B. Bennett, Leader of the Opposition at Ottawa, objected that: "This Commission that met in London certainly should have included representatives of the provinces of Canada as the provinces had the right to express an opinion there. Why? Because the British North America Act is a treaty, a pact made between four provinces, . . . and now we are told that this committee that met in London in 1929 made certain recommendations which are to be passed into law by the imperial parliament."[23] As these recommendations contemplated the removal of British supervision over the dominions' legislation, including constitutional statutes, both Bennett and his fellow Conservative, Ferguson, feared that the federal administration might secure power to amend the constitution unilaterally.

Ferguson wrote to the prime minister enclosing a memorandum[24] which, as one student says, "simply expounded a doctrine which had been accepted in its broad lines by most public men since Confederation, but which had never been so forcibly set forth at such a critical moment."[25] Premier Ferguson insisted on the right of the provinces to pass on any proposed amendments, a right which the forthcoming Statute of Westminster should safeguard. He observed:

> The Conference appears to have ignored the fact that the confederation of the provinces of Canada was brought about by the action of the provinces. Our Constitution is really the crystallization into law by an Imperial statute of an agreement made by the provinces after full consultation and discussion. The Province of Ontario holds strongly to the view that this agreement should not be altered without the consent of the parties to it.

The memorandum referred to the "Compact of Confederation," an expression which "had its sanction in the fact that the Quebec resolutions, of which the Act is a transcript, were in the nature of a treaty between the provinces which originated the Dominion." The confederation conferences had recognized the equality of the provinces, through their quality in voting, and in "the foreground of all the proceedings in the formative stage of the union, is the plain intimation that the Dominion was being created at the instance of the provinces." The province of Canada's Parliament considered and passed the Resolutions as a treaty, and a treaty it was considered by all.

The operational freedom of the federal government had been rigidly delimited by the provincial delegates according to Ferguson, who added: "It is not without significance that the British North America Act, as arranged for by the treaty and as enacted by the Imperial Parliament, did not confer upon the federal Parliament any power to amend the Constitution of Canada, although each province was given power to amend its own constitution, except as regards the office of Lieutenant-Governor."[26] Premier Ferguson quoted from decisions of the Judicial Committee of the Privy Council[27] to establish the sovereignty of the provinces and claimed the same position for all provinces, whether they had been among the original partners to the compact or created since confederation. Unfortunately, he said, a great many amendments had been made to the B.N.A. Act without the provinces having been consulted. These precedents might have undermined the provinces' constitutional rights, but in Ferguson's view there could be no conceding the claim that the federal government had the sole discretion of deciding when the provinces should be consulted. Failure to obtain provincial approval for amendments constituted an usurpation of power by the central government, he said, and the province of Ontario would continue to protest such violations of its rights. "All our personal and civil rights are now in the keeping and protection of the provinces, and any amendment that would extend the authority of the Dominion might easily be a serious menace to our national unity." The premier concluded that no restatement of the amending procedure could be accepted by the province of Ontario unless that procedure fully acknowledged "the right of all the provinces to be consulted, and become parties to the decision arrived at." The premier of Quebec, Alexandre Taschereau, protested in similar vein.[28]

ALTERING THE COMPACT

Premier Ferguson's successful intervention in 1930 sparked a powder-train into academic and socialist circles whence occurred explosions of indignation. "As a lawyer and student of history," said Professor Norman MacKenzie, "I have no hesitation in saying that the British North America Act is not a compact, and from a legal point of view could be amended by Parliament without considering the desires of the provinces." What was to him the obvious legal interpretation and the intentions of the Fathers of Confederation was, "by what is termed a constitutional convention, coming to have quite a different meaning from the original one."[29] Despite this and other extensive attempts to discredit the compact theory during the nineteen-thirties, support for it continued, apparently undiminished, throughout the following quarter-century.

French Canadian leaders saw the survival of their culture intimately bound up with the continued existence of a method of amending the B.N.A. Act that did not leave the federal Parliament with sole jurisdiction in the matter. Ferguson's stand offered the best avenue of counter-attacking those views which would give Parliament such amending power. A representative of the Quebec government told the Sirois commission: "Participant de la nature des conventions, le pacte fédératif ne peut être amendé ni modifié sans l'assentiment de toutes les parties, c'est à dire de toutes les provinces. Il n'appartient ni à une majorité des provinces, ni encore moins au gouvernement fédéral, d'y apporter des changements."[30] A retired justice of the Supreme Court of Canada, P. B. Mignault, advised the same commission of inquiry that without any question the constitution could not be modified without the consent of Quebec.[31]

While scholars objected to the assertion that unanimous provincial approval was necessary, most agreed that all provinces should assent before any amendments were passed that dealt with minority rights in language, religion, and education. One such student, Dr. Maurice Ollivier, wanted the amending power conferred on Parliament alone but thought that "il faudrait insérer dans l'act impérial une disposition décrétant qu'aucune modification de la méthode adoptée pour modifier l'Acte de l'Amérique britannique du Nord ne sera valide sans la ratification de toutes les provinces."[32] He also suggested a plan whereby the federal Parliament would enact a constitution for Canada; the amendment of certain unspecified features of this parliamentary enactment would require unanimous provincial assent.[33] Brooke Claxton, later a federal cabinet minister, proposed an amending scheme requiring unanimous provincial consent for amendments of secs. 51, 51A (Commons representation), 93 (minority education), 133 (use of French language), and heads 12, 13 and 14 of sec. 92 (marriage, property and civil rights, administration of justice). If a province failed to express its dissent within one year, it would be recorded among the approvers.[34] In testimony before a parliamentary inquiry, Professor Frank R. Scott proposed a similar method, with the exception that he would have removed property and civil rights from provincial jurisdiction.[35]

A leading student of the constitution concluded that, in amendments affecting the provinces as bodies politic, the basis for the requirement of provincial consent was "much stronger and more definite" than that given by any contract doctrine. Dr. Paul Gérin-Lajoie says:

> It is, on the one hand, law proper . . . in so far as each province is thereby constituted as a body politic supreme within its own sphere and free from interference by the federal Houses of Parliament. The complement of this legal basis, on the other hand, is found in a most definite constitutional convention in so far as a province is in no way subordinate to the United Kingdom or its Parliament and is, therefore, subject to no interference from this source.[36]

That attitude has apparently been generally accepted and is today incorporated into a working assumption for all intergovernmental conferences trying to develop a domestic procedure for full amendment of the constitution. The agreements reached in conference on the Fulton-Favreau formula and on the Trudeau-Turner formula both failed to reach fruition. The cause was the same in each case. The negotiators had agreed that adoption of the amending formula would not go ahead without the explicit approval of *each* provincial legislature and this the formulas failed to obtain in Quebec despite the Quebec premiers' apparent agreement at the conferences.

Representation in the Commons

The Senate plays such a negligible role as spokesman for the provinces that sectional representation in the lower house assumes great significance for the country's federal character. The question of

whether legislative representation should be based on population or
on section brought on the constitutional crisis in the Province of
Canada, and was thus one of the key impulses of the confederation
movement. Refusal to grant tiny Prince Edward Island more than
five members was one of the considerations that kept that province
out of the union until 1873 when she entered with the desired six
members of the Commons. Clearly, the provisions dealing with representation were an important part of the agreements of 1864-67.

The issue was raised in Parliament in 1871 when the Commons was
debating an address to Britain seeking legislation in connection with
the proposed Manitoba Act. A Liberal member, David Mills, accused
the Tory government of preparing to violate the compact by the addition of new members to the Commons. This step, he said, would upset
the particular balance of representation that the provinces had agreed
on in 1865. He urged the House to adopt a resolution "that any alteration by the Imperial Legislation of the principle of Representation
in the House of Commons recognized and fixed by the 51st and 52nd
sections of the British North America Act, 1867, without the consent
of the several Provinces that were parties to the compact, would be a
violation of a fundamental principle in our constitution," and would
be destructive of the independence and security of the provinces.[37]
The resolution was rejected, the address went forward to Britain
without consultation of the provinces, and Ottawa's request was
granted.

The federal government did not consider sectional representation
to be guaranteed but some of the provinces did. As the population
balance shifted westward, the Maritimes lost seats in the Commons.
Prince Edward Island, by 1914, had been cut from its original six
members in the lower house to three; Nova Scotia and New Brunswick had also lost seats. The Supreme Court ruled in 1903—and was
later upheld by the Judicial Committee—that Prince Edward Island
had no legal right to a fixed representation. Any redress was clearly
a political question. An interprovincial conference discussed the
issue inconclusively in 1910.[38] At the latter conference, the three Maritime provinces submitted a joint brief asserting their moral rights to
greater representation. The union's tiniest province made a special
claim that "according to the spirit of the terms upon which Prince
Edward Island entered Confederation, the original number of its
representatives should not be decreased, and that in order to carry
out the true compact that number should be restored."[39] The interprovincial conference addressed its observations to Prime Minister
Robert L. Borden, who agreed that the provinces had a right to be
consulted authoritatively in representation matters. In introducing
the 1914 redistribution bill, Borden commented that he could not see
how "it would be possible for this Parliament to attempt any alteration in the representation of the provinces without the consent of the

provinces themselves."[40] Where the courts had failed to uphold the "compact," political negotiation apparently had succeeded.

The provinces' right to be consulted about any proposed redistribution of parliamentary seats appeared to have been well-established in Ottawa—until the Second World War. The census was taken in 1941 and the constitutional statute required an adjustment of the representational base. Pleading the exigencies of the wartime situation, the prime minister announced that redistribution would be postponed. King's foes were not persuaded that the war was the real reason for postponement. The Liberal prime minister had refused to form a wartime coalition cabinet and was leading a partisan government that would have to face an election. Under-representation on the basis of population was especially acute in British Columbia and Quebec, and in the latter province the "crusade in Europe" was most unpopular. Postponement of the redistribution was but another example of the prime minister's astute political judgement.

Objections to King's move were led by the Liberal premier of Quebec, Adélard Godbout, who wrote to the prime minister in these terms: "Ce recensement décennal constitue une partie essentielle de l'entente intervenue entre les provinces de laquelle est née la Confédération canadienne, et, en consequence, la loi constitutionnelle ne peut convenablement être modifiée, sous ce rapport, sans le consentement des provinces."[41] In the Commons, Lionel Bertrand complained that the war was being used as a pretext to inflict this and other injustices upon Quebec; it was but another example of the way that Ottawa persisted in breaking the contract. Confederation was not a contract, replied Justice Minister Louis St. Laurent, it was but an entente—the provinces had given up all their rights in 1867 except those specifically reserved to them in the B.N.A. Act. Mr. St. Laurent's reply constituted the government's official position and the province's protests were to no avail. The postponement was sanctioned by an imperial statute.[42]

Four years after the war ended, Parliament secured the power to amend the B.N.A. Act in respect of matters touching the federal government alone, so long as these did not trench on provincial jurisdiction, educational and religious provisions of the Act, the use of the French tongue, or the duration of Parliament.[43] Both Ontario and Quebec protested that taking such power unto itself made the federal government guilty of a gross violation of the 1867 compact, particularly in respect of the understanding relating to the permanency of arrangements affecting the federal Parliament.[44]

The Financial Compact

The struggle over subsidies in 1864-66 denoted a critical aspect of the confederation agreement. So often have supporters of the compact theory referred to these negotiations, and emphasized the close relationship of financial resources and provincial autonomy, that the confederation settlement merits a brief review.

In return for assigning their major revenue sources to the federal authority, the provinces were relieved of their debts, and paid an annual sum of eighty cents per capita, as well as small yearly amounts —ranging from $50,000 to $80,000— to finance the cost of the provincial legislatures and administrations. A number of special grants were made to meet extraordinary problems.[45] The monetary settlement written into the B.N.A. Act was based on both the Quebec Resolutions and the London Resolutions; the latter granted New Brunswick and Nova Scotia more revenue than they would have received under the terms which had been agreed upon at Quebec. Although the agreed revenue transfers were not large, they were believed adequate. The division of legislative jurisdictions had supposedly transferred all the expensive duties to the central government, and the revenue sources remaining to the provinces were expected to be large enough to meet the cost of the "limited" local obligations when the federal subsidies were taken into account. The tenacity with which the Maritimes had fought for higher subsidies indicates that the financial settlement was a key clause of the "entente" for the English provinces.[46]

Federal-provincial financial relationships form a long and tangled chapter in Canada's history. This aspect has been well-explored[47] and requires our immediate attention simply for the purpose of sketching their connection to the compact theory. Immediately after July 1, 1867, agitation arose in Nova Scotia: Charles Tupper was accused of having sold out the province for "eighty cents a head." Eighteen of the nineteen members elected to the legislature were pledged to seek secession, and the federal leaders were pressed to grant "better terms" to Nova Scotia. On learning of this pressure, the other provinces set up a watch against any proposed alterations in the financial agreement.

The Conservative cabinet at Ottawa did contemplate granting Nova Scotia "better terms." Reaction came swiftly, and predictably. In the Ontario legislative session of 1869, the Liberal leader, Edward Blake, moved a series of thirteen resolutions protesting the preferential treatment given to Nova Scotia in "violation" of the compact. The seventh of these resolutions said that the federal authority could not, and should not, change the financial settlement of the confederation act; and the eighth resolution declared that any such amendment should require the consent of the other provinces.[48] John Sandfield Macdonald's Conservative government rejected the resolutions.

The Liberals fought a similar battle in the House of Commons. There, in 1869, Blake and Alexander Mackenzie proposed an amendment declaring that the central government had no right to act unilaterally in altering the financial terms of the confederation compact.[49]

This motion was defeated, but the struggle was carried on by L. H. Holton, a Quebec member who had opposed approval of the Quebec Resolutions in 1865. When second reading was sought for the bill to increase the subsidies to Nova Scotia, Holton moved an amendment in these terms: "That in the opinion of this House any disturbance of the financial arrangements respecting the several provinces provided for in the British North America Act, unless assented to by all the provinces, would be subversive of the system of government under which the Dominion was constituted."[50] This type of appeal to the compact theory did not occasion serious discussion for long as every province ultimately benefited from the many revisions of the statutory grants.

Economic aspects of the compact theory received renewed consideration during the early nineteen-thirties when the extent of the provinces' financial incapability of meeting their increasing social responsibilities became evident. Many commentators of the period directed their attention to the country's "constitutional impasse." The problem, in short, was that only the central government possessed fiscal resources capable of dealing with the public's demands for social assistance; the constitution, however, imposed social welfare responsibilities exclusively on the provinces. Everyone recognized the necessity of coping with the economic and social crisis—which affected the federation's different regions quite unevenly—but few could agree on a method of transferring the burden of the social service responsibilities from the provincial treasuries to the federal treasury. Some demanded that federal subsidies to the provinces should be vastly increased, others rejected this solution because it seemed to violate the principle that the government spending tax revenues should be obliged to levy the necessary taxes. For this latter group, the only solution was to transfer the constitutional obligation for social services from the provinces to the federal government, but neither the cabinet at Ottawa nor those in the provincial capitals were agreeable to making a constitutional change of this magnitude.[51]

In their search for new sources of revenue, the "compact provinces" (i.e. the four original ones of 1867) argued that the confederation financial settlement represented an agreement whereby each government was to have revenue sources appropriate to its responsibilities. In their view, what the situation called for was not higher subsidies but a reallocation of guaranteed tax sources. This view led to the concept of fiscal autonomy employed by the provinces of British Columbia, Ontario, and Quebec in their submissions to the Sirois commission in 1938,[52] and again during the federal-provincial conferences of 1941 and 1945-46. Spokesmen for these three provinces, in essence, said: let the federal government stop invading our only taxation fields, let it acknowledge provincial priority in direct taxation as the confederation compact provides, and our financial problems will disappear.[53]

A most sophisticated exposition of the compact theory of fiscal autonomy was given in the Royal Commission of Inquiry on Constitutional Problems, known as the *Tremblay Report*. The commissioners said that fiscal systems were "in intimate relationship" with the political philosophy from which they emanated. A taxation system consequently should not be judged simply in terms of the adequacy of revenue produced thereby. To have a just scheme of taxation, the commission said, "it is required that . . . this fiscal system by its inspiration and modalities shall be in harmony with the political philosophy from which the state issued and by which it should continue to live."[54] While the taxation provisions of the constitution "are, unfortunately, anything but precise," the nature of the compact is easily deduced from the obligations assigned to the parties. For every duty, the commission said, "there is a corresponding right to ways of performing it, which, in this case, means a right to fiscal resources proportionate to the extent of the obligations." Legislative competences were distributed logically to the federal and local levels of government; it follows that "each order of government should have the prior initiative as regards the taxes which correspond qualitatively to its constitutional functions."[55] The historic responsibility for levying indirect taxes on the one hand, and direct taxes on the other, was examined carefully and a conclusion drawn that the division of taxing powers required adjustment. In consequence, said the Tremblay commissioners:

> there should be assigned to the federal government (over and above indirect taxes the direct taxes which correspond most exactly to its functions, and especially those whose use by the province would tend to erect economic barriers within the country. These would be the taxes on consumption already mentioned.
>
> In the same way, there should be assigned to the provinces the taxes which, through their incidence on ways of life, institutions and social life are in closest relationship to their constitutional functions. These would include the tax on real property, already devolved to the municipalities, taxes on successions, on the exploitation of natural resources, on personal and corporation incomes.[56]

In justifying this particular division of powers, the commission said that assignment of the tax on successions should be determined by the provincial regulation of inheritance laws. Natural resources taxes provided the economic bases of provisional autonomy and are levied in areas of exclusive provincial jurisdiction; consequently, they should be left to the provinces. The personal income tax, at current rates, "contributes powerfully in the shaping of family life and the social milieu," the commission said. Income taxes also had a direct incidence on property. Therefore, the province "should be able to decide the sociological modalities, or in other words, the basic exemptions" according to family responsibilities, and educational, welfare and health costs. Corporation taxes could and should be used to shape policies relating to natural resources and social welfare. Thus, said the commission, the provinces should have the initiative in the companies' tax as well. Should adoption of these proposals reduce federal revenues below those needed for federal programs, the solution appeared obvious—Ottawa must vacate the social welfare and educational fields which it has invaded unconstitutionally. In sum, these fiscal proposals were regarded by the Tremblay commission as a "return to the Constitution."

Another economic element of the compact was developed by New Brunswick in its submission[57] to the Sirois commission in April, 1938. The province argued that it had entered the union on the strength of a firm agreement which had not been fully carried out. The province further claimed that a material portion of the "contract of Confederation" was contained in Resolution 66 which provincial delegates adopted at London in 1866: "The communications with the North Western Territory, and the improvements required for the development of the trade of the Great West with the Sea-board, are regarded by this Conference as subjects of the highest importance to the Confederation, and shall be prosecuted at the earliest possible period that the state of the Finances will permit."[58] This provision was not incorporated into the B.N.A. Act, but the province contended that the London Resolutions were binding on all parties as a "joint declaration" and formal agreement. A spokesman argued for New Brunswick that sec. 145 of the B.N.A. Act, together with federal and imperial legislation regarding construction of the Intercolonial Railway, demonstrated that the founding fathers had accepted the binding character of the London "agreement." The terms of this agreement had, in New Brunswick's opinion, committed Canada to channeling all of its trade through Maritime ports. Because this agreement had been broken, the Maritime provinces had suffered grievously and deserved compensation. Neither the Sirois commission[59] nor the federal government accepted the contention.

COMPACT FEDERALISM IN PRACTICE

Fundamental premises of compact federalism are supported by dicta and decisions of the Judicial Committee of the Privy Council that established the sovereignty of the provinces within certain spheres, and by a broad interpretation of provincial powers. This broad interpretation of local jurisdiction is based on a literal rendering of the introductory clause of sec. 92[60] in conjunction with the two general clauses in the section that vest in the provinces authority over property and civil rights in the province, and "generally all Matters of a merely local or private Nature."

Mr. Justice Mignault argued in 1938 that the expression "property and civil rights" had a very broad meaning in constitutional history, at least in the areas of New France (Ontario and Quebec).[61] This broad meaning stemmed from an edict by Louis XIV which established a supreme council at Quebec. The council was given authority "de connaître de toutes causes civiles et criminelles, pour juger souverainement et en dernier ressort selon les lois et ordonnances de notre royaume," and it was argued that this edict extended the whole of French law to New France. The jurist asserted that specific acknowledgement of this law was made by the Quebec Act, which reestablished the preConquest civil law situation, and that later statutes, including the B.N.A. Act, always had this wider meaning of property and civil rights in view. The phrase property and civil rights in the province was not expressly limited in the confederation act, Mr. Justice Mignault said. This lack of limitation meant, he felt, that the Judicial Committee was expounding the true law of the land in its decisions giving a broad meaning to property and civil rights.

Going beyond these Judicial Committee decisions, which effectively gave the residual powers to the provinces, spokesmen from Quebec resorted to a particular version of constitutional history for further support. The Sirois commission was told officially that: "Pour donner naissance à cette fédération, les provinces ont consenti à l'entinté fédérale une certaine partie de leurs pouvoirs, mais elles ont conservé, outre les pouvoirs législatifs non cédés, leur entité politique et leur constitution particulière, et elles sont ainsi demeurées, dans la sphère qui leur est propre, des Etats souverains."[62] The governments of both Ontario and Quebec objected to the unilateral establishment of the inquiry into federal-provincial relations. If the working of the compact of 1867 was to be reexamined, the central provinces argued that consultations with the provinces should have preceded the establishment of a commission of inquiry. The commission might better have been set up, it was implied, in accordance with certain procedures analogous to those used in the international sphere.

The New Brunswick brief to the Sirois commission was as firmly in the compact tradition as was that of Quebec. The provinces, as "sovereign and independent nations under the British Crown," had set up a federal agency for certain limited purposes and the B.N.A. Act "did not effect any change in their status. They are still independent sovereignties. . . ."[63] Alberta refused to submit an official brief to the commission, preferring to issue one at large to the "sovereign People of Canada." A similar attitude was manifested in 1962 when the province of British Columbia, led by a Social Credit government, refused to deal with another royal commission—the Porter inquiry into financial and banking policies. Its government contended that fiscal matters should be explored by a conference of sovereign governments.

Much of the struggle between the provinces and the federal government during the last century turned on the rights and dignities of the lieutenant-governor. The Ottawa authorities contended he was simply a political agent of the Governor-in-Council, but decisions of the Judicial Committee did not support this view. The J.C.P.C. ruled that the lieutenant-governor was a representative of the Queen for purposes of the governance of a province. The federal-provincial struggle over the office of lieutenant-governor was revived briefly during the nineteen forties. In one instance in 1945, Premier Duplessis sought a voice in appointments. He wrote to Prime Minister King that the "tradition of courtesy and sane diplomacy which is in conformity with the spirit and letter of the federal pact" required the approval of the provincial cabinet before a new lieutenant-governor was nominated. "We consider," said the Quebec premier, "that the nomination of a lieutenant-governor is comparable to that of an ambassador."[64] This battle Quebec lost although an informal practice of consultation did develop on the matter several decades later.

A partial explanation of the favour with which Quebeckers have held the compact theory in the past might be discerned in their special concern for the constitution which incorporates the religious and language guarantees of the Quebec Act of 1774. One French Canadian has termed the Quebec Act "a true social contract between us and England . . . the consecration of our natural rights."[65] The B.N.A. Act also contains all the elements of a "veritable social contract, clothed with the royal sanction," according to a Quebec view of the constitution expressed in 1918.[66] So bitter did that province feel about attacks on her native sons during the conscription crisis, that the Quebec legislature solemnly debated a resolution offering to break the "sacred compact" if the English truly felt that Quebec was not maintaining her part of the bargain.[67] During this debate one member exclaimed bitterly: "Let bygones be bygones, he says, and yet his [English] friends abide by their improper gains over our trust and fealty made by trampling upon our rights and the sanctity of our treaties. History offers no record even in ancient times of such disrespect for sacred alliances and compacts as has been openly professed and practised in this Twentieth Century on this hemisphere of ours."[68]

During Maurice Duplessis' long reign as premier at Quebec city, he perceived a great many central government "encroachments" on areas of exclusive provincial jurisdiction and he vigorously attacked them as violations of the sacred compact of 1867. British Columbia and Prince Edward Island had been confederated by order-in-council and the three prairie provinces had been created by federal statute. When negotiations for the admission of Newfoundland resumed after the Second World War, the Quebec cabinet objected that the provinces had not been consulted; it was concerned because the addition of more English-speaking members to the Commons and Senate "modifierait nos garanties constitutionnelles."[69] Compact violations were seen in the creation of the Canadian Broadcasting Corporation which broadcast both cultural and educational programs in Quebec and which denied the province permissions to establish its own broadcasting system for educational purposes. The work of the National Film Board and the federal departments of health, welfare, and labour "intruded" on provincial concerns.[70] A scholar, whose views accorded closely with those of Premier Duplessis, wrote: "Ce genre de tentative s'exécute au nom de l'unité nationale. Il s'agit d'uniformiser le code, l'école, voire la syndicalisme, et enfin la langue, bref de détruire les cadres dans lesquels et grâce aux-quels les Canadiens français conservent leur originalité de peuple."[71]

The provinces have sometimes exploited their autonomous status in other countries. In 1927 the prime minister acceded to a request by Manitoba and British Columbia that the provinces be specifically represented in the Canadian delegation to the International Labour conferences at Geneva.[72] Most provinces maintained special offices in Britain—such as Ontario House and B.C. House—whose purposes were to promote immigration and trade. Maison de Québec was established in Paris during 1961, and federal officials were openly chagrined at the head-of-state reception accorded to Quebec Premier Jean Lesage who opened the building during an official visit.[73] In the same year, Manitoba embarked on its own educational foreign aid program within the ambit of the Colombo Plan. Quebec has been sporadically active in assisting French-language schools outside her provincial borders.

Does the compact theory permit us to deduce that the provinces have the right to conclude foreign agreements? Apart from the American relationship, that has been the only significant external relations issue to appear in domestic politics during the past quarter century. The dispute grew steadily in prominence throughout the nineteen-sixties as the province of Quebec sought to extend both the breadth and depth of its relationships with France and the international French community. The Quebec government felt its objectives required the conclusion of formal understandings between the province, foreign governments, and some international bodies. That activity, and particularly the symbolic gestures accompanying it, brought the province into dispute with the federal government led by Lester B. Pearson at first and then by P.-E. Trudeau. The federal prime ministers insisted that Ottawa represented Canada's total international personality and that it possessed a monopoly of the so-called "treaty power." There-fore, they argued, there was no way in which any province could conclude a valid agreement with a foreign state unless it was done under the terms of some existing arrangement which had been negoti-ated by the federal administration. Advocates of the compact theory favoured a much more restrictive interpretation of the federal gov-ernment's powers: that Ottawa's authority consisted only in that ex-plicitly conveyed by sec. 132 of the B.N.A. Act as narrowly inter-preted by the *Labour Conventions* case. Without specifically citing the compact theory, some *Québecois* argued that the province's ex-clusive jurisdiction over education and other cultural matters carried with it a concomitant right to conclude whatever arrangements with other countries which might be required to carry out provincial edu-cational and cultural policies. The issue played a major role in the deux nations controversy which is discussed within the context of the dualist concept.

CRITICISM OF THE COMPACT THEORY

The compact theory has been widely criticized. The most thorough analysis was that of Professor Norman McL. Rogers who undertook the task in 1931 in reaction to the Ferguson memorandum. He felt that the growth of a vigorous nation had been arrested by two restrain-ing influences: the exaggerated emphasis on the claims of imperial unity and on the claim of provincial autonomy. "If it was the purpose of the first of these influences to keep us a colony," he said, "it is the tendency of the other to make us a league of provinces."[74] In failing to provide a domestic amending process, the founding fathers had committed a "sin which in scriptural fashion has now been visited upon their children even unto the third and fourth generation."

With this beginning, Professor Rogers set to work to mine the foundations of the theory. If there was a treaty, who were the original partners? Only New Brunswick and Nova Scotia could pose in this light, he said; the Act of 1867 had created the provinces of Ontario and Quebec and the federal government, so none of them could be legal parties. British Columbia and Prince Edward Island entered the union after negotiations with Ottawa, so they could not be assimi-lated to treaty partners, and the three prairie provinces had been cre-ated at the instance of the House of Commons.[75] Delegates to the three founding conferences had lacked authorization from either their own legislatures or the imperial Crown to conclude any binding agreements, and, what was more, "the task of drawing up a new constitution . . . attached to the function of legislation and did not properly lie within the field of executive action" because of the imperfect nature of the Crown in respect to the provincial executive councils. Only one legislature, that of Canada, approved the Quebec Resolutions; New Brunswick rejected them, and Nova Scotia's legislature was so hostile to the project that it was never submitted for consideration. The only discussions authorized in British North America were those "confined to the fact of union and did not extend to any specific terms," according to Professor Rogers. He pointed to changes made at the London conferences and by the imperial law clerks, changes which were not known in the provinces until after the Parliament at Westminster had enacted the constitutive bill.

The loose use of the words "treaty" and "compact" in the provincial parliament was a matter of tactics, according to this view. The history of amendments made to the B.N.A. Act also refutes the conception of the act as a compact. "To sum it up, the practice hitherto adopted with respect to the amendment of the British North America Act is definitely against the implications of the compact theory," Professor Rogers concluded.[76] After examining other federal states, he saw "no precedent whatever for the compact theory as advanced in Canada," particularly in respect of any requirement of unanimous consent for constitutional change. "Finally," he said, "on grounds of practical inconvenience the compact theory of Confederation is wholly untenable as applied to the present conditions." He admitted that political expediency might necessitate a limited measure of provincial consultation and consent for future amendments, and he urged the need of transferring the amending power to Canada. But the first thing to be dealt with, this critic felt, was the removal of "the barbed wire that has been set in our path" by advocates of the contract doctrine.

In 1945 the federal cabinet sought to remove the "barbed wire" poised by the provinces' independent taxing rights through a radical centralization of fiscal powers.[77] If the measures proposed in 1945 were extreme, the fiscal proposals of the Tremblay commissioners were equally so. The compact theory of federalism found apt expression in the Tremblay taxation scheme, but questions should be raised as to how well this fiscal plan embodied political practicality. Assigning priority in the allocation of the federation's chief revenue sources to the provinces would have led to revolutionary political changes for which there was little evidence of popular support.

Two further objections to the fiscal implications of compact federalism deserve notice. The one is that existence of wide variations of taxation standards within one federation might seriously jeopardize the exercise of economic policy necessary to meet public demands for control over cyclical fluctuations in the economy. Three types of reply have been made to this objection. The first is that of the Tremblay commission, which asserted the necessity of subordinating materialistic values to those of culture and religion. In a second type of argument, a Montreal economist, François-Albert Angers, has challenged the efficacy of such intervention in the economy when directed in accord with the "unproven and fallacious" doctrines of Lord Keynes. Administrative efficiencies, Angers said, would be greatest when any such government intervention was directed from the centres of the economic regions, a role that most provincial capitals could play.[78] Another Montrealer, Pierre-Elliott Trudeau, provided the third variety of reply with advice to his English-speaking socialist friends to cease their objections to provincial autonomy and concentrate on winning power in the provinces. From these vantage points, he said, socialist parties would be able to effect almost as much social good as they could from Ottawa. Trudeau, like Angers, also pointed to sectional aspects of the economy—in contrast to those who emphasize the centralized control of finance in Canada—and indicated the constitutional controls that provincial governments could, but did not then attempt to exercise within their borders.[79]

A second important objection is that implementing the fiscal theories of the compact doctrine would tend to accentuate the economic disparities of the constituent regions. To meet this objection, Premier George Drew of Ontario had proposed in 1945 at the reconstruction conference the establishment of a committee of the provinces which would reapportion sums contributed by the wealthier provinces. The Tremblay Report applauded this proposal and suggested an interprovincial commission that would attempt to rectify the inequity whereby one province was able to tax corporate income earned in another province. Such a commission would also make outright grants to poor provinces on the basis of fiscal need. The poor provinces might well question, however, whether the Ontario or Quebec proposals would increase their independence, which would necessarily depend on the willingness of the wealthier provinces to tax themselves for "foreign" benefit.

CONCLUSION

Salient qualities of the compact theory may be summarized with the assistance of the criteria suggested earlier for this inquiry. The concept tends to stress centrifugal forces within the union, and places emphasis on strengthening the provinces rather than the central power, which would be held in close check. This objective is best achieved through assuring the financial autonomy of the provinces. This autonomy, in turn, requires guarantees of meaningful fiscal independence and interpretations of the compact so that all provinces gain economic benefit from the effects of union. The theory insists on the need of maintaining the full political independence of the provinces within their designated constitutional spheres; federal initiative in areas of local jurisdiction must therefore cease. The exercise of competence outside the country in matters such as immigration, educational assistance, and cultural promotion is justified by the compact doctrine. Exclusive provincial responsibility for civil liberties (except for those of secs. 93 and 133) is asserted, and the legitimacy denied to extra-provincial pressures for uniformity in educational standards or for the extension of language rights. Great emphasis is placed on the right of each province to be consulted authoritatively on any proposed amendments to the constitution.

The compact theory of federalism originated during the first great period of constitutional ferment and was given lucid exposition in the *Letters* of Mr. Justice Loranger. The "provincial revolt" coincided with a long trough in the economic cycle, a diminution of the nationalist spirit that swept the country two decades earlier, and the reduction of external threats. *La survivance* was bolstered by the compact theory but the same doctrines also served the English majorities outside of Quebec. *L'ancienne province* has usually exercised a powerful influence on the party in power at Ottawa, but the doctrine of provincial sovereignty permitted both Manitoba and Quebec to resist federal pressure during the school disputes, as it did other provinces during recent attempts to extend the range of official bilingualism. The compact notion was maintained for a time in respect to provincial representation in the House of Commons, but gave way during the Second World War. This concept of federalism gave the poor provinces encouragement and justification during their campaigns for higher federal subsidies. In the fifties it was employed to support provincial demands for exclusive control over certain taxation fields that would ensure their fiscal independence. Most enduring manifestation of the compact theory has been in the veto enjoyed by all provinces in the negotiations over adoption of a new domestic amending formula.

Constitutional lawyers have effectively refuted the existence of the compact as a legal notion but it may be defended on other grounds. As Professor G. F. G. Stanley has observed:

> The legalist will, of course, reply that the intervention of the Colonial Office and the passing of the bill as an Act of the British Parliament in effect destroyed the compactual . . . basis of the historical process of confederation. Perhaps it does; to the lawyer. But to the historian the simple fact remains that the officers of the Colonial Office accepted without question the assessment of the situation given them by the colonial delegates. To them the Bill was in the nature of a colonial Treaty, even if such a treaty were not found in . . . the text books of international law.[80]

6

The Dual Alliance

Closely allied to the theory of a compact between provinces is the idea of a compact between races.* A prominent Montreal economist has said, for example, that the Canadian federation was inspired by a purpose altogether different from that which animated the American union. This purpose, as he saw it, was to safeguard the permanence and to promote the expansion of two national cultures.[1] It is here, in the essential partnership of two linguistic and cultural groups that one finds the dominant fact of Canadian nationhood. Here too, says the historian, Arthur Lower, "is the most resounding note in our history, the juxtaposition of two civilizations, two philosophies, two contra- dictory views of the fundamental nature of man."[2] To Professor Malcolm Ross, "we are inescapably, and almost from the first, the bifocal people." The characteristic prudence of the Canadian, he said, "derives from this necessity for taking second thought, for keeping one foot on each bank of the Ottawa."[3] Just as this dualism has dominated the country's history, literature, and national life, so it has been the dominant theme of more than a century of federal politics.

The coexistence of these two linguistic universes has inspired an unusual type of relationship between the two races. "The character- istic process," says Jean-Charles Falardeau, "has not been one of assimilation but one of progressive differentiation, of cultural duality within the framework of a single national political unit." As a social

---

*Valid objection may be made to this use of the word "race." It is, however, part of the Canadian vocabulary as a virtual synonym for the word "nation," particularly in the present context with which it is intimately associated.

scientist, Professor Falardeau stressed that *"unhyphenated canadianism is a fiction,"* and pleaded with all who would understand the country to begin by reckoning with its dualist nature.[4]

From this basic dualism arose the conception of confederation as a compact between two peoples, a compact that acknowledges the existence and right to life of two languages, two religions, and two ways of life. An important aspect of the dualists' perspective was described by Professor John Meisel in this way:

> Like the terms of reference given the Royal Commission on Bilingualism and Biculturalism, and like the commissioners themselves, the Canadians who make this distinction assume that Canada is a partnership between two language groups. These language groups constitute two societies which share one political union. It follows from this position that both English and French occupy a special place in the life of Canada and that both languages must be accorded special and equal status in clearly identified areas. In recognizing the two principal language groups in Canada, the adherents to the country's essential dualism recognize . . . that people of various origins, in the process of their Canadianization, become part of one or the other of the two language groups and members of one or the other of the two societies.[5]

This approach is, above all, a conception of the country which emphasizes its *cultural* duality rather than its multi-ethnic composition. The distinction between cultural group and racial origin is often slurred over or ignored altogether in argumentation that French Canadians comprise an ethnic minority similar to, and no more significant than other ethnic minorities. What in turn should not be ignored is that people holding a dualist conception of the country's culture are divided on whether it logically implies the necessity of political or structural changes beyond expanding the status of the French language generally and maintaining a place for English within Quebec.

The contractual element of the concept is traced back to the declarations of the British commanders of the occupation of 1760-63, to the Treaty of Paris of 1763, the Quebec Act of 1774, the Constitutional Act of 1791, and the Act of Union 1840. By these various actions, Britain granted to its French-speaking citizens the right to speak their own tongue and to practise their own religion. This was an agreement, it is said, which the Canadians fulfilled by their loyalty to the crown during the American revolution and the invasions of 1812-14. The compact between races found political expression in the quasi-federal politics of the Province of Canada, and by 1865, it was virtually a commonplace notion. "It influenced both the political thinking and the political vocabulary of the day," says Professor G. F. G. Stanley, and "it was already on the way to become a tradition and convention of our constitution."[6]

The equality of the French and English was acknowledged from the beginning of the union. As early as 1849, the fiery Nova Scotian, Joseph Howe, had lectured a prominent Upper Canadian that no respectable British subject would have any part of a union designed to submerge any portion of the population, or to create a group of second class citizens.[7] These egalitarian sentiments were apparently shared by the Fathers of Confederation. Sir John A. Macdonald made his view clear during the bitter school and language battles, when the prudent course of intra-party politics would have dictated saying nothing. "There is no paramount race in this country," he told the House of Commons in 1890, "there is no conquered race in this country; we are all British subjects, and those who are not English are none the less British subjects on that account."[8] An acknowledgement of the cultural duality of the country was, for Macdonald, the first condition of the union's birth and continued existence. Whatever else Canadian federalism might have meant in 1865, "it was clear," says Dean Frank R. Scott, "that it had to be free from any reasonable suspicion of being a device to bring about the assimilation of French Canada."[9]

While affirming loyalty to their own nation, the leaders of French Canada did not hesitate to encourage their kinsmen in a larger loyalty to the federation as a whole. Sir Wilfrid Laurier, the national leader of the Liberal party, chose the important feast day of Saint Jean Baptiste in 1889 to declare this larger fealty. "We are French Canadians, but our country is not confined to the territory overshadowed by the citadel of Quebec; our country is Canada." Could it not be believed, he asked, that, when the fate of arms turned against Montcalm and the *Canadiens* on the Plains of Abraham, "it entered into the designs of Providence that the two races, enemies up to that time, should henceforth live in peace and harmony?" This, he thought, was the inspiration of the whole scheme of confederation.[10]

In later years, Laurier was replaced in the affections of many militant Quebeckers by Henri Bourassa. He too preached of a Canadian nationalism founded upon the duality of races and mutual respect. "The fatherland is all Canada," he said, "that is, a federation of distinct races and autonomous provinces." Bourassa made this declaration during a battle with Jules-Paul Tardivel who espoused a more limited patriotism. "For us," said Tardivel in 1904, "our compatriots are the French Canadians; for us our fatherland is—we do not wish to say precisely the Province of Quebec—but French Canada." Tardivel had but a limited following at this time, but his sentiments were those of many in Quebec, and they were to become more important as the duel between the two cultures waxed hot, now cold, but was never entirely extinguished.

SCHOOLS AND CONSCRIPTION

A contention frequently advanced during the last third of the nineteenth century was that the use of the French language was guaranteed by the Act of 1867 to French Canadians throughout the country.[11] The issue became critical as the prairies were populated, and the hope arose in Quebec that the west might become another bastion of French culture. The French language was used officially in the North West Territories, and the Manitoba Act of 1870 had apparently guaranteed both language and church school rights to the French-speaking Red River settlers. But English, rather than French, came to predominate throughout the west, and agitation arose during the eighteen-eighties to have done with "popery" and the "inferior" French tongue. Accordingly, in 1889, the Manitoba legislature passed a statute depriving the French of rights which they thought had been guaranteed by the Manitoba Act. "That it had been the intent of the Act to maintain those rights is morally beyond dispute," said one observer, "but its wording was vague and the Privy Council refused to declare the new school law *ultra vires*."[12] Thus, the strong issue of federal versus provincial rights was added to the powerful mixture of race and religious prejudice that was already brewing.

Laurier won office in 1896 largely as a result of the political struggles that ensued, and a compromise school arrangement was patched up. The compromise proved to be shortlived. In 1916, the Manitoba legislature moved once more to do away with teaching in the French tongue.[13] French Canadians saw this action as a gross violation of the Laurier compromise and of their status as equal partners in the federation. In his history of Manitoba, W. L. Morton had commented that: "the bitter sense of betrayal felt by the French members drove them on to assert the whole claim of their people, their historical, moral and constitutional right to have denominational schools and to have equality of the French language with English; to assert, in short, the principle of duality. . . . The bill, the French members declared, was a violation of the 'pact,' or 'treaty' of Confederation, which had recognized the equal and distinct status of the French in Canada."[14]

In 1913 the Ontario government issued the notorious Regulation 17 which prohibited the use of any language other than English in the schools. The storm that arose in French Canada was charged with emotion. The premier of Quebec, Lomer Gouin, had been noted for his insistence that the provinces be allowed to exercise their constitutional powers free of all outside pressures, but even he felt constrained to intervene. In 1915, he appealed to the government of Ontario "pour le verbe français, le droit de résonner sur les lèvres des écoliers d'Ontario qui veulent l'apprendre et le parler."[15] The Abbé Arthur Maheux has said that the Regulation 17 issue was a graver danger to Canadian unity than had been either the First World War or the navy issues, because neither of the latter issues had put the two cultures in direct opposition.[16] When, more than a decade later, Ontario Premier G. Howard Ferguson rescinded Regulation 17, he was praised as a man whose name would long be honoured for this service to the two cultures.[17]

The school struggles were manifestations of the constant tensions between the French and English in Canada. Twice within a generation, inter-cultural conflict threatened to rip open the fragile seams that held the two nations together in one federation. European wars brought on both crises. The first came in 1917. Three years of fighting and war casualties had inflamed English Canada's identification with Britain's causes, but the same three years had only persuaded the French Canadians of the idiocy of sending their sons to die in foreign wars. Despite violent protests throughout Quebec, English-speaking Canadians put devotion to imperial duty ahead of unity at home and imposed conscription on Canadians and *Canadiens* alike. The suspicions and outright hostilities bred by the 1917 crisis became a continuing sore of the body politic.

Interracial tensions again became critical in the Second World War. Here, Canadians of British descent identified themselves with Britain's interests, but French-speaking Canadians did not. Neither did they identify themselves with the concerns of the other homeland, France, for that country had abandoned the *Canadiens* to their own devices centuries before. During the early days of the war, the Liberal prime minister, W. L. Mackenzie King, sought and won French Canadian voting support, partly on the strength of a promise never to impose conscription. The government changed its mind on that point and introduced conscription—after a national plebiscite in which the prime minister asked the majority to free him from the no-conscription promise which he had made to the minority linguistic group. The results did not strengthen French Canadian faith in the majoritarian political process as any kind of guarantee for their rights. The two world wars furnished only two examples of a number of occasions in this century when consensus on important issues of external relations has been notably lacking between the two cultural groups.

LA CRISE DU FEDERALISME

During the nineteen-forties, intercultural disagreement was revealed on the methods to be used in pursuing the state's objectives. The federal cabinet, which was dominated by the English-speaking Mackenzie King, C. D. Howe, and James G. Gardiner, believed that the federal government's resources should be employed in matters of national interest. French Canadians believed the constitutional distribution of powers should indicate which order of government should carry out any particular task. King's government enacted measures directly affecting social security and education. Maurice Duplessis protested "on behalf of all true French Canadians" that the federal government was acting unconstitutionally. In 1945, the central government persuaded seven of the nine provincial governments that the major taxing powers should be concentrated in Parliament's hands. Premier Duplessis objected that the independence of the provinces would be destroyed if this should happen.[18] In 1949, Parliament added to its competence the unhindered right to amend the B.N.A. Act in respect of nearly all central government areas of jurisdiction. Again, the Duplessis government in Quebec objected strenuously; giving Parliament this power, it was said, was incompatible with the basic principles of federalism.

French Canadians also saw their culture threatened by the absence of genuine concern for federalism in the other provincial capitals. At first, seven provinces, then eight, and eventually all nine English-speaking provinces signed tax rental pacts with the Ottawa régime, and only the province of Quebec retained unimpaired possession of its fiscal rights. *L'ancienne province* also felt isolated in constitutional matters. A number of provincial cabinets and a great many private groups were agitating for the early adoption of a Canadian procedure for amending the B.N.A. Act. But French Canada had always had faith that the existing arrangement would give its culture a little additional protection against the English-speaking majority, and no urgency about constitutional amendment was felt in Quebec City. None of the methods proposed in English Canada at this time met Quebec's minimum requirements, and the province's spokesmen felt that acceding to such amending procedures would endanger *la survivance*.

Such was the impact of these economic and political pressures on Quebec that by 1952 one student of the constitution, Paul Gérin-Lajoie, was writing of "la crise du fédéralisme au Canada," an expression which he felt was quite appropriate.[19] La Chambre de commerce de la province de Québec had a similar impression. In 1952, this influential organization declared that the whole province was alarmed by the issues stirred up by these English Canadian movements. La Chambre called on Premier Duplessis to establish a royal commission to inquire into the pertinent constitutional and financial questions.[20]

The crisis of federalism bore a cultural as well as a political aspect. The cultural concerned the preservation and encouragement of French Canada as a nation both within and without the provincial boundaries of Quebec. In the past, despite their strident insistence on provincial autonomy, Quebec politicians had seldom hesitated to demand the restriction of other provinces' independence for the sake of assuring maximum rights to French minorities.[21] In 1928, the Quebec legislature had asserted its right to take an interest in the education of French Canadians in other provinces; it enacted a measure encouraging school commissions to help support French-language schools in Ontario. In accordance with this legislation, special funds could and were raised "pour les fins patriotiques, nationales, ou scolaires, et dans les limites de la province ou ailleurs."[22] Strong and successful pressure was exerted from Quebec during the nineteen-thirties to force the Canadian Broadcasting Corporation to permit establishment of French-language radio stations on the prairies, despite strong resistance from officials and only slight evidence of local demand. The logical incompatibility between the compact theory underpinning provincial autonomy and dualist tendencies was often painfully obvious. One conference at the University of Montreal, for example, heard a plea from a delegate from the Maritimes: "N'insistez pas trop sur le principe de l'autonomie provinciale. Il joue contre nous."[23] Within Quebec, the growth and spread of industrialism combined with the increasing effectiveness of the mass media to invigorate the impulses of social change. Some of these impulses found expression in anti-clericalism, while others reflected the spreading influence of the materialist values attributed to Anglo-American civilization. Associations rooted in the traditions of French Canadian culture sought to gather strength through an appeal to the "national" loyalties of *Canadiens* everywhere. But the same forces that were at work in Quebec were even stronger outside the province. The French Canadians of the "dispersion" were being anglicized rapidly.[24] A great increase in the missionary work that Quebec institutions had traditionally carried out in these scattered colonies was needed lest the French Canadian settlers be lost completely to the English Canadian culture.

Leaders of French Canada faced a dilemma. The political imperatives of their society were centred in Quebec City, but their cultural imperatives spanned the federation and urgently demanded the creation of institutions that could transcend provincial boundaries.[25] If greater language and school privileges could be won for the isolated French colonies, the gradual dissolution of these minorities into the majority culture might be halted. But any insistence on expanding, or even protecting, existing minority rights elsewhere would undermine Quebec's demand for the greatest possible degree of provincial independence. Put another way, Quebec had to assert its own sovereign status to ensure protection of the cultural heartland, but the expansion of the French culture required restricting the autonomy of the other provinces.

A Two Nation State

A possible solution of the problem had been suggested a quarter-century earlier by Henri Saint-Denis. In 1933 he had argued that the founding fathers had made the protection of the two cultures the chief object of confederation. Where this end had been willed, he said, it must be assumed that the necessary means had also been willed. Those means involved the creation of political institutions which would properly express the state's basic dualism. The question of how to justify and, then, of how to attain such institutions perplexed a number of French Canadian thinkers during the early nineteen-fifties. Some of them sought new definitions of federalism. François-Albert Angers, for example, said that federalism was not "une simple formule intermédiaire entre l'anarchie et la Nation-Etat centralisée," as many English-speaking persons assumed, but rather, it was "une réalisation du pluralisme considéré comme la seule véritable forme de démocratie organisée."*

This thinking seems eventually to have crystallized into a conception of the federation as a dyarchy. The reason why Canadian pluralism should be expressed in a dualist polity lies in the collaboration of but two races in the founding of the state. As a national group, the French Canadians were different; the view that they were just the same as other ethnic minorities on this continent "is contrary to history and sociologically erroneous," according to Professor Falardeau.[26] As a "charter member minority," the French Canadians were said to have peculiar survival abilities and the particular right to realize them.[27]

But if the state is a type of dual monarchy, where are the two political heads? The answer is suggested in these comments by Professor Michel Brunet:

Pour les Canadiens français, le gouvernement d'Ottawa ne peut être que le gouvernement central d'une fédération unissant Québec au

---

*Essai, p. 109. Federalism was said to be more democratic as a state form because it permitted more local decisions than did a unitary state, and this, it was claimed, resulted in fewer dissatisfied minorities in a country which had deep cultural divisions. Ibid., p. 110. Little consideration is evident in this argument of any important distinction between federal government and decentralized unitary government.

Canada anglais. Une collaboration étroite et harmonieuse peut et doit exister entre les autorités provinciales et fédérales. Cependant, le gouvernement chargé de défendre et de promouvoir le bien commun de la nationalité canadienne-française est celui de la province où habite l'immense majorité des Canadiens français. C'est pourquoi Québec de doit pas être considérée simplement comme l'une des dix provinces. Elle a le droit de réclamer un statut spécial dans la fédération canadienne puisqu'elle est le porte-parole et le défenseur de la minorité.[28]

Ottawa is not and cannot be a focus for the interests of French Canada, because the entire governmental apparatus is dominated by the English culture. Even in those departments of government where French is the normal working language, English methods prevail over those of the French culture. The only alternative focus of French Canada's culture is the province of Quebec and its capital city.[29] This type of reasoning has brought some intellectuals to develop the proposition that Quebec City is the site of a "national government" which should be acknowledged as the equal partner of Ottawa in a dualist federation.

The two nations thesis was taken up by a Quebec barrister, Philippe Ferland, in a presentation to the Tremblay commission which was later published in the widely-read *L'action nationale*.[30] He said the federal-provincial tax rental agreements which the English provinces had signed had, for all practical purposes, created a legislative union of all English-speaking Canada. Now, he said, all could see that the Canadian federation had evolved into two national political units, one centred in Quebec City, and the other in Ottawa. Quebec alone had not signed an agreement and now the two nations stood in clear relief. The Act of 1867 and the existing financial structure were highly centralizing, M. Ferland said. If the French-speaking were to save their national life, the constitution must be revised. All federal controls over provincial laws should be abolished, he said; judges for the provinces should be appointed by the provinces, the Quebec Court of Queen's Bench should be the final interpreter of the civil code, and all Quebec-Ottawa conflicts should be settled by a three-man arbitral board. Complete provincial control over interior trade and commerce and adequate fiscal powers for Quebec were also proposed. He felt that these new arrangements should be entrenched by means of an Ottawa-Quebec "entente," partaking of the nature of a formal treaty between nations.

A 1954 taxation conference between Prime Minister Louis St. Laurent and Premier Maurice Duplessis gave M. Ferland another opportunity to explore the dualist theme.[31] In an article published in *Thémis,* the law journal of the Université de Montréal, M. Ferland observed that the "neutral" city of Montreal was the site for a dramatic confrontation that brought the country back to confederation's first point of departure. Now, he said, the two original parties had come face to face, "l'Etat canadien-français et l'Etat canadien." The one party represented legislative union, the other a cultural community that wished to improve its chances to survive as a nation. Throughout his exposition, M. Ferland posed the antithesis: "Deux Etats, deux conceptions, deux peuples."

THE TREMBLAY COMMISSION

Of all the manifestations of the dualist concept that might be cited, the most remarkable is the *Report of the Royal Commission of Inquiry on Constitutional Problems,*[32] commonly known as the *Tremblay Report* after the name of the commission chairman. This document is, as Professor Alexander Brady has said, "a landmark in the literature of federalism,"[33] and in it is found the most explicit and detailed statement available of the dual alliance theory. Here the theory is justified in history, law, philosophy, politics, and economics. Most engaging are the philosophical and fiscal conceptions, some of which had been expressed several years earlier in articles by a member of the commission, the Rev. Richard Arès.[34]

The Tremblay commission surveyed the past and analyzed the present to discover French Canada's particular role in the development of confederation. The commission's report discussed the survival of the minority culture in the face of economic depression, world war, urbanization, and militant English Canadian nationalism. An examination of constitutional history from Quebec's viewpoint was undertaken[35] and this conclusion drawn: "By reason of its history, as well as of the cultural character of its population, Quebec is not a province like the others, whatever may be said to the contrary. It speaks in the name of one of the two ethnic groups which founded Confederation, and as one of the two partners who officially have the right to live and expand in this country. It is the only one able to represent one of these two partners."[36] After inquiring into difficulties of public finance, and condemning both conditional grants and federal spending in "forbidden" areas, the commission dealt with the problem of the two national communities.

"The term bi-cultural as applied to Canada designates a reality far more complex than most of those who use it seem to think," the commission declared.[37] It then simplified this complexity by dividing the country into the French Canadians, who have in common their French origin, the French tongue, and Roman Catholicism, and the Anglo-

Canadians, who are of Anglo-Saxon origin and "in the great majority" Protestant. "Now the French-Canadians," said the commission,
"are the only group whose religious and cultural particularism, as
sociological facts, almost exactly coincide." A given cultural milieu,
the commission says, is always marked by the religious conception
which inspired it, no matter how remote the religious background
might appear today. From this intimate association of culture and
religion there flow serious political consequences. "In the first place,
by the fact that being of differing essence, order and object, they
cannot be confounded, religion and culture comprise, each for its
own, the whole Canadian problem."[38] The fact that culture and religion are so closely related—they are said to meet on the plane of
humanism—gives each group in Canada "an almost monolithic homogeneity."

Only federal government makes it possible for two such homogeneous nations to coexist in the bosom of a single state, according to
the commission, and so federal government must be thoroughly
understood. This state form is usually examined in its political and
juridical senses, but it also has important sociological and philosophic
aspects. Chief among these is an appreciation of federalism as a
system of social organization that is built on four bases: "The Christian concept of Man and society; the fact of variety and complexity
in social life; the idea of the common good and the principle of every
society's suppletory functions."[39]

The commission characterized the two national communities in
accordance with their religio-cultural bases. The genius of the French
Canadians was declared to be their logicality, that of being "inclined
to reason from principles as a base." The Anglo-Saxons' genius was
seen as their pragmatism and a resulting disinclination to be concerned
with theoretical principles. The two groups represent distinct tem-
peraments which differ in their understanding and experience of life.
Even their conception of order differs. By making religion a strictly
personal affair, the commission said, "Protestantism withdrew its
social morality from all ecclesiastical discipline and liberated socio-
political thought from any reference to a transcendent order. For a
Catholic . . . the social order is the arrangement of society according to
an organic method, founded on the dignity of the person and tending
toward the common good. . . . Liberty defines itself with respect to this
order."[40] But, according to the commission, the Protestant concept
has no reference to a transcendent order, and it makes liberty pre-
eminent. In consequence, the two cultures hold two quite different sets
of values.

Without challenging English Canada's right to pursue its set of
values, identified as the acquisitive instinct of Calvinist materialism,
the Tremblay commission asserted the necessity of guaranteeing the

freedom of cultural groups to survive and expand. Only through a flourishing social culture, it was argued, could the individual develop his finest personality. A plea was made for the country as a whole to return to the conceptions of Christian humanism from which both cultures sprang. In returning to these conceptions, the central government would be led to determine its policies with greater respect to cultural imperatives than to materialist impulses. The partnership of the two cultures should be reaffirmed as the basic premise of Canadian life, the *Report* said, for, whatever the sphere of its manifest action, a national life can develop better through diversity than through uniformity.

The commission mounted a resolute attack on the "new federalism" of Maurice Lamontagne,[41] which was said to be destructive of cultural pluralism and out of harmony with French Canadian thinking. Mr. Lamontagne's federalism was, to the commission, synonymous with "unitarianism," defined as "the doctrine and policy of unity at all costs translating itself concretely as the progressive transfer to the central government of functions and powers exercised by the Quebec government."[42] The commission said that "new federalism" tended to aggrandize the powers of the central government, and in so far as a provincial government was concerned, it tended "to reduce the latter to insignificance after having reduced it to beggary from the financial and fiscal viewpoint."

In the political and legal sense, true federalism was defined as "the system of association between states in which the exercise of state power is shared between two orders of government, co-ordinate but not subordinate one to the other, each enjoying supreme power within the sphere of activity assigned to it by the Constitution."[43] This definition was elaborated with an outline of A. V. Dicey's essential characteristics of federations.[44] As a political system, federalism might vary according to its inspiration. "When its sole objective is to adapt the political system to the geographical and economic diversity of any given country, it can be more or less flexible and relaxed," said the commissioners. But when federalism aimed at ensuring the parallel development of distinctive cultures within the framework of a single state, its structure must be extensive and rigid.[45]

Where two nations exist within one federal state, it is more imperative than ever that the central authority recognize its true position as but one order of government that is in no way superior to the other level of government. This means, in the commission's view, that "the federal order, to be soundly constituted, must be built from the bottom upwards and must therefore rest, as on a base, upon the local collectivities, that is to say, on autonomous and fully living communes or municipalities."[46] The federal structure must aim at strengthening the corporate lives of both the whole and the part. But the inevitable question that arises is, as formulated by Professor Brady, "what division of power has the most logic in a given situation?"[47]

The Tremblay commission had a ready answer—the division spelled out in the confederation document drafted in 1865 and assented to by both races. This constitution, which the Judicial Committee of the Privy Council had upheld and safeguarded, "assigned to the two orders of government those prerogatives which correspond to the objectives of cultural federalism." Phenomenal aspects of Canadian life have changed since 1867, but the same federal principles were required. There must be restored to the two levels of government, said the commission, "the functions which the sociological reality respectively assigns to them today, just as it did in 1867." But it sometimes seemed that the authorities at Ottawa, instead of following his sound rule of federalist politics, almost deliberately tried to misinterpret the basic principles of Canadian federalism. The commission detailed the "sins" of encroachment committed by the federal government, commented sarcastically on the viewpoint of the supporters of the Massey commission's recommendations,[48] and referred frequently to the "centralizing proclivities" of politicians and officials at Ottawa.

These centralist tendencies, which parts of English Canada appeared to favour, had brought the country to the point where its political leaders would have to choose a set of principles by which the state would regulate its dealings with its citizens and the social order. Two alternatives were presented. The first comprised the principles of the "traditional personalist concept" which accords primacy to Man. The second set of principles were those of "the totalitarian concept, either of socialist or fascist type, in which the state has primacy."[49] If the federation were to choose the first alternative, then care must be taken not to adopt fiscal and other policies that properly belonged to inspirations of the second alternative, the totalitarian. The commission proposed that this choice be made deliberately by a conference of governments.

Adopting the first alternative, it was argued, would involve setting out to put the constitution into greater harmony with the principles that guided the Confederation Fathers and the Judicial Committee in their dealings with the B.N.A. Act. A return to the personalist concept would also involve eliminating the practice of discovering auxiliary powers to add to the central authority's competence. Instead of empire-building, said the *Tremblay Report,* federal officials would seek to establish propitious circumstances that would enable the provinces to play the major role envisioned for them by the Act of 1867. For this role, the provinces require adequate fiscal powers. The commission proposed that the governments of Canada jointly determine and specify a maximum tax burden in terms of the national income. The powers of direct taxation should then be distributed according to the effects of a particular tax field on the cultural system. With this redistribution accomplished, the burden of social security could be shifted entirely to the provincial sphere where it belongs constitutionally.[50]

The poor provinces were to be assisted through a plan established in consultation with the other provinces. Assistance would take the form of equalization subsidies and schemes for equitable sharing of the provincial levies on corporation income and estates. While the commission felt that provincial stability and economic progress depended upon the progress of the country as a whole, the commissioners still had reservations about equalization schemes. "If equality of services between the several parts of a federative state is desirable," and the commission granted that it was, "it cannot, however, be considered an absolute. Consequently, it cannot be established as a permanent system for the redistribution of funds nor, more especially, can it be sought to the detriment of the higher interests of one or more groups."[51]

To the claim that the federal government needs access to all important tax fields to maintain high employment and to counter economic fluctuations, the commission suggested that its proposals would not impair such stabilizing operations. The Tremblay plan would leave to the central government all the major business taxes (except for the corporations levy which might, or might not, be shared), and it would, in addition, make the central government's financial responsibilities considerably lighter, thereby creating greater room for manoeuvre in the national sphere. Flexible devices, such as the purchase tax used in the United Kingdom, might well be tried out, the *Report* said. What is more, the new spirit of cooperation which would infuse all levels of government after such a structural reorganization could encourage close coordination of provincial policies for counter-cyclical efforts. Economic stabilization plans would also become more effective with the increase in provincial revenues and the provision for the provinces of Bank of Canada credit which the commission proposed. To facilitate intergovernmental cooperation, the commission proposed the establishment of a permanent secretariat for federal-provincial conferences and the creation of a permanent Council of the Provinces on the model of the American Council of State Governments.

The commission returned repeatedly to its theme that, "with regard to French-Canadian culture, the Province of Quebec assumes alone the responsibilities which the other provinces jointly assume with regard to Anglo-Canadian culture."[52] If, as is its legitimate ambition, Canada should at some time give rise to a true nation harbouring two groups living in friendship and fruitful cooperation, then "the role of the Province of Quebec, as national focus and first political centre of one of the two groups, will be a truly great one . . . while the rest of the country has every interest not to underestimate the importance of its role."[53]

If the commission seemed to have dealt with the constitutional problems chiefly in fiscal terms, it was because these problems originated in fundamentally different interpretations of the nature of confederation, according to the *Report*. "We are firmly of the belief that the entire constitutional system is bound up with the question of taxes and of the allocation of taxes." These questions also involved the fundamental liberties and political future of both the citizen and the two cultures.[54] No alarm should be felt at the proposed rearrangements, said the *Report*, for all that they contemplated was an "integral return to the Constitution in social and fiscal matters, and, in conformity with the federative principle, one which restores to each order of government the plenitude and exclusivity of its functions."[55]

LAW AND THE CONSTITUTION

An essentially dualist approach to the Canadian federation bears significant consequences both for the law and constitutional change. Both civil and common law jurisdictions were established by the British North America Act, and Parliament has provided that the governor in council should nominate at least three of the nine justices of the Supreme Court from the Quebec bar.

These provisions give rise to the possibility that appeals taken in civil law cases may be finally decided by justices who are not learned in the civil law. While this system of appeals greatly troubles Quebec nationalists, its implications are more important in constitutional law. Not one, but two, sets of jural postulates are needed for interpretation of the constitution. "Two occasionally opposing sets of values operate within the same territorial frontiers," as Professor Edward McWhinney has pointed out.[56]

One of the problems posed for the legal scholar is the question of the extent to which French Canada's special way of life justifies the establishment of a double standard of interpretation as between cases arising in Quebec and those arising in English-speaking provinces. Of central concern is the different status of the individual which is recognized by the common law on the one hand, and by the civil code on the other hand. For example, when jurists deal with civil law appeals involving public speech, they must decide whether to defer chiefly to the Anglo-Saxon, or to the French Canadian, conception of the rightful place in society of individuals and private associations. In deciding cases from Quebec, the six justices of the Supreme Court of Canada might well feel obliged to elevate the rights of the individual at the expense of the rights of society.

These issues have been critical ones when the Supreme Court has decided such important cases as *Saumur* v. *City of Quebec*.[57] In this instance, an English-Protestant majority of the court overturned a unanimous decision of the Quebec Superior Court. The Quebec jurists had upheld a conviction of a member of the Jehovah's Witnesses for distributing sectarian literature without the police permit prescribed by a municipal bylaw. The highest court ruled that the sect—which explicitly declared in court that it was not a religion and was, in fact, opposed to religions—was entitled to the protection of a provincial statute guaranteeing freedom of worship, and that such a right would prevail even in the absence of such a statute. This right was created, it was said, by reason of principles of the British constitution which were imported into Canada by the B.N.A. Act. Among those who dissented was Chief Justice Thibaudeau Rinfret. His opinion clearly showed his scandalized reaction to the vilification of the Roman Catholic Church which filled the sectarian literature in question. Such was his outlook that it "does not appear to me necessary," he wrote, "to demonstrate that a municipality whose population is 90% Catholic not only has the right but the duty to prevent the dissemination of such infamies." A similar incident which inflamed the emotions of both English and French-speaking was the enactment and enforcement of the Quebec Padlock Act, which was declared *ultra vires* by the Supreme Court of Canada in 1957.[58] While the Supreme Court did not divide neatly along linguistic lines, in both instances the values of the majority of the population were judicially held to prevail over those of the French-speaking minority.

Besides the courts, the constitution in a federation must be of major concern to a beleaguered racial minority. If that is too easily changed, it may be defenceless. But if both majority and minority races were equal in status and loyalty, and if both had been parties to an agreement on the terms of union, then it followed that those terms could not lightly be altered without the assent of both groups.[59] Premier Maurice Duplessis wrote this viewpoint into the Speech from the Throne with which the lieutenant-governor opened the legislative session in 1945. The speech declared: "The Government considered that it belongs neither to the majority of the provinces nor the Ottawa Government to bring about changes in the Canadian Constitution." "I firmly believe," the lieutenant-governor continued, "that the British North America Act is a pact of honour between the two great races; my government intends to respect it, it exacts that respect."[60] In matters of constitutional amendment, the Tremblay commission did not go beyond deploring changes that had been made in the B.N.A. Act without Quebec's consent. The commissioners' general approach

implied that Quebec—as the representative of one of the two nations
—should have the right to veto any proposed amendments affecting
the French culture.

DUALISM ON THE LEFT

The most explicit statement of the "two nations" approach to constitutional amendment which we have arose from within the socialist movement whose traditional centralism had for many years precluded the possibility of its making much headway in Quebec. To
remedy their lack of appeal to French Canadians, leaders of the New
Democratic Party went far to try and provide their Quebec supporters
with ideological support. A study guide produced for the new party's
founding convention in 1961 set forth, as a fundamental socialist
principle, belief in the proposition "that no political party can do a
job for Canada unless the two main streams of our population play a
role of equal importance."[61] This principle went beyond those of the
party's predecessor, the C.C.F., which had emphasized the right of the
majority to a centralized government if that should prove necessary
to the realization of social objectives.

The 1961 program adopted by the founding convention said that
the New Democratic party "strongly affirms its belief in a federal
system which alone insures the united development of the two nations
which originally associated to form the Canadian partnership, as well
as that of other ethnic groups which later made Canada their home."[62]
The program added that true unity must be based on recognition of
the two national cultures and a firm respect for minority rights. These
declarations resulted from a hard fight at the convention by Le
nouveau parti démocratique de Québec. In a brief submitted to the
convention,[63] the Quebec socialists asserted that confederation should
be considered not only a pact between provinces, but an agreement
between the nations as well. They added that the "federal government
should fully assume its responsibility in educational matters which is
to safeguard the rights of school minorities in a province of each
of the original partners of Confederation," and asked that minorities
in other provinces be guaranteed the same rights accorded to the
English in Quebec. This demand that French Canadians be granted
a special status everywhere in the federation was not recognized in
the party platform.

The French-speaking socialists made two other proposals that concern us, even though the convention did not act on them. According
to one proposal, the Senate should be transformed into a Confederation Council, with rights equal to that of the Commons, and a membership elected in two groups—one-third at federal elections, and

two-thirds at provincial elections. Nominations to the Supreme Court should also be subject to ratification by the new upper house. The other proposal urged that the B.N.A. Act be made susceptible to being amended in Canada with each of the original partners of confederation having the right to veto any proposed amendment. A few months later, the Quebec socialists made their views on constitutional amendment even more explicit and obviously dualist in response to a speech made in January, 1962 by T. C. Douglas,[64] national leader of the New Democratic Party. Mr. Douglas had stressed the need of transferring the amending power to Canada, and of devising a procedure which would express "regard for the fact that Canada is a bicultural state." He praised the dual alliance, spoke of the necessity of preserving the integrity of both cultures, and advocated incorporation into the B.N.A. Act of a bill of rights that could be amended only with the approval of Parliament and all the provincial legislatures. But, said Mr. Douglas, "a country's constitution can never be sacrosanct," and the property and civil rights clause must not be entrenched. He suggested one important restriction: no amendment to the property and civil rights clause should apply to a civil code province without its expressed approval.

The Douglas speech provoked great concern in the ranks of Le nouveau parti démocratique de Québec. A week later there appeared a "Declaration of principle on the Canadian constitution" which had been unanimously adopted by the provisional council of Le nouveau parti.[65] This declaration said—almost defiantly—that Mr. Douglas certainly didn't wish to close the question for the party, and that the Quebec provisional council felt it necessary "à souligner que des précisions supplémentaires sont requises afin de garantir les droits de la province de Québec" in any amendment formula.

A suitable formula must embody several basic principles, according to Le nouveau parti. First of all, it must recognize the existence of a French Canadian nation possessing the right to determine the conditions on which it will remain in the union or withdraw from it. Secondly, and more importantly, "il y a la conception de la Confédération comme pacte entre deux nations. A ce titre, il est inadmissable qu'une de ces nations puisse modifier ce pacte sans le consentement de l'autre nation." Le nouveau parti's third fundamental principle might almost have been drawn directly from the *Tremblay Report*. It read: "L'histoire politique du Canada a consacré l'Etat du Québec comme l'expression politique la plus parfaite de la nation canadienne-française." It added that the preceding century of federal history should give no surprise to anyone (*i.e.,* T. C. Douglas) to learn that "les Canadiens français considèrent de plus en plus l'Etat du Québec comme la principale consécration politique et l'expression juridique la plus importante de leur fait national."

The French-speaking socialists urged Quebec's spokesmen at the constitutional conferences to insist on an entrenched clause in the constitution that would guarantee the coequal status of French as a working language in all federal bodies. The amending procedure itself should be subject to the unanimous consent of the provinces. Recognition of the two nations should be made in the establishment, structure, composition, and powers of a constitutional court, and none of these aspects of the court should be altered without unanimous provincial assent. Any amendment formula, Le nouveau parti said, must permit Quebec to maintain all its rights under secs. 92 and 109 of the B.N.A. Act (not merely head 13 of sec. 92 as Douglas proposed); Quebec should also be protected against suffering any financial loss through refusal to transfer powers which other provinces might be willing to give over to the federal government. The statement concluded by insisting that Parliament's present amending powers must be revoked before a general amending procedure was adopted. In the light of these principles, the party felt obliged to oppose the formula proposed by Justice Minister Fulton, because, "en faisant de la province de Québec une province comme les autres, elle nie l'évidence et met en danger l'avenir de l'Etat national des Canadiens français."

Throughout the sixties and early seventies, the English-speaking socialists responded to the dualist demands from Quebec in mixed voices. The party leadership was beset by two sets of influences. Agreement with the claims for country-wide bilingualism combined with recognition of French-Canadian economic grievances and with the need to develop the long missing base of popular support in Quebec. In opposition, however, was the party's strong tradition of centralization (inspired by egalitarian, economic control, and some nationalist ends) and an electoral base critically dependent in certain areas on communities which were self-consciously multi-cultural and hostile to French-Canadian claims for special status. The resulting policy compromises always stopped a considerable distance short of a dualist stance. Not so inhibited was a young, strident left-wing group within the party whose leaders were largely academics from Toronto, Winnipeg, and Montreal. In challenging the New Democratic Party to return to socialist principles, this group put great emphasis on the values involved in anti-colonialism, national self-determination, state control, and worker participation. This led them first to acknowledge the "right" often proclaimed in Quebec to have the province's constitutional status determined by general plebiscite, and secondly, to express faith that the likely and desirable outcome would not be separatism but a dualist constitution. The most explicit expression of these attitudes was that formulated by Gad Horowitz, a political scientist then at McGill. In an article in *Canadian Dimension* in 1965, he discussed the rise of a French-Canadian nation and called for creation of its logical corollary: "There must be an English Canadian nation (not a mere collection of English-speaking provinces) in partnership with the French Canadian nation. . . . It is time to dignify French Canada's demands, to recognize them as normal human demands, by making the same demands for ourselves. Harmonious interpersonal relations can exist only among fully developed persons. The same applies, not metaphorically but strictly, to nations, whether they are within a single state or not."[66] From this Professor Horowitz went on to conclude that it was time for a new federative statute, one which would provide two parliaments equal in status, one for each nation. It should also establish a joint body whose task it would be to arrange the inter-nation (but intra-state) relations between the two and any other tasks assigned to it.

Eventually the Waffle, as the radicals were known, broke away to form an independent socialist group. While the "constitutional question" was a secondary point of difference between the N.D.P. and the breakaway group, it was an important one, as a symbol at least to the one group of the depth of one's commitment to democratic principles.

DUALISM ON THE RIGHT

The decade of the nineteen-sixties was continuously being described as a period of the greatest crisis Confederation had yet encountered. At Ottawa a crisis of legitimacy persisted as federal cabinets, fired by activist ambitions, found themselves in double minority positions following the federal general elections of 1962, 1963, and 1965. They enjoyed neither the confidence inspired by majorities of the popular vote nor the assurance inspired by partisan majorities in the House of Commons where they were forced to rely on shifting combinations of minor party supporters. By contrast, one perceived in the provincial capitals strong premiers and strong governments backed by able public services, all of them making forceful demands and often good cases for increased financial resources and untrammeled legislative room. To Ottawa's pleas for more administrative and political cooperation, the English-speaking premiers responded in language bespeaking greater provincial independence and a renewal of a coordinate style of federalism. French-speakers in Quebec seemed to employ a multitude of voices. While most Liberal party leaders used what were essentially strong coordinate concepts, other voices on the ideological right as well as on the left spoke in terms of "two nations," "special status," "associated states," and of outright secession from the federal union. Perhaps the most important of these was Daniel Johnson, leader of the Union nationale party both in opposition and in government.

Through Daniel Johnson, the premises, philosophy, and recommendations of the Tremblay commission found better expression in the political arena than has any comparable royal commission in Canada. While not as publicly devoted to religious considerations as the *Report,* Johnson clothed the commissioners' criticisms of the existing federal regime in appealing rhetoric and vigorously reinterpreted every daily development in the light of his dualist principles. As leader of the opposition, he appeared always ready to exploit to the maximum fears in the rest of Canada about Quebec separatism, but his denunciations and demands seldom appeared without at least a thin gloss—the expression of his faith in the willingness of "the other nation" to discuss a reformulation of the entire confederation settlement. Alone among all other politicians on stage at that time, he consolidated his rhetorical and reasoned analyses of Quebec's place in Confederation into a book published in 1965 under the title *Egalité ou indépendance.* This basic position was somewhat elaborated in a later paper which he presented to the Confederation of Tomorrow Conference in Toronto in 1967 when he was premier of Quebec. The two works together give a fair representation of several hundreds of speeches he made on the subject before his death in 1968.

In place of a meaningful guarantee of the rights of the French Canadians, which Johnson saw as a major purpose of the original act, the actual constitution of the fifties and sixties provided only for a constantly changing situation, one in which majority wishes always predominated and that, by definition, meant the wishes of the English linguistic culture every time. This could not be real federalism, he wrote, "car il est de l'essence même du fédéralisme que les pouvoirs de l'Etat soient partagés, par une constitution écrite, entre deux ordres de gouvernement dont chacun est maître chez-lui."[67] Cooperative federalism was simply a disguised move toward the centralized state, and instead of a solid, reliable, constitutional statute, the federation now had as its supreme authority an institution not even mentioned in the B.N.A. Act, the federal-provincial conference in which Quebec had no more rights than Newfoundland. Quebec had quite properly rejected the Fulton-Favreau formula because it would have imposed a straight-jacket ("camisole de force") on the province allowing others, even Prince Edward Island, to veto amendments which would deny her necessary cultural powers. The B.N.A. Act, now having been proved incapable of fulfilling its original intention, must be replaced by a federating document which both reallocated legislative powers and explicitly recognized the founding of the state on the equality of two cultures, those of the two nations. One could not have cultural equality without cultural autonomy, he argued, and cultural autonomy was not possible without political autonomy. If that could not be achieved politically in Canada as a whole then the only choice was that of an independent Quebec. How serious Johnson was about separatism here may well have been indicated by his next statements: "Je sais bien que c'est là une solution extrême, une solution de dernier recours. C'est un peu comme la grève. Mais pour un syndicat qui entreprend des négociations, il ne serait pas sage d'exclure au départ le recours à la grève, même s'il espère bien l'éviter. Si la sécession devenait pour les Canadiens français le seul moyen de rester eux-mêmes, de rester français, alors ce ne serait pas seulement leur droit, ce serait leur devoir d'être séparatistes."[68] He defined a truly binational Canada as one in which "l'on puisse aimer et servir en anglais ou en français, avec les mêmes responsabilités, quelle que soit la province ou la région que l'on ait choisi d'habiter." He thought it necessary for each nation to define and specify its objectives within the new federal state and that these objectives then be incorporated through a Constituent Assembly in a new constitution so structured as to guarantee and effectively protect in every way the juridical equality of the two nations. He went on: "Cette constitution devrait, à mon sens, être conçue de telle façon que le Canada ne soit pas uniquement une fédération de deux nations égales en droit et en fait."[69] A charter of individual rights was required as was a charter of national rights, both of which should be written into the new constitution. An ancient wrong would also be righted: wherever they found themselves in a minority situation parents of either group would be able to have their children educated at public expense in institutions conforming to their culture (a phraseology which avoided the vexatious religious school question). The basic test of whether any constitutional proposition met the test of equality between the cultures was the application of exactly the same rules to either cultural group wherever it was in a minority situation.[70]

While Johnson kept demanding that the new constitution should be specific about the rights of both nations, he was relatively vague on what they should be and how they should be provided for institutionally. Continually he mentioned the right of "auto-détermination pour la nation canadienne-française" but usually he avoided saying whether this meant the unilateral right to secession which was asserted by others in the debate. The powers he thought each nation should have he indicated indirectly at this time as including: the regulation of radio and television, tariffs affecting "certain vitai industries," immigration, credit, natural resources on taxation, succession and estate duties (which were undermining the economic regime ancillary to the civil code), constitutional court appointments, and all other matters bearing directly on the protection and expansion of the nation's cultural life. The formulation virtually comprehended the whole of the powers exercised by modern government if read broadly. That it should be read broadly seemed indicated a few years later when he told the Confederation of Tomorrow Conference: "We believe that, as is the case in most federations, provinces or member-states of Canada must retain all powers not expressly granted to the central government."[71] In specifying that all welfare, educational, economic development, labour, and municipal affairs must be within the powers of the two nations, he left little to the new central government besides the control of currency and that was subject to inter-nation consultation when it came to setting or changing monetary policy. A two-nation constitutional tribunal, a truly bilingual public service, extensive minority school rights throughout Canada, and a formal structure for intergovernmental consultation and negotiation completed the list. As a procedure, he proposed that these powers be granted initially to all provinces together with a power of delegating some to the central government so that the other (English-speaking) provinces could decide for themselves what should be the relationship between the federal government and themselves. He thought the situation proposed was "not incompatible with federalism." English-speaking commentators also thought his proposals were not incompatible with outright separatism. To what extent they were intended as a negotiating position and to what extent as an ideal federal structure, we do not know.

Summing all of Johnson's ideas into one collectivity, as has been done in the previous paragraph, brought one to what was known in the sixties as the Associate State doctrine. It has been crystallized in these words:

> The essence of this alternative . . . is to create two virtually sovereign states, one English and one French, and then to provide for the delegation by them to a new confederal body of certain defined and limited powers. Some of the advocates of this approach would assign to the confederal body roughly those powers given up by the members of the European Common Market; others would assign it broader powers including trade and monetary policy and international relations.[72]

To this is added the following observations by Professor Ramsay Cook, of the University of Toronto:

> The sovereignty of the two national states would be limited by an agreement to establish a common central government, the unique feature of which would be equality of representation for each nation. The jurisdiction of this government would be narrowly limited to such matters as foreign and defence policy, international

trade, postal services, transport, perhaps monetary policy and the transfer of equalization payments from rich to poor sections of the Confederation.[73]

Of great importance, according to Professor Cook, was the proposed method of binational policy-making in which, according to the Société Saint-Jean-Baptiste of Montreal, "No law would have force without being approved by a double majority, being a majority of the representatives of each associate state."[74]

The Associate State doctrine was the most extreme of the many proposals short of outright separatism which were mooted in Quebec during the sixties. In part, these proposals were stimulated by the calling of a new Estates General of the French Canadian nation by the nationalist Société Saint-Jean-Baptiste and in part by establishment of a special Quebec legislative committee on the constitution. In the sessions of both groups dualist proposals were examined at great length.

A more federalist, less extreme version of the dualist proposals was that designated *Statut particulier*. Here all existing conditional grant programs would be wholly taken over by the Quebec government, together with tax compensation, and the federal government would withdraw completely from all health and social welfare areas, again providing Quebec with appropriate financial compensation. The right of the Quebec government to make international treaties within constitutional areas of provincial legislative jurisdiction was to be recognized, and that government was also to receive extensive rights to meaningful consultations on federal policies relating to economic management such as tax levels, international trade, tariffs, and the supply of credit. This approach was popular with members of the Lesage Liberal administration in Quebec during the first half of the decade and manifested itself in many of the specific demands which were made by Quebec City on the Liberal régime at Ottawa.

CRITICISM OF THE DUAL ALLIANCE

Sharp criticism of the dualist concept has come from French Canadian separatists who wish to see Quebec become an independent state, and from English-speaking politicians and intellectuals. Apart from a few isolated comments,[75] the English-language press devoted little attention to the most scholarly exposition of dualism, that of the *Tremblay Report,* and the commission's views apparently disturbed few people in French Canada other than the separatists. For some premiers of

Quebec, such as Jean Lesage and Daniel Johnson, the two nations theme provided solid underpinning for their insistence on a greater measure of provincial autonomy. In this sense the treaty between the races simply reinforces the compact theory.[76]

The first contemporary separatist to criticize the idea was Marcel Chaput; to him the dual alliance idea was nonsense, and, if such a compact did once exist, it has long since been shattered by the untrustworthy English. He argued that there was no hope for the French-speakers outside Quebec—they were being assimilated too rapidly. One of the tragic facts of history, he said, was that "le Québec dans la Confédération n'a jamais réussi à protéger—ni même essayer de protéger—les minorités privées de leurs droit."[77] But one should not mourn, these are French Canadians who desert their national homeland voluntarily. Other separatists since Chaput have developed the theme in essentially the same way.

Professor Frank R. Scott mounted his attack on several occasions during the late fifties.[78] As he has pointed out, the two nations concept speaks of a treaty between races; the treaty is said to be consecrated in a number of British statutes, and consummated in the confederation act, the chief purpose of which is supposed to be that of permitting the two cultures to develop side by side in equality and harmony. If the B.N.A. Act is so regarded, said Professor Scott, "and if the further supposition is made that the government of Quebec is alone authorized to speak for the French race, then some radical conclusions can be rapidly reached." The races being equal, their representative governments are equal, and Canada becomes a dyarchy. Quebec is made to take on a particular French and Roman Catholic character, in opposition to the particular English and Protestant character attributed to Ottawa. The reduction of the federation from eleven states (one federal and ten provincial) to two stands in stark contrast to the original theory of confederation. But the B.N.A. Act did not conceive of governments as representing races or religions, said Scott, and the fortuitous territorial concentration of racial and religious majorities has not legally imparted any special character to the state machinery which must serve all citizens impartially. "The Quebec government is as much the government of the English minority in that province as of the French majority," and the obverse is true of the government at Ottawa.

The two nations idea makes no provision for the governance of the half-million Quebeckers who speak English and presumably should be ruled in local matters by an English majority. Neither, Dean Scott observed, does the theory show how the French Canadians in other provinces authorized the Quebec government rather than their own governments to speak for them. Since Dean Scott made his criticisms, the Acadians have edged into a more significant position in New

Brunswick and, by the elections of 1960, helped to place the French-speaking Louis Robichaud at the head of the council table at Fredericton. Premier Robichaud was not among those subscribing to the dualist concept.

And, if the cabinet at Quebec City should actually speak for all French Canadians, the parallel proposition cannot be made for the federal cabinet. The British Columbian, to take one example, has been accustomed of late to having his politics shaped in terms of choices to be made between the policies of the provincial government and the policies of the federal ministry. The Nova Scotian, whose province made the first attempt to leave confederation, would be as surprised as the British Columbian to learn that it is the federal government that truly speaks for all English Canadians. As Dean Scott pointed out, federalism was imposed on the country by centrifugal tendencies inherent in a continental geography and regional loyalties, regardless of what the feelings of the Lower Canadians may have been. These are factors which the dualist concept neglects altogether.

French-Canadian analyses of the English-Canadian *mentalité* frequently mention a dominating economic orientation but little concern for economic considerations has been manifested in most formulations of the dualist concept. Dr. A. W. Johnson focussed his attention on this area in his critique of the special status approach. Economic management through either expenditure or taxation functions would be virtually impossible, he thought, under a constitution which made one major government like Quebec's virtually independent of the others in economic matters. The degree of cooperation required was too much to expect in an arrangement whereby one government represented essentially one economic region and the other government(s) represented four or more different economic regions. Neither was it possible for him to visualize English-Canadians granting veto powers to Quebec in some important matters but denying them to their government(s). He also foresaw great difficulties in the field of health and welfare, wherein "the logical conclusion of the system proposed is either for Parliament to refrain altogether from trying to stimulate new country-wide health and welfare programs or for Parliament to extend an unconditional fiscal benefit to Quebec only."[79] He also worried about the effect of the Quebec example on the other provinces. Would not their leaders be driven to demand comparable powers, powers which in logic could not be denied to them but which would lead to the effective dissolution of the federation? Other questions he posed related to the continuance of federal redistribution payments (equalization) and to the practical difficulties of the anomalous status of Quebec representatives in a federal Parliament which dealt with one range of things with respect to Quebec and a much larger range of matters with respect to the rest of Canada. Most of these difficulties would be solved, he thought, with the Associate State approach provided it was carried to the point where one no longer had a federal but a loose confederal arrangement. Similar criticisms of the dualist concept have been made by academics such as Professors D. V. Smiley and Ramsay Cook,[80] and by other commentators such as the Rt. Hon. P.-E. Trudeau (both before and during his term as prime minister), and Dr. Eugene Forsey (a founding member of the C.C.F. who refused to join its successor party primarily because of an insistence at the N.D.P. convention on using the phrase "two nations"). The celebrated opposition of the Rt. Hon. J. G. Diefenbaker to the *deux nations* phrase is discussed in the next chapter.

The conception of confederation as a dual alliance is French in origin and expression, and primarily French in terms of support in political circles. Many have been the flights of English oratory devoted to the glories of the dual cultures, but few have been the English-speaking supporters for the political implications of the theory. A comment by Professor J. A. Corry may typify the extent of English Canadian sympathy for the dualist concept. Most competent lawyers would deny that there was any compact between provinces, he said, but, "if we speak in moral rather than strictly legal terms, there is ground for saying that Confederation was a compact, not between the several provinces but between the two races, English and French, which agreed to associate together in the Dominion of Canada on terms of mutual tolerance and respect."[81] To alter the constitution in respect of language, religion, or basic social relationships might not be a breach of contract, said Professor Corry, "but it would be a breach of faith to insist now on withdrawing such matters from the jurisdictions of the provinces without their consent."

This critical distinction marks virtually the whole of the English language academic comment on the dualist concept: almost unanimously the commentators accept the definition of Canada as a bilingual country. Many also accept it as a country that is primarily bicultural, that is, comprising two linguistic communities each with distinctive traditions and outlooks and receptive to newcomers whatever their mother tongue. Here, the critics part company with the advocates. They reject the assertion that a man's cultural allegiance must be the primary determinant of his political arrangements. Almost unanimously the equality of individuals is urged as a value superior to the dualists' claim for the equality of the cultural nations. To the dualist who protests that majoritarian democratic practices will overwhelm flimsy statutory protections for his minority culture, the critic of dualism expresses faith in the possibilities of non-structural reforms enshrining the values of liberal individualism. At the extreme, some English-speaking critics join company with some

French-speaking and denounce dualist conceptions as impossible to achieve, logically inferior, and less desirable for both cultures than outright separatism of Quebec from Canada.

CONCLUSION

This discussion of the dualist concept may be summarized briefly. In the face of the French Canadians' determination not to be assimilated, a view of Canada as a bicultural country has taken root and permeated its history, its literature, and its politics. French Canadian expansion outside the borders of Quebec created island colonies within an ever-growing English-speaking majority. Industrialism, economic fluctuations, vast increases in social service demands, and a militant English Canadian nationalism increased the impulses of centralization. French Canada sought a system that would bolster the independence of the province of Quebec and, at the same time, justify intervention into the affairs of other provinces to ensure the survival of the French minorities outside Quebec.

The solution suggested by the Tremblay commission involved an assertion that the Canadian union had as its primary purpose the protection and expansion of two nations: the Anglo-Canadian, which found its focus in Ottawa, and the French Canadian, of which the province of Quebec was its most perfect political expression. These nations were equal in historical and cultural dignity and ought to be accorded equal political status, according to this viewpoint. A number of governmental adjustments were proposed—chiefly in the fields of finance, minority rights, and constitutional amendment procedures. Adherents of the dualist concept included French-speaking socialists. Le nouveau parti de Québec sought to persuade the New Democratic Party leadership that the two nations idea should be institutionalized in a procedure of constitutional amendment. One Quebec socialist notably absent from the supporters of this concept was Dean Frank R. Scott. He centred strong criticism of the notion on the basic postulate of the federation's purpose, on the untenable proposition that the country was divided culturally and politically into two sharply-differentiated and homogeneous groups, and on the impracticability and undesirability of realizing the concept in practice.

Consideration of the dualist concept in accordance with the criteria adopted for the inquiry will indicate the idea's chief points of distinction from the other concepts. An initial difference relates to the varied impressions of the federation's origin. While the centralist theory dismisses the idea of partnership altogether, the dualist concept agrees with the other three that the federation resulted from a partnership, but it argues that the partners were races, not provinces. Where the objective of the centralist idea is essentially an integration of the various policy-making areas, the compact theory seeks to enhance the independence of the eleven governments. The dualist concept, for its part, would transform the constituents of the federation from territorial divisions into national units based on language and two capital cities.

Both the centralist and administrative concepts favour the centralization of major fiscal powers, a step opposed by the coordinate, compact, and dualist concepts which emphasize the right of the provinces to exercise their legal taxing powers to the full. Only the centralist would attempt to consolidate the control of all major finances; the dualist and the other three concepts advocate methods guaranteeing the constituent groups adequate finances for their constitutionally-assigned tasks. Both dualist and compact theories agree that provincial cabinets must be politically independent and left to determine civil rights for themselves, but they part company on the question of national guarantees of language and separate school rights for French-speaking minorities. The compact theory, alone among all the concepts, insists on unanimous provincial assent for all constitutional amendments; the dualist concept is content with requiring unanimity on amendments directly affecting the French culture.

CHAPTER

7

The Deux Nations Controversy

Questions involving the federal structure pervade Canadian political debate but only twice have they been transformed into popular issues and presented to the voter for apparent resolution. The federal general elections of 1896 and 1968 both revolved around the rights and place of French Canadians in the federal union. The first of these is well marked as a critical point in development of the party system. In 1896 Wilfrid Laurier and the federal Liberals succeeded in surmounting (and sometimes capitalizing on) the anti-French racism of the English-speaking while approving of their provincial autonomist passions. Simultaneously, Laurier won over Quebec voters with an *appel du sang* that he was the one leader who could best be trusted to safeguard the linguistic heritage of French Canadians outside Quebec (and especially in Manitoba). These events provided the political seal for the period's fast-coalescing legal, economic, and social forces of regionalism, which eventuated in development and acceptance of the compact concept as the working theory of confederation for thirty years or more.

The deux nations campaign of 1967-68 may well prove to be as important a bellwether for the future shape of the federal system as 1896 was for its time. Even more than in the nineteenth century contest, politicians and commentators across the country debated the real, imagined, and ideal shapes of the federation and argued about the presumed consequences of changes in attitudes at Ottawa.[1] Once again, a French-speaking Canadian led the federal Liberals to victory by winning both the support of English-speakers infuriated by French Canadian demands for justice and that of French-speakers apparently more persuaded by yet another *appel du sang* than by a Conservative leader offering them what Quebec's leading spokesmen had said they must have.

The preliminary skirmishes had been conducted several years earlier by Lester B. Pearson, then prime minister, and John G. Diefenbaker, Progressive Conservative leader and the former prime minister. "Some talk today about Canada being two nations," Mr. Diefenbaker observed at one point. That to his mind was not at all what John A. Macdonald and George-Etienne Cartier had had in mind a century before: "The aim and purpose of the Fathers of Confederation was to bring about a united nation. The Fathers of Confederation did not believe in a Canada of two nations."[2] Mr. Pearson felt this was a distortion of the two nation concept. "There is a special difficulty . . . over the word 'nation'; and this difficulty, which leads to confusion, comes from the identification of nation and state." While some countries like France were one nation and one state, others like Switzerland and Belgium were not, he said.

> In this sense many nations do not have, nor do they desire, political sovereignty. The term "nation" . . . belongs to sociology, to history and tradition. It indicates a way of life, a group of human beings, a group with common language, traditions, culture, customs, feelings and above all, the will to live together as a group. Surely . . . this justifies and explains the validity of the concept of a French Canadian nationality. . . .
>
> I believe we should recognize that in the historical and linguistic and cultural sense our country is basically composed of two nations which must have equal rights and equal opportunity in our land.[3]

The Liberal leader did not thereby dispel his rival's fundamental dislike for the idea which Mr. Diefenbaker returned to attack vigorously throughout the winter and spring of 1967-68.

Montmorency and the Tories

The controversy first took public shape in 1967 at the Montmorency (Que.) policy conference sponsored by the Progressive Conservative party. The major spokesman on constitutional affairs was a Quebec businessman and writer, Marcel Faribault. Assigned by the organizers to discuss the concept of nations, he referred to disputes which had arisen among intellectuals about Canada's *deux nations* in much the same terms as Mr. Pearson had used years before: it was largely a problem of semantics. Carefully, Mr. Faribault cited two authorities for the sense in which he understood French-speakers used the word nation. The first authority, Robert's French Dictionary, was quoted: "Nation—a group of human beings, generally quite large, which is characterized by its consciousness of its unity and the wish to live in common." The philosopher Duvillier was quoted as well: "Nation implies the idea of spontaneity; State implies an idea of organization which can be more or less artificial. A nation can survive even when it is divided into several States; a state may be composed of several nations." From this Mr. Faribault went on to assert that "there is nothing in the two nation concept that is opposed to a federal political regime."[4] In another, more informal address to the conference, Mr. Faribault specified that the preamble of a new constitution would have to include recognition that the country was comprised of "two founding people." He went on: *"You put that down.* We might translate it in French 'two nations.' You will translate it 'two founding races of people' if you want. We cannot say 'people' because 'people' in our case doesn't mean nation, the same as 'nation' in English doesn't mean 'nation.' But let us be reasonable and admit that I can tell you this, and you can listen, and hear, and understand." Following this and other discussions in committee, the general assembly of the conference adopted a resolution:

That Canada is, and should be a federal state;
That Canada is composed of two founding peoples (deux nations) with historic rights who have been joined by people from many lands;
That the Constitution should be such as to permit and encourage their full and harmonious development in equality throughout Canada.[5]

The French phrase had been deliberately inserted into the English text to demonstrate to both language groups exactly what was intended and to obviate any possibility of misunderstanding. Following hard on it was a consequential recommendation that the equality of French and English languages should be constitutionally provided for, together with Canada-wide provision of the same rights for French-speakers as English-speakers enjoyed in Quebec. This conference, one commentator predicted, would loom in history either as "a monumental mistake or a monument to progressive conservatism."[6] In using the phrase deux nations, the meeting produced what he called "one of the worst misunderstandings in Conservative party history, a misunderstanding which was deliberately aggravated by the Liberal Party, which was only fair, and by John Diefenbaker, which was not." Far from advocating the establishment of "two nations" in Canada, anybody who would read the key paragraph of the recommendation "finds that the Conservatives approved no such establishment and those who implied that they did were either ignorant or mischievous or probably both."

A Progressive Conservative leadership convention followed at Toronto the next month. In a successful drive for the leadership, Robert L. Stanfield managed skillfully to endorse both "deux nations" and special status, while carefully redefining them in his own terms. His thesis both for the leadership convention and for the later election campaign had its first of many enunciations in a speech delivered in Montreal on August 31.[7] In it, he said:

> What French-speaking Canadians outside Quebec seem to want is to possess the mechanisms necessary to safeguard their identity and, when it is practicable, to be able to use their own language in their dealings with public bodies. These are surely not unreasonable requests. In endorsing them, however, let it be clear that I am not suggesting that the federal government ought to become involved in matters of provincial jurisdiction. What I wish to do is to establish my belief that we should try to define these matters clearly and precisely in the constitution.
>
> There appears to be a consensus in Quebec in support of what is called a special status for the province within Confederation. . . . The notion that any group of Canadians should enjoy some rights or privileges which are not enjoyed by other Canadians is entirely unacceptable. But I do not believe this is what the people of Quebec mean. I believe that what they seek is only that measure of authority in respect to social and economic affairs which will enable them to fulfill themselves as French-Canadians. The people of Quebec view their provincial government as the logical instrument for the execution of this authority.
>
> This desire of Quebec for these provincial responsibilities is not shared to the same extent by Canadians in other provinces. Implicitly, therefore, the requirement of Quebec is for some kind of different arrangement in the distribution of authority, in respect to social and economic matters.
>
> At first sight this may appear to many Canadians in other provinces to constitute a threat to the federal government's ability to fulfill purposes related to the federation as a whole. I do not accept the view that this is in principle the case. It seems to me that we must first determine the full range of the matters over which Quebec considers it essential to exercise its authority. Then we must give serious study to the extent to which these requirements can be met without impeding the authority of the federal government to perform its essential function.

The Montmorency policy conference recommendation was endorsed by the more general conference in September and this, together with the views of Mr. Stanfield quoted above, constituted the party's official position on what was called the national unity or constitutional issue during the winter of 1967-68 and during the 1968 election campaign.

The "Second Class Citizen" Version

Many members of the public, including Progressive Conservative candidates and party workers, took the official policy to be something quite different and unacceptably so. They assumed it to be that version of deux nations specially fabricated, stuffed with straw, and fiercely demolished by John G. Diefenbaker in his desperate attempts to retain a leadership position. He injected a wholly novel element into the dualism debate and made it a central point for many. At a press conference on Sept. 1, 1967, he put it this way:

> When you talk about "two nations" that proposition will place all Canadians who are of other racial origins than what is wrongly described as English and French in a secondary position. All through my life one of the things I've tried to do is bring about in this nation a citizenship which was not dependent on race or colour, or blood counts or racial origin, but a citizenship whereby each and everyone of us was a Canadian. I'm not going back on that—and support a proposition that will place these Canadians, six or seven million strong today, in a position of being a secondary, second-class citizen in a nation that we're trying to build strong and united.[8]

"Nation" meant "independent state" in both languages, he asserted; to pretend otherwise was subversive subterfuge. Throughout that winter and the ensuing election campaign, Mr. Diefenbaker argued that to talk about two founding people, cultures, or nations in any sense would "balkanize" Canada, relegate all "Third Force" Canadians to second class citizenship, and lead inevitably to an independent Quebec. Such was his version of the two nations concept and his followers attributed it to the new Conservative leadership of Robert Stanfield and Marcel Faribault. As Mr. Diefenbaker's biographer and former speech-writer put it, the former prime minister felt that contracting out, two flags, two pension plans, "Two Nations and all the other baggage of political dualism was ushering Quebec out of Confederation on the instalment plan."[9] The writer, Thomas Van Dusen, went on to say that, however it was worded, Mr. Diefenbaker would accept no theory of two nations "because it would make of those neither French nor English second-class citizens." What the former prime minister did, essentially, was to twist the linguistic cultures base of deux nations into a wholly racial one. As the father of the Canadian Bill of Rights, his claims were often taken as authoritative.

They also confirmed all the worst suspicions of the many, especially in the West, whose fears for their own equal place in Canada had been aroused and long sustained by the inquiries, hearings, and reports of the Royal Commission on Bilingualism and Biculturalism.

To fears of second class citizenship were added concerns that the new Conservative leadership intended to make the English-speaking provincial governments inferior in status to that of Quebec. In attacking the Conservative convention policy, the influential *Winnipeg Free Press* discussed deux nations wholly in terms derived from speeches by the Quebec separatist leader, René Lévesque. "He wants a two-nation Canada allied not in a federal system but in the limited relationship of the Benelux countries," the Liberal newspaper said on September 21. "His two-nation theory is one in which he wants Quebec out of Canada with all the economic benefits of being in." To this and other criticisms, Mr. Stanfield rejoined with a continuing series of speeches which emphasized that "we must face the simple facts that Canada exists, and Quebec exists, and there are tensions," as he told an audience at Clear Lake, Manitoba. Those problems must be dealt with and it would be extremely difficult to do so, in his view, until French had acquired additional rights in the rest of the country. "To refuse to recognize this would make Quebec a French ghetto," he said. "It is not only desirable but necessary that French acquire increased rights outside of Quebec."

The NDP and "Particular Status"

Canadian socialists seemed to interpret the current tensions similarly. Under the impetus of a newly-organized Quebec wing, the New Democratic Party moved its constitutional policy a long way from the centralism of its socialist forebears in the C.C.F. In 1967, the party literature argued that the Liberal government's practice of abandoning shared cost programs seriously inhibited federal government activity in areas such as secondary education which nine provinces would probably welcome. The answer was to design a particular status in the federation for Quebec.[10] This view found its way into the official party platform for the 1968 election which said:

> Our federal system must have the flexibility to recognize the particular position accorded to Quebec since 1867 as the centre of the French-speaking community in Canada. She must have the right and the funds to fulfill government responsibilities which affect the community such as social security, education, town planning and community development.
>
> By accepting this particular situation, Canadians elsewhere can seek federal action in these fields without creating misunderstanding, frustration and intolerable strains to our confederation.[11]

To this, T. C. Douglas, the party leader, added in a press conference in Sudbury on May 21 that his party believed a strong federal government was more necessary than ever if it was to grapple with modern problems effectively. But Canadians had a commitment to Quebec which could not be ignored. "Thus, it may mean that in any area such as education and housing, where Quebec feels that a strong federal program may erode provincial rights, it may be necessary to have two programs—one for English-speaking Canada and one for Quebec."[12]

The Anti-Nationalist Liberal Position

The central government's champion in the campaign was Pierre-Elliott Trudeau. An impressive intellectual debater, he had formulated his classical concepts of federalism and views of Quebec's place within Confederation during years of struggle against the reactionary nationalism of the Maurice Duplessis régime. His elevation to the federal justice ministry and responsibility for constitutional questions provided him with a new platform from which to wage the old battle against Duplessis' successors, both political and doctrinal. His ideological foes, such as Daniel Johnson, Jean-Jacques Bertrand, and Michel Brunet were conservative nationalists who tended toward organic views of society and the state. Mr. Trudeau was dedicated to the values of liberal individualism, the only philosophy in his view congruent with federalism and the preservation of individual liberties. Where they argued for equality of societies, he argued for the equality of individuals. Where they fought for acknowledgement of Quebec as the homeland and spokesman for all French Canadians, he fought for improved recognition of French outside Quebec to ensure that all French Canadians could call all Canada their homeland and Ottawa their government as well. When Quebec nationalists demanded special status for their province, Pierre Trudeau insisted on the jurisdictional equality of all provinces. To Premier Johnson's demands for an entirely new federal constitution, Mr. Trudeau responded that the existing legislative distribution was more than adequate to accommodate legitimate French Canadian ambitions, provided that the federal government retreat from its repeated invasions into areas of exclusive provincial jurisdiction and respect them strictly in the future. (Movements in this direction had been initiated by the last Pearson government in which he was a significant influence.) For Mr. Trudeau, nationalism (whether Quebec-based or not) was tantamount to outright racism and was ever a "clear and present danger" to liberty. For Premier Johnson and his colleagues, liberal individualism was but fool's gold for a French Canada floundering in a sea of dollar-driven Anglo-Saxons; liberal individualism simply provided spurious justification for English cultural oppression in the past and would guarantee assimilation in the near future. This was the French Canadian "family" dispute that was overlaid on the Canada-wide election campaign of 1968 and virtually inundated the opposition's constitutional position.

Both in his speeches[13] and in his many essays, Mr. Trudeau developed and espoused an "anti-nation" and strictly coordinate view of federalism which he carried into the election campaign. In December 1965, he had argued at Loyola University that special legislation "would make of Quebec a minority like all the others in Ottawa." In March 1967, he said that "splitting established authority solely for ethnic reasons opens the door to intolerance and all kinds of abuses," and in the same month he told the Canadian Club at Montreal: "I'm convinced that any political platform based on ethnic considerations is not progressive but reactionary." In January 1968, he declared in a CBC television interview that constitutional change was not needed; such demands were simply elaborate excuses for not doing some of the many things that needed doing and could be done under the existing constitution. "The accommodation we are looking for is not in the entrenchment of two nations, as it were, one of them to be represented by the Quebec government and the other by the other governments. This is a conception we completely repudiate." Four days later he posed the constitutional question as a simple one of more rights for French Canadians or more power for the province of Quebec. Not particular status for the province but equal status for all French Canadians in all of Canada was the only possible answer, he told the Quebec conference of the Liberal Federation. "We must not confuse the rights of French Canadians with the legitimate or illegitimate desire of a provincial government to build itself a little empire," he argued. When a few days later in February, he confronted Premier Johnson of Quebec at the Constitutional Conference, he put the same points to the Quebec leader and the national television audience with equal bluntness. Giving Quebec the powers demanded was basically separatist, he said. It could not be done without reducing Quebec members of Parliament at Ottawa to second class status; it called for the severance of all direct relations between the central government and the citizens in Quebec. Secession would be the logical and inevitable outcome. More rights for the French language outside Quebec but no more rights for the government of Quebec than for any other province.[14] That was Mr. Trudeau's hard and fast line. It won him much applause in English-language newspapers and he maintained the same stance throughout the election campaign that followed hard on his subsequent selection in April 1968 as Liberal party leader and prime minister in succession to Lester B. Pearson.

Agreements and Differences

On questions relating to federal structure, the 1968 campaign saw an almost complete reversal of party form. During the sixties, no party had been more flexible in acknowledging and dealing with provincial grievances than the governing Liberals; nobody had been more "hard line" than Mr. Diefenbaker.[15] Mr. Trudeau, however, had spent years crusading in opposition to the power of a strong provincial government, while Mr. Stanfield had been a strong premier of Nova Scotia in sympathy with the opposition to Ottawa's traditional paternalism in dealing with the provinces. After the double changes in party leadership, Mr. Stanfield's policy looked much like an endorsation of Mr. Pearson's flexibility and cautious innovation in relations with Quebec. For his part, Mr. Trudeau seemed to have taken over the "one Canada" vocabulary popularized by Mr. Diefenbaker, the deposed Progressive Conservative leader. Curiously, where both major party leaders now favoured the policy of expanding bilingualism, it seemed to work to Mr. Stanfield's serious electoral disadvantage but not at all so for Mr. Trudeau. A second common theme marked the constitutional speeches these men delivered during 1968: Canada needed both strong central and strong provincial governments, secure in their powers and vigorous in their exercise. Their difference in emphasis, however, was in the willingness or otherwise to consider the possibility of changing any aspect of the ways in which the various provinces remained legally and constitutionally equal to each other. While fundamentally both were committed coordinate federalists, Mr. Stanfield was prepared to *consider* the argument for limited special status, but Mr. Trudeau had long ago decided firmly against it.[16]

Just as Mr. Trudeau's policy favouring an "evolving status quo" never varied, so his real political target remained constant as well. Whatever the message Robert Stanfield and his allies sought to convey to the voters, it was their fate throughout 1968 to be Mr. Trudeau's proxy target for Premier Johnson and his associate states concept.

More important than the content of the federalist issues, so far as the contest's personality nature left any room for a major policy battle, was their context. So radically different were the Liberal and Conservative strategic positions that contextual dissimilarities encouraged the press to represent as wildly dissimilar what were virtually the same substantive positions respecting the federal structure. As the prime minister, Pierre-Elliott Trudeau was able to speak for his party with unchallenged authority, and he was defending what by 1968 amounted to an established federal government policy. The Pearson régime had initiated an expansion of bilingualism some years ago, extensively reshaped the form of Ottawa's involvement in provincial affairs, and even developed a face-saving formula which permitted

Quebec (and other provinces) to enjoy the delights of symbolic assertion of their international sovereignty in areas of provincial jurisdiction such as education.[17] These things were done and Mr. Trudeau favoured them. His plans to extend and give statutory form to country-wide bilingualism in government service were believed by French Canadians and apparently ignored by English-Canadians who liked his hard line on Quebec and his promise of a new politics. By contrast, the Progressive Conservative leader had an impossible task. His advocacy of bilingualism was frequently seen as a betrayal of the anti-French attitudes favoured by his party's electoral base and associated with his predecessor, Mr. Diefenbaker. A colourful and passionate figure, the former Conservative prime minister won more public attention for his attacks on his distorted version of deux nations than the quiet and cautious Mr. Stanfield could muster for his official policy. While his Quebec ally, Marcel Faribault, was an undoubted federalist, he delighted in fine-spinning linguistic and constitutional distinctions which seldom survived the hazards of transmission and the centralist preferences of the English language mass media. The open support vouchsafed to the Progressive Conservatives by Daniel Johnson's Union Nationale organization also made it easy for opponents to associate the Stanfield policy with the Johnson associate states views, which were both notorious and unacceptable in English Canada.

Weak, indecisive, too soft on Quebec. These had been the common images of the Pearson Liberals in English Canada. An incisive personality, Mr. Trudeau was able to cut himself completely adrift both from the Liberal government record and its unfavourable titles. Leech-like, the same images[18] were fastened on Mr. Stanfield as he struggled to effect a premature union of recalcitrant elements into a new Conservative coalition. Among other things, his task involved trying simultaneously to: 1. Establish his authority over the party; 2. Hold the traditional Conservative electorates; 3. Indicate to French Canadians that he had made a clean break with the party's anti-French past; 4. Avoid alienating his disparate allies in Quebec; and 5. Stabilize the yawning fractures in his party and candidate ranks. In this he did not succeed in time for the June 26 election. The complexity of his strategic position made his policy statements hopeless as mass media competitors against the unyielding and popular simplicity of Mr. Trudeau's position. The New Democratic Party's policy, although more explicitly "special status" in inclination than the Conservative, largely remained out of the line of mass media attention during the election battle; it thus escaped both the confusions and the abuses visited on the latter. In the event, the voters, whether English-speaking or French, preferred Mr. Trudeau and his policies over those of Mr. Stanfield and Mr. Douglas. The prime minister was re-elected with a majority in the House of Commons (the first since the 1958 election) and a popular vote distribution of: Liberals 45 percent; Progressive Conservatives 31 percent; N.D.P. 17 percent; and Créditistes 5 percent.

Bilingualism Married to Multiculturalism

Whatever might have been the real significance of the issue itself,[19] Mr. Trudeau took it that the 1968 election returns had validated his conception of Canada as a federal state with ten equal provinces, two languages, and a multiplicity of cultures. His government's return resulted as he had promised it would, in the passage in 1969 of the Official Languages Act. It decreed that: "The English and French languages are the official languages of Canada for all purposes of the Parliament and Government of Canada, and possess and enjoy equality of status and equal rights and privileges in their use in all the institutions of the Parliament and Government of Canada." The Act made the two languages co-equal for the federal civil service, all Crown agencies, and the federal courts in "bilingual districts." Bilingual districts were to be those in which the minority language group, whether English or French, constituted at least ten percent of the population or, where, being somewhat less than ten percent, there was historical precedent or a substantial number of minority language speakers. In strongly supporting passage of the act, the opposition party leaders applied the whips to their parliamentary colleagues. All voted for the bill on the critical second reading with the notable exception of John G. Diefenbaker and sixteen other Conservative rebels who cast negative votes. Their opposition was not carried through to the third and final reading.

A few months later, in October 1969, the New Democratic Party met in convention at Winnipeg where, despite the 1968 election results, the party again endorsed its policy of special status for Quebec. The resolution called for a flexible federal system within which Quebec's relations might differ from those of other provinces in matters such as social security, town planning, education, and community development. What was not accepted at the convention was an attempt by one party faction to substitute a resolution calling for recognition of the "right of Quebec to self-determination."

For the two major parties, however, deux nations disappeared after 1968 as a question of partisan division. This development was undoubtedly facilitated by the election defeat of the Union Nationale government in Quebec in 1970, its replacement by a Liberal government more concerned with things economic than things symbolic, and by the prime minister's assault on the revolutionary nationalists which began in October 1970. Whatever the causes, the federal structure issue disappeared and was not even discussed at length during the

1972 general federal election. Resolutions from Progressive Conservative party conventions together with speeches by Mr. Stanfield seemed
to indicate his party's essential agreement with a conception of
Canada put in these words by the prime minister:

> It was the view of the Royal Commission, shared by the Govern-
> ment and, I am sure, by all Canadians, that there cannot be one
> cultural policy for Canadians of British and French origin, another
> for the original peoples and yet a third for all others. For although
> there are two official languages there is no official culture, nor does
> any ethnic group take precedence over any other. . . . A policy of
> multi-culturalism within a bilingual framework commends itself
> to the Government as the most suitable means of assuring the
> cultural freedom of Canadians.

Analysis

A clear battle between two concepts of Canadian federalism? That the
deux nations campaign was not, although some English-speakers
might have thought the policy component of the election contest
amounted to something comparable. The voters were not offered a
choice on the question of expanded bilingualism. Although a prime
feature of the dualist concept, this policy was favoured by all the
elected party leaders. Just the same, the widespread antagonism
which the issue generated served terribly to confuse debates and
judgements on the equal or special status question. A political pragmatist rather than a constitutional theoretician like his opponent,
Robert Stanfield had deep personal experience of the inequalities of
the provinces in social, political, and especially, economic fact. The
provinces all had different, unequal needs. To consult, negotiate, and
discover whether Quebec had particular needs requiring constitutional
change was to him only reasonable. Never though, despite being
pressed many times by interviewers, did Mr. Stanfield commit himself
in advance to the desirablility of any particular redistribution of jurisdictions in the federation. That would depend on circumstances to be
investigated calmly and coolly away from the hurly-burly of a general
election.

For many voters, the Stanfield policy of flexibility toward Quebec
was either unacceptable or too uncertain, too fuzzy. Sharpness of outline there was in the associate states concept promoted by the Johnson
forces, as well as in the racist misinterpretation of deux nations vili-
fied by the Diefenbaker camp, but neither found an electoral focus.
This left only the hard simplicity of the Trudeau approach and that
had the added attractiveness of being the next closest thing to the
status quo available.

The 1968 campaign result made it clear there would be no constitutional accommodation of those forces seeking symbolic recognition for the unique place of Quebec within Canada. In this, it helped to bipolarize the Quebec citizenry into those who were Liberal and federalist and those who were non-Liberal and separatist. That the bipolarization was not quite complete was demonstrated by the Quebec results in the 1970 provincial and 1972 federal general elections. Between these two events came the Victoria constitutional conference. To that affair, the legacy of 1968 was surely the impossibility of agreement. Indeed, the major outcome of the deux nations campaign as a whole was to render the dualist approach illegitimate as a concept which could find formal expression in a Canadian federal constitution during the nineteen-seventies and possibly beyond.

Two Nations or More?

The continuance of Canada as a state demonstrates how man may use his political inclinations to overcome the seeming imperatives of geography, resource economics, and the clash of rival cultures. More notable than the bare existence of this state, however, has been its character as a liberal democracy which persists despite John Stuart Mill's dictum. "Free institutions are next to impossible in a country made up of different nationalities," he wrote. "Among a people without fellow-feeling, especially if they read and speak different languages, the united public opinion, necessary to the working of representative government, cannot exist."[1] Mill published his observations in the eighteen-sixties, during the birth-pangs of the Canadian federation whose subsequent measure as a stable and democratic government may well have depended on two factors not taken into Mill's calculations. For most of the Confederation century, only one or the other but seldom both levels of cabinet government were strong and activist across a wide front. Equally important as the stability arising from the relative lack of sustained inter-governmental conflict is that French-speaking people for long were regular, though not continuous members of the shifting majorities supporting the central government. Not until recently was there suggestion that French Canadians might have become a permanent minority on all federal questions important to them—a development completely inimical to representative democracy as the great English liberal saw so well.

Like all shotgun weddings, that of parliamentary government to federalism which gave birth to Canada was an uneasy one—no matter how unavoidable. Without the forceful leadership provided by a cabinet system at the centre, the dominion could never have been stitched together; without the self-government of federalism, the country would have been ripped apart by sectional interests and racial antagonism. Never a simple blend of her British and American heritages, Canada has been a heterogeneous mixture to which is added French Canada, a constituent too often misinterpreted both at home and abroad as implying little more than linguistic inconvenience. The assertive reinforcement of a vibrant French-Canadian culture by a strongly interventionist political régime gives the state a dynamic dimension utterly lacking in the Anglo-Saxon federations. The difference is critical. That dynamic today provides both catalyst and component for the turbulent interaction between regional interests, almost exclusively expressed by militant provincial governments, and a central régime in which the executive impulses of both cabinet government and rationalized bureaucracy have virtually triumphed over the representative features of Millsian liberalism.

REFLECTIONS ON THE METHODOLOGY

The readiness with which we compare aspects of one federation with another, and especially with the American, indicates the character of such studies as a branch of comparative politics. That alone should alert us to the centrality of methodology if much validity is to be attributed to comparative statements—whether they involve two federations or the same state at two points in time. So long as comparative federalism was founded on public law, the political scientist, being largely ignorant of jurisprudence, could follow the master, K. C. Wheare, with some confidence. From this point of reasonable precision, research efforts have departed widely in the search for more complete explanations. These have included attempts to develop or incorporate a sociology of territorial diversity, notions of administrative behaviour, governmental interdependence, integration theory, and newly-popular approaches such as political behaviour and comparative political culture, the latter so much a departure from the institutional beginnings that it almost denies the existence of the subject. Unburdened by such sophistications, this study has sought simply to produce a better understanding of the country by inquiring into the structural preconceptions of the major political actors and commentators, and, in seeking them, it has been largely issue-oriented and classificatory. Not all political problems are useful for this type of inquiry and the utility of any one set of issues depends on their importance to the specifically federal aspects of the polity. The pattern of persisting or recurring issues in Canadian politics suggested eighteen criteria[2] on the basis of which five concepts have been distinguished and elaborated. Selecting other criteria might have produced other types or numbers of concepts, so that both the selection and general methodology should be assessed on the basis of logicality and the extent to which the results conform to informed understanding of Canadian politics. The whole approach presumes, of course, that structural conceptions of the federation, both "real" and ideal, are significant influences in political behaviour. At this stage it would seem useful to consider briefly the methodology used in the study.

In a federal state, a number of diverse polities subsist and preserve much of their individuality through the exercise of a degree of significant governmental authority, a pluralist structuring of the state which is the exception rather than the rule. What purpose is this special structure supposed to serve? Opinions vary, naturally, and the responses available have been classified either as unitary or pluralist. The unitary or integrative point of view holds that while federalism might at one time have been necessary, it should facilitate the creation of a new nation-state providing a common identity for once disparate peoples and imbuing them with greater consensus on social goals and the means of attaining them. As greater unity is achieved, the regional governments might be reduced gradually to administrative sub-units of the central régime. The attribution of this "purpose" to confederation characterizes and is the most distinctive feature of the centralist concept. Two concepts, the dualist and the compact, find much of their rationale in denying the legitimacy of integrative objectives. The pluralist objective involves the initial assumption that the lively persistence of individualist societies within the federation is both just and appropriate; mutual benefits are said to accrue from the cooperation and cross-fertilization of variant but sympathetic communities. Less often than in the integrative conception are these benefits said to be materialist in character: stress more frequently has been put on intangible cultural, religious, and political values such as participation. Despite such professions, pluralist arguments are also exploited in order to extract monetary or other economic benefit for the provinces.

On inquiry, the purpose-oriented criteria were found to be limited, leaving distinctions still to be made between the pluralist concepts; the methods proposed for attaining desired objectives were found useful for these distinctions. The distribution of financial resources proved to be a specially useful tool for separating concepts, and two ideas, fiscal autonomy or financial independence for the provinces, may be seen as important cross-roads in the thickets. Fiscal autonomy, it will be remembered, means a distribution of taxing powers designed to enable a normally vigorous province to raise enough money by its own efforts to meet its minimum constitutional responsibilities. The usual method proposed was that of giving the provinces exclusive rights to some fruitful tax field, a proposal generally found in dualist and compact federalism. The notion of financial independence depends on intergovernmental goodwill for its workability and involves seeing that provincial treasuries are guaranteed minimum revenues adequate to duties imposed on the provinces and seeing that their governments remain free to determine their spending priorities. These minimum revenues might consist entirely of central government subsidies assured by statute or convention; they could also be derived from limited provincial taxes supplemented by guaranteed subsidies— the general Canadian case. Administrative and coordinate concepts of federalism incorporate financial independence of the province as a basic condition, with centralists having no patience with the notion of either provincial fiscal autonomy or financial independence.

Provincial governments must perform some significant political functions in practical independence for the system to be a federal one.

Table 5 **Correlation of Differentiating Criteria and five Concepts**
(Canadian Concepts of Federalism)

	Centralist	Administrative	Coordinate	Dualist	Compact
(A) Objective					
1. Monist (unitary)	•	•			
2. Pluralist (mutual strengthening)		•	•	•	•
(B) Problem-Solving Methods					
Economic Control:					
3. Centralized finance	•				
4. Centralized taxation	•	•			
5. Finance independence		•	•	•	•
6. Fiscal independence				•	•
Political Initiative:					
7. Centralized	•				
8. Central supervision	•	•	•		
9. Provincial autonomy		•	•	•	•
Cultural responsibility:					
10. Central civil rights	•	•	•		
11. Prov. civil rights		•	•	•	•
12. Fedl. school stdrds.	•	•			
13. Prov. school stdrds.			•	•	•
14. Fedl. lang. guarantee	•	•	•	•	
15. Prov. lang. guarantee					•
(C) Constitutional Amend.					
16. Canadian majority	•				
17. Concurrent regions		•	•	•	
18. Confederal (Unanimity)					•

For this study, the practical enjoyment of rights to initiate new policy was taken as a workable gauge and a scale was derived that permitted differentiation among concepts as indicated by Table 5. Legal structures might be expected to become problems or potential issues of federalism whenever: (a) concepts prevail elevating the sovereignty of the constituent units; (b) important judicial posts become elective or political offices; and (c) situations arise in which the courts are asked to settle what are for the society essentially political rather than legal questions on a regular basis. This inquiry did not require developing indices relating to the system of courts, but it seems clear that some would be necessary if the scheme were to be useful for other federations. The authority to amend the federal constitution is the lynch-pin of a federation. If that pin is firmly set, and if it is accepted as a fact by the constituent units, then constitutional amendment may never be an issue in federal politics. But it is one in Canada, and the classification scheme required indices relating to the ability of territorially concentrated minorities to have a say in amending proposals. Disputes over appropriateness for amendments of country-wide or regional majorities allow us to distinguish compact theorists from dualists, and especially from centralists, with coordinate and administrative federalists usually sharing agreement on the desirability of some mixed list (Fulton-Favreau) or concurrent majorities system (Trudeau-Turner). While other states might well find a greater number of issues significant for the purpose, within the cultural field attitudes toward linguistic rights, education, and fundamental liberties seemed to be adequate for differentiating the five concepts.

THE FACTORS OF CHANGE

The dominance at different times of the centralist, compact, and coordinate concepts, together with the sometime coexistence of the administrative and dualist ideas, suggests the continuing instability of the centralizing and decentralizing[3] influences in the society, economy, and government. In this area the notion of a "pendulum theory" has occasionally been advanced. Here, the balance of power within a federation is said to swing back and forth between the central authority in one period and the provincial in another, with the rising government—such as the provincial during the Pearson period—achieving enhanced status at the expense of the other's lawful jurisdictions. But seldom in law or in practice do particular powers which are being exploited exclusively by one government get transferred from one jurisdiction to another.[4] What happens appears to be a three-fold process. In the absence of other action dealing with a problem, one regime moves into novel forms, new areas, or higher levels of governmental activity, conveys a general impression of being more "activist," "enterprising," or "responsive," and begins to displace the other centre of government in public awareness. (Who really dominates whom in a federation is surely impossible to answer conclusively.) Apparent ascendancy may also reflect the relative state of play in a continuing contest between governments to add popular powers to their armouries. The game is usually additive rather than zero-sum;[5] throughout Canada the only powers which governments tend to surrender altogether are a few relating to areas of private conduct. If it were taken to be explanatory or analytic, the pendulum theory would be misleading; as it is, it may furnish some description of the comparative public salience of various governments.

Particular configurations of centripetal and centrifugal forces within the federation may still be expected to be closely related to the vitality of individual concepts. Specifying the forces with precision might well yield elements basic to construction of an explanatory theory but, unfortunately, the necessary precision is missing. What, then, can be said about such influences? First, they can be classified under virtually all headings of social study: constitutional, political, economic, geographic, demographic, and social psychological. Second, some are permanent, others transitory, and still others epiphenomenal. Third, for some people, times, and places, the same factor may tend to be nationally integrative while for others it tends to confirm or strengthen regional community feeling. Some examples may be in order. Among the more permanent centralizing influences are: the central government and the powers conferred on it by the B.N.A. Act, the leadership and policy processes of the political parties and country-wide interest groups, the banking institutions, federal-oriented élites, egalitarian aspects of the culture, and nationalist sentiments like non-Americanism. With several exceptions, there are comparable factors sustaining decentralist impulses on a durable basis; for example, provincially-oriented economic élites (largely resource- and service-based), pride in community achievements, etc. In addition one sees the traditionally recognized topographical inhibitions to cross-Canada mobility, divergent regional economic interests, historical experiences, some sub-cultural differentiation (especially in the political sphere), and, of course, French-language concentrations.

For limited term or transitory influences one might examine social movements such as rural depopulation, the periodic "tides" of immigration, the Canadian Pacific Railway, the building of a reformed, functionally superior bureaucracy at Ottawa (and replication of that change in the provincial capitals decades later), the tax-rental and tax-collection structures, one-party dominance, and possibly certain programs such as public health and medical care insurances. While their classification as limited term or epiphenomenal influences is unimportant, individual political personalities have been highly significant in terms of centralization or decentralization; the categorization of prime ministers and premiers as great men is commonly made in terms of the extent to which they "built up Canada," or "stood up against Ottawa." Epiphenomena influencing attitudes toward the federal structure have included the Riel Rebellion and the world wars, (which generated a variety of influences), foreign threats, scandals, provincial adoption of long term planning in different sectors, monetary or credit crises, and the accidental contrasts of politics which confront the public with a succession of minority governments at the centre with a plethora of strong premiers in the provincial capitals.

Certain factors have often been judged highly influential and unidirectional but these claims seldom stand up under examination. The external Canadian tariff, for example, may well have bonded Ontario and Quebec closer to the federal capital and thereby been judged centralizing, but its effect on Outer Canada was almost certainly contrary in all important political senses. The concentration of corporate finance in Toronto and Montreal was thought by some to be centralist in effect but that estimation ignored the growing access to foreign capital in the provinces—particularly during the post-Second World War period. Physical communication systems may work in both directions, a belief exemplified by Ottawa's encouragement of Air Canada and a fast air mail service and by the provinces' subsidies for provincial air services and development railways. Despite efforts by the Canadian Broadcasting Corporation and the Canadian Radio-Television Commission, the mass communication system tends to be either highly parochial (radio and newspapers) or highly diffuse where not foreign (television) in content and, presumably, effect. Intergovernmental financial transfers would be a highly unreliable device for any Ottawa government seeking to widen its influence over the provinces. Conditional grants almost certainly look centralizing but the resentments they may eventually generate in the recipients may well cancel out that effect and contribute to decentralist sentiments. Indeed, unconditional grants—and especially those so well established they acquire semi-constitutional sanctity—strengthen provincial régimes immeasurably and their levels come to comprise constant grudges against the centre, sentiments which may well be conveyed to sizable populations during election campaigns.

THE INSTITUTIONAL DIMENSION

A potentially important omission from the considerations to this point have been factors related to particular institutions, their composition, functioning, and evolution. As Professor Alan Cairns has demonstrated so well, the features of institutions such as the systems of judicial interpretation and popular elections may determine not simply the shape of the issues, but whether they will be brought to attention and dealt with at all. The composition and functioning of the Supreme Court of Canada has been a continuing sore point with French-Canadian commentators, although it is more a symptom than a cause about which complaints are made. Professor Smiley has pointed to the lack of cross-fertilization between federal and provincial legislatures in terms of personnel and questions whether it remains true that the central cabinet today performs the regionally representative tasks previously attributed to it. We know little of the existence, operation, and virtually nothing of the influence, of voluntary associations and interest groups. Conspiratorial reasons may be appropriate here, although better explanations will likely be found in factors like the limited access permitted by cabinet government, the relatively unrepresentative nature of the Canadian Commons (in contrast to the British example), and in the difficulties of organizing from a comparatively small resource base in a large federal country to deal with a multiplicity of parliamentary régimes as is often necessary on a single issue. The earlier devotion of socialists to centralist ideas underwent change, not simply as a result of exposure to some general secular trend, but in important part because of changes in the party's internal influences and structure resulting from the experience of power at the provincial level—and not at the central. At Ottawa, the moves from the opposition to the treasury benches and back again together with the length of tenure in each place have exercised a large influence on whether the party espoused centralist or other conceptions of the ideal federation. Since confederation, the task of representing the provinces at the centre has fallen not simply to cabinet spokesmen but to the second largest party which has traditionally based its opposition attacks on provincially-oriented critiques in preference to abstract ideals.

The extent to which the provincial institutions exhibit manifestations comparable to the central ones is less clear. That cabinets are executive-dominated and action-oriented[6] can only be stated as a general impression but that the governing parties in the provinces identify themselves firmly with provincial interests is axiomatic. The usual pattern of single party dominance creates situations in which the opposition party is often scarcely visible and the ground on which they loyally oppose is a constantly shifting one, with the defence of federal interests against parochial regional governments being a chancy and occasional tactic at best. Only the situation in Quebec can be stated with much assurance. As Professor Vincent Lemieux put it: "From the end of the nineteenth century up to the late 1950's one of the two main provincial parties of Quebec was relatively autonomist and the other relatively federalist; since the 1960 Liberal victory, this distinction no longer applies. The two parties are both autonomist and have proposed greater powers for Quebec within the Canadian confederation."[7]

Ideally, an issue-oriented scheme would take into account influences exerted on the subject by institutional features such as those mentioned. The reality of limited resources has denied us such comprehensiveness.

Whose Concepts, When, and Why?

In seeking to unravel the skein of Canadian politics by drawing out major threads so far largely neglected,[8] this work has employed an analytic and taxonomic approach. To go further, to undertake explanatory theory-building would require answers to several important and rather difficult questions: how do concepts come into being, who comes to hold which ones, and why do they? Complete answers must await further research and so must the theory, if indeed it is possible to arrive at viable explanations through such a route. The chart, "Time Lines for Concepts of Federalism," suggests roughly the

CHART

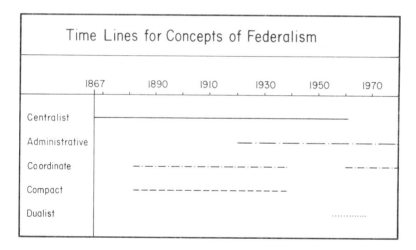

periods in which the different ideas seem to find public expression which is both of a prominent and a continuing nature, but it does not attempt the much more difficult task of indicating which of several might have been dominant at particular times. If the broad picture is reasonable, it permits the construction of hypotheses relating the life cycle of the concepts to other known cycles, whether economic, cultural development, international events, etc.[9] To the questions, who and why, the simplistic but probably valid answers lie in the political roles performed by élites articulating the varied concepts. The centralist concept requires and justifies the further concentration of public authority—an end in itself for the power-conscious, a definition of a "strong Canada" for some patriots, and useful means to goals as diverse as increasing social equality, building a more efficient common market, and synthesizing a "real" Canadian culture by assimilating the minorities. The concept is compatible with, if not often required by, the roles associated with those of federal prime ministers, social reformers, Keynesian economists, cultural nationalists, and racists. It seems impossible to disentangle the development and articulation of the compact theory from the defensive problems of provincial government leaders and supporters. The dualist idea, latent for decades in oratory and literature, was fleshed out politically and elevated to prominence with the disintegration of the compact theory position and the ensuing redefinitions of the danger, circumstances, and possibilities of French Canada, together with the roles this imposed on her leaders. The coordinate concept is similarly representative of judicial proclivities in the Anglo-Canadian culture combined with a fully adequate justification of the role tensions and situations of strong-minded premiers and prime ministers. The association of the administrative concept with senior bureaucrats and its manifestations in terms of their role objectives is also persuasive. In one sense, our present inquiry has been almost entirely élitist and what role theory does not satisfactorily explain is the important and virtually unexplored popular dimension of the question. For instance, it is usually assumed that the prototypical person who is English-speaking, Protestant, Anglo-Saxon in origin, and resident in the old provinces, is highly centralist in inclination, intolerant toward dualism, ignorant of administrative relationships, and (at least in the seventies), impatient of expressions of provincial sovereignty such as compact or coordinate federalism. The evidence for this image is almost totally absent. Only very recently have scholars such as Professors Mildred Schwartz, Donald Blake, and Richard Simeon begun to probe deeply and comparatively into the regional dimensions of mass attitudes and behaviour. While one does not expect any general distribution of popular attitudes toward such abstract questions as alternative concepts of federalism, no observations of the kind can be made with much confidence until this regionally-oriented research has been completed and analyzed.

IMPLICATIONS FOR THE FUTURE

Much of the country's political debate is conducted in terms more relevant to the academic analysis of concepts of federalism than to the more comprehensible discussions of hockey's Hot-Stove League and its equivalents. While that may not be surprising, and politicians do not usually make such mistakes during general election campaigns, their inter-election vocabularies and preoccupations are often intelligible or interesting only to the most dedicated *aficionado*. The air of irrelevance or unreality that marks most conferences of prime ministers and premiers was well illustrated by the meetings in May, 1973. One able political journalist, Geoffrey Stevens, put this interpretation on the proceedings: "The leaders are talking about several things but what most of them boil down to is money. It's not even real money: it's bureaucrats' money. Specifically, the main issue involves the financing of health programs; how much money should come out of the pocket of the federal Government and how much out of the provincial pockets. The taxpayer might be excused for concluding that when his leaders are finished talking all the money will come out of the same pocket—his."[10] For some functional specialists, what was involved was truly revolutionary: the proposed elimination of federal conditional health grants and their replacement with unconditional grants which would grow with changes in the Gross National Product; the federal government was also proposing to limit its "thrust fund" initiatives in the field to block grants. To the public the discussions must have appeared to be petty quarreling. The consequences for the political system of this gulf in understanding may be immeasurable but they cannot be negligible. At the least, the inherent tendencies of politics to be élitist are considerably encouraged in a political culture in which deference to authority is already counted a major feature. The tendency toward federalist jargon not only reduces markedly the possibility of public interest, it considerably isolates important areas and debates from public scrutiny or influence. The latter is a most persuasive argument against any attempt to expand administrative federalism or to reinstate it as the major means of intergovernmental problem-solving.

Creative Politics and Canadian Unity

Whether a preoccupation with federalist disputes causes, or results from the recurring unity issue is probably unanswerable, although some there are who see the situation as deliberately created by conservative interests for their own ends. Professor John Porter, for example, has argued that the country has suffered a lack of "creative politics" as a result. As he sees it, the polity must be polarized into left and right if the society is to become more equal and progressive, a development which has been side-tracked into unwarranted concern for Canadian unity. In his view, the social fabric is really much tougher than political scientists and politicians alike would have us believe. The judgement on cohesiveness depends in part on the fundamental view of man: is he to be seen chiefly as Hobbesian or sociable in nature? Canada's framework is legalist and the polity is liberal individualist in public tone. The reflex-like campaigns to discredit the slightest manifestation of nationalism as "racist" and evilly predestined is an example. The attitude fits in well with Ottawa's insistence on the formality of legal equality for all provinces, on giving policy priority to a Charter of Human Rights, and on the technocratic overhaul of the central administration. Despite the importance of these views, it should be remembered that the legal rationalism which inspired modern federalism was "liberal" on the question of community; indeed, the federal institution is founded on the notion of providing a single state umbrella for a number of communities even if, and perhaps especially where, they were not all alike in philosophical temperament. If, at heart, Canada is still best characterized, in Eric Nicol's terms, as "a railway in search of a country," one in which "the ties that bind are creosoted and six feet long," then Canada as a whole remains too fragile a community for the federalist concerns to be abandoned in favour of the more explicit ideological conflict preferred by Professor Porter. Whatever its cost in other terms, the concentration on unity is itself a failing exercise according to some views. Toward the end of the turbulent nineteen-sixties, Professor Michel Brunet painted a sombre picture:

> Canada and its population are just beginning to realize that the country is engaged in a process of partial disintegration. The ideals and objectives that gave birth, two hundred years ago, to a British kingdom in North America have little appeal to the imagination of most of today's Canadian citizens. Sixty per cent of Canada's inhabitants . . . are not of British origin. Organized in opposition to the United States, Canada is becoming every day more closely linked to its powerful neighbour with whom it forms willy-nilly an economic and military continental union. The basis upon which the country rested since the establishment of the Canadian federation in 1867 is in a state of gradual erosion because many of its regions have the conviction that they do not receive their fair share of the economic loaf, because a great number of its citizens lack a common national consciousness and because the Québecois no longer accept the leadership of the English-speaking majority.[11]

Although few agree on its definition, most commentators would concur on the absence of an overarching pan-Canadian nationalism: "we have conceived the immaculate non-nation," as Professor John Holmes put it once. The multiplicity of concepts of federalism and their general good health may be evidence to support the observation, but neither phenomenon is proof of a complete absence of national feeling and the promise of inevitable disintegration invariably associated with it. There *is* a characteristic national sentiment but its dissimilarity from comparable foreign feeling (except possibly the Swiss), its diffuseness, and its political rather than socio-cultural base has misled most non-literary commentators. That characteristic is one of pride in a common political nationality[12] and a generalized tolerance. Confronted with the failure of their determined efforts to assimilate the French-speaking, the majority English were forced to accommodate themselves to the considerable presence of a different way of life within the bosom of the single state. That accommodation and tolerance became a major feature of the political culture at the official level. Just as an ideological spectrum much wider than the contemporary American achieved legitimacy, so varied visions and interpretations of the ideal structural arrangements have come to be the norm. In practice denying the development of a single, official ideology,[13] Canada carried her unAmerican activities to the extreme of political tolerance in which even advocacy of the state's dismemberment was acceptable so long as the means proposed were peaceful.

Problem-Solving and Diplomacy

So extensive were the intergovernmental consultations involved in the recent moves away from centralist paternalism toward a more coordinate concept that federal-provincial diplomacy became a new art and a negotiation process was established that slowly grew formal, institutionalized, and more central to certain policy-making. "The pattern, indeed, is one of the distinctive characteristics of Canadian federalism," according to Professor Simeon. Although an admitted "complication" in comparison to unitary systems, he argued that the new process comprised a valuable device for policy development in such a decentralized state. What was more, he said, "there is little evidence that it has frustrated widespread public demands in recent years."[14] Professor Smiley has reacted to the same phenomenon quite differently. The society remains intractably federal "in a most elemental way," he observed, yet significant regional interests, being denied effective expression through Ottawa's institutions, have been forced to find exclusive outlet through provincial governments. Under such circumstances, in which "the most important of public policies are made by processes of joint federal-provincial decision," he concluded that "Canada cannot be effectively governed."[15]

Such an argument has been popular but it is not universally compelling. The mass media and academics alike are much impressed by the multitude of issues "left unsolved" by the process of negotiations between near-equals, but such situations seldom pose the threat to the country's survival that is imagined by liberal intellectuals and those caught up in the afterbirth of yet another aborted conference. Many problems that appeared critical at the time have simply "gone away" despite nothing successful apparently having been done about them. Other problems became manageable or less pressing when they changed shape or were factored into smaller issues. The New Deal decisions combined with the Depression to produce a burning "constitutional crisis" which was never really resolved; the rejection of the postwar Reconstruction proposals appeared to be similarly threatening, but both proved to be less than fatal to the federation. Issues like those of the energy crisis in 1974 are often invested with great mass media attention and all the trappings of full intergovernmental conferences, but those trappings do not always, or even generally, make the negotiations of critical significance for Canada's survival. True, the product is usually a short-term solution, and these irritate would-be long-range planners, but short-term solutions are typical of processes centring on elected politicians and are seldom fit cause for prophecies of doom.

Frustrated by apparent constitutional or political rigidities, public authorities in the past have devised means of injecting enough flexibility into the system not only to keep it working but to keep the voters reasonably satisfied. Conditional grants, intra-party accommodations, equalization, delegation to executive agencies, "opting out," and political rather than judicial settlements are all examples. Should these methods prove unsatisfactory for future problem-solving, the federation may still find new sources of flexibility—perhaps through developing interest group systems (supplementing or replacing ineffectual party functioning), through new forms of administrative decentralization from Ottawa, or through bureaucratic stimulation of new channels of public representation and action such as poverty, neighbourhood, and local incentive programs. During the first Trudeau administration (1968-72) there were signs that it was exploring the criminal law authority in search of additional power which it thought necessary to control pollution, prices and wages, and multinational corporations. Adjusting the incidence by region for certain taxes was another method explored in the search for economic flexibility. In any case, whether such searches were successful or not, only a thoroughly committed centralist would argue that every new problem requires resolution through an expansion of the central power; and what is flexibility to a pragmatist in the majority often proves to be illegitimate aggrandizement to the person in a minority seeking rights and protection by means of a firmly understood and predictable distribution of power. Little in the country's experience demonstrates the necessary inferiority of policies emerging either from the provincial political systems (most of which have been undergoing rapid change, even democratization, since 1960), or from a process of intergovernmental bargaining between near equals whose agreement indicates country-wide support for a policy and facilitates its implementation.

Salvation by Constitution?

If ever a time arrived when an explicit choice was to be made between a centralist, coordinate, or dualist conception of the union, it would be during the drafting of a fundamentally new constitution. While the constitutional conference seemed at times during the sixties and early seventies to be Canada's verbal substitute for civil war, the sessions were chiefly limited to amendment procedures, financial matters, and civil liberties rather than concerned with fundamental redrafting. Although there were a few individual attempts,[16] the only comprehensive effort by a public body was that reported in 1972 by the joint Senate-House of Commons special committee on the Constitution, but its conclusions involved radical rewriting in only two limited senses: institution of a basic bill of civil liberties together with a proposal to assign social welfare exclusively to the provinces and broad economic management powers to the central government. While the specific topics of the many intergovernmental meetings varied somewhat in the period up to 1971, the failure of the process to produce agreement even on domestic amending procedures disheartened the participants and disillusioned many observers. The reasons are not hard to find. Constitutional conferencing during the Pearson-Trudeau period turned into rituals seeking a virtual trans-substantiation of the great number of conflicting priorities and real problems that bedevilled the various Canadian and provincial political systems during the period. Some of the dissatisfaction arose as well from the very conception of the constitutional exercise. Redrawing a federal instrument involves changes in the basic rules determining what business is public and how it should be conducted. New rules for the game cannot be agreed, however, if essential players insist on fundamentally different rules or decide they are not really interested in playing the game with each other at all. The rule redrafting is hard enough in Canada where certain parties conceive of the field in quite different terms. It was immensely complicated by the injection of demands that the occasion should be taken to solve all of the country's political problems as well as design new rules for determining the federal framework within which they were to be tackled. Curiously, the constitutional conferences of our time were able to agree—and then only for a brief period —on a domestic amending formula and on a truncated bill of rights, both matters which had not been thought necessary a century before.

Canadians who have been alive to their social surroundings and who have lived for long in more than one region understand that "one nation" falls far short of describing their country. So too does "two nations," unless the term is appreciated in the significant sense of being two linguistic cultures, one of which every new Canadian incorporates into his psyche regardless of whether he makes his first arrival by ship, plane, or cradle. Overdue but reasonable recognition of this dualist aspect of the state was given in the Official Languages Act of 1969. While the political features of the dualist concept may conform admirably to the French Fact, it fails utterly to fit the fact of the heterogeneous English-language communities. In similar fashion, the centralist concept ignores completely the implications of impracticality inherent in the creation, development, and flourishing of whole, new, and separated provincial communities, a marked contrast to the sporadic and uncertain course of the "nation-building" attempted on a Canada-wide basis during the same period.[17] In an age in which governments are activist and interpenetrating at all three levels, the compact theory is anachronistic. Only a modified coordinate approach seems to offer the possibility of a federal polity that facilitates an optimum mixture of the major competing values of the day.

Those values in tension at the time of writing and of most relevance to the federal quality of the political structure would seem to include: nationalism, majoritarianism, equality, participation, and responsiveness. Nationalism seems to demand a tighter-knit society and varieties of it compete with each other and with local identifications. Majoritarian questions revolve constantly on the point of what kind of majority of which people, or area, or community is most appropriate to settle which kinds of disputes. The type of equality favoured is also important. Where, for example, equality was thought of in terms of like measures (of services or funds) for everybody, then country-wide action in social services was threatened or made impossible by regional differences in inequalities, needs, and attitudes. Where there are no *a priori* reasons for expecting one political system to be more open relative to another, effective citizen participation and governmental responsiveness appear to be inversely related to the size and complexity of the society—an argument favouring strong provinces. The respective influences of these values varies over time, but for the immediate future the most feasible compromise between them may well involve recognition that Canada is a country of not one, nor two, but many "nations."

Special Status for All

Without either delegation or symbolic recognition of the two founding cultures, the present constitutional arrangements are unsatisfactory even if they should eventually include something like the Trudeau-Turner amending formula. Although the working conditions already incorporate delegation in some areas, the whole question has been confused by the deliberate misleading of the English-speaking voter on the issue of "special status." Their politicians sold them a goldbrick labelled "equal status for every province" and its glitter blinded many to its worthlessness. The whole course of federal-provincial relations through this century demonstrates that every province has sought and wanted special status for itself. The demand has, of course, been worded slightly differently: "special consideration" for the particular problems of the Atlantic Provinces, of the Prairies, of British Columbia, particular problems which people in Ottawa were asserted to be incapable of understanding. Not only has every province wanted treatment different from the others; they have been enjoying it in fact. Each has had a unique combination of agreements and joint programs with the federal government; the Canada Assistance Plan (C.A.P.), for example, was a mere umbrella treaty sheltering different welfare arrangements between the provinces and Ottawa. There could be no status more special than that of Prince Edward Island where the economic development agreements of the sixties virtually turned the entire province into a federal receivership. There is no meaningful way in which the Island people could have been politically equal to the people of either British Columbia or Quebec, each of which had federal subsidy, tax, and grant arrangements varying greatly from the other's. The facile arguments rejecting special status for Quebec because of pedantic legalisms dealing with alterations in the status of federal MPs looked more ostrich-like than serious in their contribution to understanding.

The most promising route to what might be an acceptable federal reconstitution—if that proves unavoidable—lies through developing the delegation idea. With such a process, the constitution could give formal recognition to today's working arrangements and go beyond them as well where provinces wished. If New Brunswick and Prince Edward Island wish to negotiate to have Ottawa manage all of their welfare and economic promotion functions, why should they not do it with constitutional and popular approval? If the Western provinces can persuade the federal government to take over university education in exchange for a freer hand in natural resources, why not? (In the absence of an agreed and explicit set of national values, any national interest objection in such cases is impossible to sustain because of its basic definition in situational expediency.) More fruitful avenues of constitutional reform are open to us than has been the case until now through variations on the delegation procedure, through extension of umbrella arrangements such as the Canada Assistance Plan, and even through extending the list of concurrent powers which might apply to all or only to some provinces.

The consequences of a more open, less rigidly structured constitution are no easier and no more difficult to foresee than are those of maintaining the present system with its wide divergence between formal provisions and the working reality. A constitutional order in which the citizen's relationship with the central government changed as he moved from province to province would not be a simple one. Neither would taxation arrangements be simplified, but they would be possible. Complexity is not new to Canadian politics; it is the best one word description of the system in use today following a quarter-century or more of intense federal-provincial diplomacy.

In one respect the changes proposed for consideration would reduce an important element of flexibility in the present system—the freedom of most premiers and cabinet executives to conclude virtually whatever agreements they like with other governments, free from the effective scrutiny of the legislature and the public. The potential gain would counterbalance that loss. Since the need for intergovernmental arrangements would remain, political leaders would be impelled to seek at least enough public support to make their proposals stand up to some examination in the legislature and, possibly, in the occasional election campaign as well. Would delegation procedures mean more or less decentralization? We cannot predict with certainty. It could mean both. Assessment of the probabilities is affected by one's time-bound judgements about the relative strengths and ambitions of those at Ottawa and in the provincial capitals. A mixed result seems likely: greater centralization of some functions and decentralization of others together with variations from region to region. A formal delegation procedure—such as that in the Fulton-Favreau formula or something a little less rigid—would certainly facilitate public awareness of changes in governments' responsibilities and that, in turn, would probably make some easier and others harder to achieve.

Two objections more might be made to such a permissive federal constitution. First, the result would not be a "true federal constitution"; it would not conform neatly to any of the concepts which have formed the subject of this book. Conformity to an abstract model is, however, basically irrelevant to the way in which people do their public business together, and there is nothing inherently more desirable about a federal rather than a confederal or a mixed form of government. Secondly, it might be objected, such a constitution might permit Quebec to negotiate her way right out of the the Canadian Confederation. If that is what the majority of the people of Quebec really want (and safeguards can be instituted to determine those wishes reliably), then why should they not have it? Negotiated divorces are preferable to shotgun and gelignite divorces. More to the point, such a constitution should make divorce much less attractive to Quebeckers; it might go far to demonstrate that Canadians as a whole have abandoned racial nationalism altogether in favour of mutual trust and genuine tolerance.

NOTES

1. No official record was kept of the 1864 meeting at Charlottetown. Journalists were barred, and even *The Globe* of Toronto, whose editor was a leading delegate, reported only social notes and rumours from the conference. The chief sources of information for scholars are the Colonial dispatches filed by the lieutenant-governors on the basis of reports made to them by delegates in their capacities as executive council members. Sparse, but official, notes were made at the Quebec City conference and at the London meetings by Colonel Hewitt Bernard. These are preserved in Joseph Pope, *Confederation, being a Series of hitherto unpublished Documents bearing on the British North America Act* (Toronto, 1895). Of only slight value is the record made by J. H. Gray, who observed the conference rule of avoiding substantive reports: *Confederation: or the Political and Parliamentary History of Canada, from the Conference at Quebec in October, 1864, to the Admission of British Columbia, in July, 1871* (Toronto, 1872). Debates on the Quebec Resolutions in the New Brunswick legislature were not reported. The most valuable source for the intentions of the Confederation Fathers is the record of debates in the Parliament of the Province of Canada when the Quebec Resolutions were presented for approval: *Parliamentary Debates on the Subject of the Confederation of the British North American Provinces* (hereinafter cited as *Confederation Debates*) (Quebec, 1865).

2. Alan C. Cairns, "The Judicial Committee and Its Critics," *Canadian Journal of Political Science*, 4 (1971): 301-45.

3. The word "confederation" as the traditional name for the union gives superficial support to those who argue for the sovereign character of the provinces. The term, however, meant little to men like John A. Macdonald, who freely admitted that he would adopt any phrase that would permit him to achieve his design of a British North American union. See his speech in *Confederation Debates*, 30 ff.

4. A. R. M. Lower, *et al., Evolving Canadian Federalism* (Durham, N.C., 1958), 5. Some American scholars dispute this interpretation of their country's constitutional background.

5. See Gad Horowitz, "Conservatism, Liberalism, and Socialism in Canada:

An Interpretation," *Canadian Journal of Economics and Political Science,* 32 (1966): 143-71.

6. Professor Lower has commented: "Although grave decisions have had to be made in Canada in the past, it may be doubted whether the people of this country as a whole have ever grappled with the task of hard, serious, political thinking. Things come too easily for us for that to be necessary." "Canadian Unity and its Conditions," in Violet Anderson ed., *Problems in Canadian Unity* (Toronto, 1938), p. 1.

7. *The Constitution of Canada* (Toronto, 1922), p. 405.

8. I owe this insight to D. V. Smiley who unfortunately has not yet given it the development that it merits. See, however, his *Canada in Question: Federalism in the Seventies* (Toronto, 1972).

9. "Parliamentary government rests on the doctrine that a single parliament, containing representatives of the voters, is the final organ through which public will is expressed in the country. Federalism requires a multiplicity of representative legislatures, most of them representing but a section of the country, with the consequence that the expression of public will is dispersed through several agincies." H. McD. Clokie, *Canadian Government and Politics* (3rd ed., Toronto, 1950), p. 56.

10. *Liquidators of the Maritime Bank of Canada* v. *Receiver-General of New Brunswick* (1892) A.C. 437, at 441.

11. G. P. Browne, *The Judicial Committee and the British North America Act* (Toronto, 1967), esp. 29-32.

12. *The Government of Canada* (2nd rev. ed., Toronto, 1954), pp. 38, 89.

13. "Constitutional Trends and Federalism," in Lower, *et. al. Evolving Canadian Federalism* at 95.

14. Smiley, *Canada in Question,* chap. 1, and R. L. Watts, *New Federations* (Oxford, 1966), p. 13.

15. W. S. Livingston, *Federalism and Constitutional Change* (London, 1956), p. 9.

16. "Federalism in the Commonwealth," in John D. Montgomery and Arthur Smithies, *Public Policy,* 14 (1965): 355.

17. "Some Forms and Limitations of Co-operative Federalism," *Canadian Bar Review,* 45 (1967): 410.

18. *Federal Government* (4th ed. London, 1963), p. 214.

CHAPTER 2   THE CENTRALIST CONCEPT (pp. 21-61)

1. "Centralization and Decentralization in Canadian Federalism," *Canadian Bar Review* (hereafter cited as C.B.R.), 29 (1951): 1098.

2. "Proposed Additions to the New Canada Bill for a General Government," in H. E. Egerton and W. L. Grant, *Canadian Constitutional Development* (London, 1907), pp. 107-10.

3. Ibid., p. 108.

4. The reaction of the Duke of Kent, to whom this proposal was addressed, is preserved in the *Report* of Lord Durham. See Sir C. P. Lucas, ed., *Lord Durham's Report on the Affairs of British America* (3 vols.; Oxford, 1912), 2: 320-21.

5. Letter to R. W. Horton, under-secretary of state, in Egerton and Grant, pp. 147-48.

6. Donald Creighton, "Conservatism and National Unity," in R. Flenley, ed., *Essays in Canadian History* (Toronto, 1939), p. 36.

7. Lucas, 2: 288-89.

8. Joseph Pope, *Memoirs of the Right Honourable Sir John Alexander Macdonald* (2 vols.; Ottawa, 1894), 1: 71.

9. Ibid., pp. 71-72. Another biographer of Macdonald seriously questions the warmth of his support for the federation proposal at this time. Professor Creighton suggests that the Kingston resolution was likely passed "to Macdonald's surprise and probably against his will." Donald Creighton, *John A. Macdonald: The Young Politician* (Toronto, 1958), p. 145.

10. Howe to George Moffatt, president of the B.N.A. League, in J. A. Chisholm, *Speeches and Public Letters of Joseph Howe* (2 vols.; Halifax, 1909), 2: 25. Howe would, however, have no part of a union designed simply to "swamp the French."

11. Creighton, *Young Politician,* p. 150.

12. O. D. Skelton, *Life and Times of Sir Alexander Tilloch Galt* (Toronto, 1920), p. 171.

13. Ibid., p. 213.

14. The sections had equal weight in the legislature, but it must be admitted that the idea that the premier should resign when he lost the confidence of only a minority part of the membership of the legislature is, of course, outside present federal practices. On the other hand, contemporary commentators commonly question whether it would be legitimate for a party, such as the Progressive Conservatives, to contemplate trying to govern the country without substantial support from a number of Quebec members of Parliament. Compare the similarity of opinion columnists on this point following the general elections of 1957 and 1972.

15. Skelton, p. 215.

16. Ibid., p. 216.

17. In July, 1858, before he entered the Government, the legislature had taken no action on a resolution that Galt moved in these terms: "It is, therefore, the opinion of this House that the Union of Upper and Lower Canada should be changed from a Legislative to a Federative Union by the subdivision of the province into two or more divisions, each governing itself in local and sectional matters, with a general legislative government for subjects of national and common interest; and that a Commission of nine members be now named to report on the best means and mode of effecting such constitutional changes. That a general Confederation of the provinces of New Brunswick, Nova Scotia, Newfoundland and Prince Edward Island with Canada and the Western territories is most desirable and calculated to promote their several and united interests by preserving to each province the uncontrolled management of its peculiar institutions and of those internal affairs respecting which differences of opinion might arise with other members of the Confederation, while it will increase that identity of feeling which pervades the possessions of the British Crown in North America; and by the adoption of a uniform policy for the development of the vast and varied resources of these immense territories will greatly add to their national power and consideration." Ibid., pp. 219, 220.

18. The best account of these changes is Creighton, *Young Politician,* chap. 11.

19. Letter to Sir E. B. Lytton, in Skelton, *Galt,* pp. 242-44.

20. Ibid., p. 243. Note the phrase "thus affording the means of remedying any

defect" and the reference to the American amending provisions. The Confederation Fathers gave more consideration to the amending procedures than is usually suggested.

21. Creighton, *Young Politician,* p. 373.

22. Preserved in Joseph Pope, *Confederation: being a series of hitherto unpublished documents bearing on the British North America Act*; hereafter cited as Pope, *Confederation* (Toronto, 1895), pp. 1-38, 53-88.

23. Creighton, *Young Politician,* p. 377.

24. In this connection, see the explanatory letter from William McDougall, provincial secretary of Canada, to the Governor-General, dated May 4, 1865, in Pope, *Confederation,* pp. 298-300.

25. Letter from Macdonald to Brown Chamberlin, M.P., dated October 26, 1868: "I fully concur with you as to the apprehension that a conflict may, ere long, arise between the Dominion and the 'States Rights' people. . . .

"My own opinion is that the General Government or Parliament should pay no more regard to the status or position of the Local Governments than they would to the prospects of the ruling party in the corporation of Quebec or Montreal. . . .

"It is impossible, of course, that the elective franchise should be at the mercy of a foreign body." Noted in Joseph Pope, *Correspondence of Sir John Macdonald* (Garden City, N. Y., 1921), 74-75. Tupper quotation from Donald Creighton, *John A. Macdonald: The Old Chieftain* (Toronto, 1955), p. 427.

26. Mowat's motion assigned to the provinces, among other things, "5. Property and civil rights, excepting those portions thereof assigned to the General Legislature" (Pope, *Confederation,* p. 27), which phraseology was carried over by the North Americans through the London Resolutions (see ibid., p. 134). The limiting words were dropped by the English law clerks who made the first draft of the Bill; they contended that the omnibus phrasing of sec. 91 made this provision superfluous. The same Mowat later became premier of Ontario and led the provincial rights battle that hinged so much on the lack of restriction on the property and civil rights clause. Pope, *Confederation,* p. 27 (motion); pp. 84-87 (discussion).

27. Province of Canada, *Parliamentary Debates on the Subject of the Confederation of the British North American Provinces* (hereafter cited as *Confederation Debates*) (Quebec, 1865), 34, 41.

28. Pope, *Confederation,* p. 87.

29. W. P. M. Kennedy, *The Constitution of Canada* (Toronto, 1922), p. 301.

30. R. MacGregor Dawson, *The Government of Canada* (2nd ed., rev.; Toronto, 1954), p. 42. Compare W. F. O'Connor, *Report to the Honourable the Speaker of the Senate on the British North America Act, 1867* (Ottawa, 1939), who says at p. 11: "I have reached the conclusion that there are not any material differences between the scheme of distribution of legislative powers between Dominion and provinces as apparently intended at the time of Confederation and the like legislative powers as expressed by the text of Part VI of the British North America Act, 1867. . . . I hold also that the terms of that Act, properly construed are thoroughly consonant with the corresponding terms of the London Resolutions and express their full intended effect."

31. Creighton, *Young Politician,* pp. 457-58.

32. Dr. O. D. Skelton in his *Life and Times of Sir Alexander Tilloch Galt*

shows the close correlation between the Quebec Resolutions and the scheme Galt outlined in 1858 in a tabulation at pp. 371-72.

33. One of those making this assertion was Lord Watson who claimed, in *Liquidators of the Maritime Bank of Canada* v. *Receiver-General of New Brunswick*, (1892) A.C. 437: "The object of the Act was neither to weld the provinces into one, nor to subordinate provincial governments to a central authority, but to create a federal government in which they should all be represented, entrusted with the exclusive administration of affairs in which they had a common interest, each province retaining its independence and autonomy." Commenting on this statement, Professor A. R. M. Lower said: "A plainer misstatement of what everyone in 1867 had said was the object of the Act could hardly be made." *Evolving Canadian Federalism* (Durham, N.C., 1958), p. 34.

34. W. M. Whitelaw, *The Maritimes and Canada Before Confederation* (Toronto, 1934), passim.

35. Pope, *Memoirs*, 1: 269-70.

36. *Confederation Debates*, 33, and similarly at 30, 40, 41.

37. Pope, *Confederation*, p. 85.

38. Donald Creighton, *Dominion of the North* (new ed.; Toronto, 1957), p. 310.

39. *Confederation Debates*, p. 859.

40. Ibid., p. 250.

41. Ibid., 1002. Professor Scott has compiled an extensive list of authorities for the proposition that the Confederation Fathers intended to create a highly-centralized federation. See his "Centralization and Decentralization," 1108-1109.

42. This distribution was deliberate. See *Confederation Debates*, 41.

43. Canada, *Report of the Royal Commission on Dominion-Provincial Relations* (hereafter cited as the *Sirois Report*), (3 vols.; Ottawa, 1940), 1: 33.

44. *Confederation Debates*, 42.

45. Pope, *Confederation*, p. 150.

46. John T. Saywell, *The Office of Lieutenant-Governor* (Toronto, 1957).

47. Ibid., p. 174.

48. Ibid., p. 29. Howland did not perform according to Liberal expectations; he followed parliamentary custom and called on Mowat to be premier.

49. Creighton, *Old Chieftain*, p. 238.

50. Ibid., pp. 238-39, 260-62; *Lieutenant-Governor*, pp. 233-48. Only one other lieutenant-governor has been dismissed, McInnis of British Columbia, a Liberal who was discharged by Laurier for political behaviour contrary to the Laurier conception of the spirit of the constitution. Ibid., pp. 249-56.

51. J. R. Mallory, "The Lieutenant-Governor's Discretionary Powers," *Canadian Journal of Economics and Political Science* (hereafter cited as *C.J.E.P.S.*), 27 (1961): 518. Legally, assent to provincial bills is given in the name of the governor general. Saywell, *Lieutenant-Governor*, pp. 8-9.

52. G. V. La Forest, *Disallowance and Reservation of Provincial Legislation* (Ottawa, 1955), pp. 47-48.

53. Ibid., p. 15.

54. Calculated from appendices in La Forest, pp. 83-115.

55. C. R. Biggar, *Sir Oliver Mowat* (2 vols.; Toronto, 1905), 1: 338-62; Creighton, *Old Chieftain,* p. 378. As it turned out, the struggle had been in vain from the beginning, for the Judicial Committee of the Privy Council, in 1884, decided in favour of the Liberal lumberman without benefit of Mowat's legislation. Ibid., p. 379.

56. *Confederation Debates,* 1: 108.

57. In the twentieth century the practice of disallowing *intra vires* legislation on grounds of alleged injustice fell into disuse until the federal cabinet was confronted with the Social Credit legislation from Alberta. Two of these measures seem to have been disallowed on grounds of injustice although both were also "contrary to the clear intentions of the B. N. A. Act." La Forest, 100. See also J. R. Mallory, *Social Credit and the Federal Power,* (Toronto, 1954).

58. Creighton, *Old Chieftain,* p. 19.

59. Bora Laskin, *Canadian Constitutional Law* (2nd ed.; Toronto, 1960), p. 432; also Frank R. Scott, "Section 94 of the B. N. A. Act," *CBR,* 20 (1942): 525.

60. A not-unusual view of the establishment of the Supreme Court is that of the noted Quebec historian, Robert Rumilly, who said: "C'était une mesure centralisatrice et unificatrice, dangereuse surtout pour la province qui possédait un code civil particulier—la province de Québec. Celle-ci perdait le privilège d'interpréter ses lois en dernier ressort." *L'autonomie provinciale* (Montreal, 1948), 14. Rumilly's views were echoed in the Report in 1956 of the (Quebec) Royal Commission of Inquiry on Constitutional Problems, in Daniel Johnson's *Egalité et indépendance* (Montreal, 1965), and in other documents of the period. Some concession was made to this feeling in the Victoria Charter of 1971 which proposed a role for the provincial governments in the appointment process. See chap. 4 below.

61. Bora Laskin, *Constitutional Law,* p. 497.

62. Frederick P. Varcoe, *The Distribution of Legislative Power in Canada* (Toronto, 1954), pp. 141-42.

63. *Toronto* v. *Bell Telephone Co.,* (1905) A.C. 52.

64. *Attorney-General for British Columbia* v. *C. P. R.,* (1906) A.C. 204. See also *Attorney-General for Quebec* v. *Nipissing Central Railway,* (1926) A.C. 715.

65. *In re Regulation and Control of Radio Communications in Canada,* (1932) A.C. 304.

66. *Attorney-General of Ontario* v. *Winner,* (1954) A.C. 541. "The jurisdiction declared by the *Winner* case to reside exclusively in Parliament was administratively returned to the Provinces by delegation under the Motor Vehicle Transport Act, 1954 (Can.), c. 59." Laskin, *Constitutional Law,* 516. During the sixties the federal government decided to try and recover this authority from the provincial governments but difficulties both political and administrative had forestalled this effort right up to the end of 1972.

67. Varcoe, p. 79.

68. (1882) 7 A.C. 829.

69. *Sirois Report,* 1: 56.

70. Donald Creighton, "Conservatism and National Unity," in R. Flenley, ed., *Essays in Canadian History* (Toronto, 1939), 175-76.

71. Quoted in Norman McL. Rogers, *Mackenzie King* (Toronto, 1935), pp. 30-31.

72. Canada, *Parliamentary Debates of the House of Commons* (hereafter cited as Hansard), 78 (1906): 1035.

73. (1925) A.C. 396. According to Lord Haldane, one of the questions was "whether regulation of civil rights or invasion of property rights in the fashion provided by the Act . . . could be valid in view of the exercise of the powers given to the Provinces. . . . The circumstance that the dispute might spread to other Provinces was not enough in itself to justify Dominion interference, if such interference affected property and civil rights." Ibid., 415.

74. W. P. M. Kennedy, "The Interpretation of the British North America Act," *Cambridge Law Journal*, 8 (1943): 150-51.

75. With but one important exception—the *Radio Case*, (1932) A.C. 304.

76. *Hansard*, 132 (1918): 115ff.

77. P. C. 815, April 4, 1918.

78. Varcoe, p. 83.

79. *Co-operative Committee on Japanese Canadians* v. *Attorney-General of Canada*, (1947) A.C. 87, at 101.

80. *The Dominion-Provincial Conference* (Toronto 1945), 13-14.

81. *The Road to Nationhood* (Toronto, 1946), xi.

82. The best discussion is in Denis Smith, *Bleeding Hearts, Bleeding Country* (Edmonton 1972).

83. See R. L. Watts, *New Federations* (Oxford 1966), chap. 12.

84. *Canadian Problems as seen by Twenty Outstanding Men of Canada* (Toronto, [1933]), pp. 256, 257.

85. *Hansard*, 196 (1933): 2510-11.

86. Rogers, *King*, pp. 164-65.

87. J. Castell Hopkins, *The Canadian Annual Review of Public Affairs 1935 and 1936* (hereafter cited as *CAR* with year) (Toronto, 1936), 15.

88. Ibid., 29. See also A. H. Birch, *Federalism, Finance and Social Legislation* (Oxford, 1955), pp. 159-64, 185-88.

89. (1937) A.C. 326; (1937) A.C. 355; (1937) A.C. 377. Comment in *CBR*, 15 (1937): passim.

90. J. B. McGeachy, "One Country or Nine," in Violet Anderson (ed.), *Problems in Canadian Unity* (Toronto 1938), 35-36. Summaries of the provincial briefs will be found in Eggleston, chap. 3.

91. Anderson, p. 41.

92. Reprinted in David Lewis and Frank R. Scott, *Make This Your Canada* (Toronto, 1943), appendix.

93. "Social Reform and the Constitution," *CJEPS*, 1 (1935): 434-35.

94. *Social Planning for Canada* (Toronto, 1935).

95. Ibid., 345-46.

96. Lewis and Scott, p. 104.

97. Ibid, p. 151.

98. M. J. Coldwell, *Left Turn, Canada* (New York, 1945), p. 180.

99. Ibid., p. 185.

100. M. J. Coldwell, *Canadian Progressives on the March* (New York, 1944), pp. 11 ff.

101. L. C. Marsh, *Report on Social Security for Canada* (Ottawa, 1943).

102. Ibid., p. 113.

103. Michael Oliver, ed., *Social Purpose for Canada* (Toronto, 1961).

104. Frank R. Scott, "Social Planning and Canadian Federalism," in Oliver, p. 394.

105. *Canadian Problems,* p. 248. Professor MacKenzie did not make clear whether he meant that Parliament could amend the B. N. A. Act without any action being taken by the United Kingdom Parliament.

106. Maurice Ollivier, *L'avenir constitutionnel du Canada* (Montreal, 1935), p. 77.

107. *Hansard,* 251 (1949): 2621.

108. *Social Planning,* pp. 504, 507.

109. See: "A Review of Saskatchewan's Position Regarding a Basis for the Amendment of Our Constitution in Canada," in Paul Fox, ed., *Politics-Canada* (Toronto, 1962), 94-98.

110. The federal submissions were originally published separately between green covers. They may now be found in Canada, *Dominion-Provincial Conference* (1945), *Dominion and Provincial Submissions and Plenary Conference Discussions* (Ottawa, 1946), 55-118.

111. Ibid., 76.

112. Just as the social security features of the plan bore close resemblances to the *Marsh Report,* so the plan's financial aspects bore close resemblances to the "ministerial statement on Employment and Income with particular reference to the initial period of reconstruction" which was laid before the House of Commons by the minister, C. D. Howe, in April, 1945.

113. Dawson, *Government,* p. 64. Other comment may be found in Eggleston, chaps. 5, 6; Birch, pp. 196-203; A. E. Buck, *Financing Canadian Government* (Chicago, 1949), pp. 240-43; and J. Harvey Perry, *Taxes, Tariffs and Subsidies* (2 vols.; Toronto, 1955), 2: 541-46.

114. J. A. Maxwell, *Federal Subsidies to the Provincial Governments in Canada* (Cambridge, Mass., 1937), p. 186.

115. *Hansard,* 184 (1930): 1227.

116. Birch, p. 77.

117. Quoted, from the order-in-council establishing the Massey commission, in Canada, The Royal Commission on National Development in Arts, Letters and Sciences, *Report* (Ottawa, 1951).

118. Ibid., 8.

119. John Meisel, *Working Papers on Canadian Politics,* (Montreal, 1972), p. 196.

CHAPTER 3   ADMINISTRATIVE FEDERALISM (pp. 63-112)

1. *Attorney-General for Canada* v. *Attorney-General for Ontario* (*Labour Conventions* case), [1937] A.C. 326, at 354.

2. Should any student insist that federalism necessarily involves a strict separation of two orders of government, each independent of the other within cer-

tain fields, then it must be admitted that administrative federalism does not correspond to this "classical conception." J. A. Corry, "Constitutional Trends and Federalism," in A. R. M. Lower, *et. al., Evolving Canadian Federalism* (Durham, N.C., 1958), 96.

3. "The Five Faces of Federalism," found in P. A. Crépeau and C. B. Macpherson, eds., *The Future of Canadian Federalism* (Toronto, 1965), pp. 9-10.

4. *The Canadian Forum,* 44 (1964): 206-10.

5. Commission on Intergovernmental Relations, *A Report to the President for Transmittal to the Congress* (Washington, 1955), 2.

6. See, among others, Richard Leach and R. S. Sugg, Jr., *The Administration of Interstate Compacts* (Baton Rouge, 1959); Arthur W. Macmahon, "Functional Channels of Relationship," in his *Federalism, Mature and Emergent* (Garden City, New York, 1955), 267-77; William Anderson, *Intergovernmental Relations in Review* (Minneapolis, Minn., 1960), pp. 145-66; Robert H. Connery and Richard H. Leach, *The Federal Government and Metropolitan Areas* (Cambridge, Mass., 1960), and Jane Clark Perry, *The Rise of the New Federalism*, (New York, 1939).

7. *Evolving Canadian Federalism*, p. 123.

8. D. V. Smiley, "The Structural Problem of Canadian Federalism," *Canadian Public Administration,* 14 (1971): 331.

9. See generally: G. Campbell Sharman, "The Courts and the Governmental Process in Canada," unpublished Ph.Dd. dissertation, Queen's University, Kingston, Ontario, 1972.

10. W. P. M. Mackintosh, "Federal Finance," *Canadian Tax Journal,* 1 (1953), 335-40, 417-30.

11. "By 1913 they were obtaining only about one-fifth of their total revenues from corporation, inheritance (succession), and personal income taxes." A. E. Buck, *Financing Canadian Government* (Chicago 1949), p. 16.

12. Ibid.

13. Canada, *Parliamentary Debates of the House of Commons* (hereafter cited as Hansard), 251 (1946): 2911.

14. The different arrangements are best followed in A. Milton Moore, J. Harvey Perry, and Donald I. Beach, *The Financing of Canadian Federation: The First Hundred Years* (Toronto, 1966), in the annual editions of the Canadian Tax Foundation's *The National Finances,* published at Toronto, and in Richard M. Bird, *The Growth of Government Spending in Canada* (Toronto, 1970).

15. Another levy was permitted to equalize discrimination caused by the corporations tax levied by provinces refusing to enter the agreements.

16. If, following their election victory, the Conservative government had wished to repudiate the agreements, the provinces would have been unable to force effective compliance with the terms of the agreements. (In *re Taxation Agreement Between Saskatchewan and Canada,* (1946) 1 W.W.R. 257.)

17. "Fact and Opinion," *Canadian Tax Journal,* 9 (1961): 80. In view of the central government's substitute proposals, it would have been more accurate to say that thus ended an era in which a largely successful attempt was made to centralize the *levying* of all major taxes in Canada.

18. This part of Finance Minister Fleming's speech is at *Hansard,* 24th Parliament, 4th session, 9 (1960-61): 6654-57.

19. It should not be thought that no federal-provincial tax cooperation existed prior to the wartime and postwar arrangements. After 1936, four provinces —Ontario, Manitoba, Prince Edward Island, and Quebec—arranged with the cabinet at Ottawa for the federal collection of income taxes, and three provinces permitted federal taxes to be deducted for purposes of computing liability to provincial levies. Buck, p. 17.

20. "The Structural Problem," p. 331.

21. *Federal-Provincial Fiscal Relations,* Studies of the Royal Commission on Taxation, No. 23, Ottawa, 1967, 32.

22. George E. Carter, *Canadian Conditional Grants Since World War II* (Toronto, 1971), p. 28.

23. *Proceedings of the Constitutional Conference of the Federal and Provincial Governments, January and September, 1950* (Ottawa, 1951), 24.

24. D. V. Smiley characterized the change as one from "functional federalism," under which program specialists from two levels of governments come to agreements and administer them in relative independence from higher, more generalized authorities, to one of "political federalism," in which "the most crucial of intergovernmental relations are those between political and bureaucratic officials with jurisdiction-wide concerns," such as finance departments, first ministers and their staff, etc. See his "The Structural Problem," pp. 331-32.

25. The best analysis is that by D. V. Smiley and R. M. Burns, "Canadian Federalism and the Spending Power: Is Constitutional Restriction Necessary?" *Canadian Tax Journal,* 15 (1969), 467-82.

26. E. R. Black and A. C. Cairns, "A Different Perspective on Canadian Federalism," *Canadian Public Administration,* 9 (1966), 27-45.

27. Ibid.

28. Bird, p. 169.

29. Often neglected is the fact that not all of these appeals were civil cases; a few were criminal.

30. L. M. Gouin and Brooke Claxton, *Legislative Expedients and Devices Adopted by the Dominion and the Provinces* (Ottawa, 1939), p. 9. Another study made for the commission that arrived at somewhat similar conclusions was that of J. A. Corry, *Difficulties of Divided Jurisdiction* (Ottawa, 1939).

31. Canada, *Guide to Canadian Ministries Since Confederation* (Ottawa, 1957), p. 8.

32. Canada, *Dominion-Provincial Conference 1935: Record of Proceedings* (Ottawa, 1936), p. 9.

33. Canada, *Report of the Royal Commission on Dominion-Provincial Relations* (3 vols.; Ottawa, 1940), 2: 68.

34. *The Dominion-Provincial Conference* (Toronto, 1945), 18.

35. [No author cited], Ottawa, 1945.

36. At this writing, the R.C.M.P. acts in this capacity in eight of the ten provinces. Only Ontario and Quebec have their own provincial police forces.

37. Reference may be made to *Dominion-Provincial Co-operative Arrangements* for a complete listing of cooperative arrangements existing at that time.

38. These powers were set forth in the "Green Book" proposals discussed earlier in this study at pp. 53-54.

39. R. M. Burns, "Co-operation in Government," *Canadian Tax Journal,* 7

(1959); 12. See also his *Report: Intergovernmental Liaison on Fiscal and Economic Matters* (Ottawa, 1969).

40. Burns, "Co-operation," 14.

41. Institute of Public Administration of Canada, "Joint Dominion-Provincial Administration," *Proceedings of the First Annual Conference* (Toronto, 1949), 128-65.

42. Ibid., 143.

43. Ibid., 148-58.

44. "Co-ordination in Administration," Institute of Public Administration of Canada, *Proceedings of the Ninth Annual Conference* (Toronto, 1957), 255.

45. See generally: Wilfrid Eggleston, *The Road to Nationhood* (Toronto, 1946), passim; H. McD. Clokie, *Canadian Government and Politics* (3rd rev. ed., Toronto, 1950), p. 230; J. A. Corry, *Democratic Government and Politics* (2nd ed., Toronto, 1951), p. 567; R. MacGregor Dawson, *The Government of Canada* (2nd ed.; Toronto, 1954), pp. 94, 128-31, 147-48, 355; Canada, *Dominion Provincial and Interprovincial Conferences from 1887 to 1926* (Ottawa, 1951); *Précis of Discussions, Dominion-Provincial Conference November 3 to 10, 1927* (Ottawa, 1928), and, *Dominion-Provincial Conference 1935, Record of Proceedings* (Ottawa, 1936).

46. Canada, *Proceedings of the Federal-Provincial Conference 1955* (Ottawa, 1955), passim.

47. *Law and Policy* (Toronto, 1959), p. 62.

48. D. V. Smiley, *Canada in Question: Federalism in the Seventies,* (Toronto, 1972), p. 60.

49. (Toronto, 1972.)

50. Richard H. Leach, "Interprovincial Cooperation: Neglected Aspect of Canadian Federalism," *Canadian Public Administration,* 22 (1959): 84. Despite preoccupation of many Canadian politicians with economic matters, little was done for many years, for example, in the field of interprovincial fiscal relations. Not until the nineteen-forties, did the provinces of Ontario and Quebec enter an agreement to prevent double taxation of estates. "Earlier agreements of a similar nature had been laboriously arranged by some of the other provinces," said one competent observer, "only to be discarded when the wealthier provinces showed no interest in co-operating," Buck, p. 21.

51. Leach, p. 86.

52. The Canadian Education Association's early work in inter-governmental collaboration is detailed in Freeman K. Stewart, *Inter-Provincial Co-operation in Education* (Toronto, 1957).

53. *Dominion Provincial and Interprovincial Conferences from 1887 to 1926* (Ottawa, 1951).

54. Hereafter referred to as the Tremblay commission and the *Tremblay Report* (4 vols. in 5 books; Quebec, 1956).

55. Ibid., 3 (2). 302.

56. The premiers of the Atlantic provinces had begun meeting regularly a few years earlier.

57. *Intergovernmental Liaison,* pp. 220-21.

58. (1883) 9 A.C. 117. One of the contentions which the Judicial Committee

affirmed in this case was the right of the Ontario legislature to delegate quasi-legislative authority to subordinate public boards.

59. Bora Laskin, *Canadian Constitutional Law* (2nd ed.; Toronto, 1960), pp. 35-36. See also John Ballem's note on the *Willis* case ([1952] 2 S.C.R. 392) in *Canadian Bar Review*, 30 (1952): 1050.

60. J. A. Corry, *Difficulties of Divided Jurisdiction* (Ottawa, 1939), appendix.

61. *Attorney-General of Nova Scotia* v. *Attorney General of Canada* (*Nova Scotia Delegation* case) [1951] S.C.R. 31.

62. Mr. Lamontagne left his post at Laval University in 1954 to become deputy-minister of northern affairs at Ottawa. Later he became a prominent member of the staff of Lester B. Pearson, and, eventually, after some electoral misadventuring, a federal cabinet minister, and a Senator.

63. See for example: Michel Brunet, *Canadians et Canadiens* (Montreal, 1955), pp. 153-73; Emile Bouvier, "Un nouveau fédéralisme s'impose-t-il au Canada?" *Relations*, no. 165 (September, 1954), 248-51; Pierre Harvey, "La centralisation inévitable?" *L'Actualité économique*, 30 (1954): 533-38; and the *Tremblay Report*, 2: 268-71. The one English review, by Wilfrid Eggleston, praised the book. *Canadian Historical Review*, 36 (1955): 162-63. French Canadian reviews of this book would lead one to believe it advocated a thorough-going centralization of the federal system. Serious doubt is cast on the validity of this characterization by a careful reading of the whole work, and, particularly, of pp. 247-49, 270, 272, 275-80.

64. *Le fédéralisme canadien; évolution et problèmes* (Quebec, 1954), p. 275.

65. "Texte du discours prononcé par l'honorable Lester B. Pearson," November 6, 1961, mimeographed [Ottawa, 1961], 7.

66. "Discours prononcé par Maurice Lamontagne," January 17, 1962, mimeographed, [Ottawa, 1962], 6.

67. Oliver, p. 385.

68. *Evolving Federalism*, p. 122.

69. Montreal, September 3, 1963.

70. (Translation), *The Canadian Forum*, 44 (1964): 206-10.

71. Smiley, *Conditional Grants and Canadian Federalism* (Toronto, 1963), p. 72.

72. *The Government of Canada* (2nd rev. ed., Toronto, 1954).

73. *Federal Subsidies to the Provincial Governments in Canada* (Cambridge, Mass., 1937).

74. "The Impact of New Tax Policies on National Unity," a paper for the Institute for the Quantitative Analysis of Social and Economic Policy, (Toronto, 1968). Quoted in Bird, p. 173.

75. Ibid., p. 296.

CHAPTER 4   THE COORDINATE CONCEPT (pp. 113-48)

1. *Introduction to the Study of the Law of the Constitution* (5th ed.; London, 1897), p. 166.

2. A. R. M. Lower, *Evolving Canadian Federalism* (Durham, N.C. 1958), p. 6.

3. See J. A. Corry, "Constitutional Trends and Federalism," in Lower, *et. al., Evolving Federalism*, esp. pp. 93-96.

4. *Federal Government* (3rd ed., Toronto, 1953), pp. 32-33.

5. The provinces were subordinated to the governor in council through the office of the lieutenant-governor, through the powers of disallowance and reservation, and by means of the financial arrangements. The central authority was to legislate generally for the "peace, order and good Government" of the country, and its valid legislation was to override provincial statutes in a jointly-occupied field. Neither were the provincial governments equal to each other in sovereign dignity. Their representation in the House of Parliament differed widely; the separate school provisions imposed different burdens on the various provinces, Quebec was compelled to grant minority privileges not required of the other provinces, and, for many years, Parliament controlled the natural resources of the prairie provinces.

6. W. P. M. Kennedy, *The Constitution of Canada* (Toronto, 1922), p. 411.

7. Three vols.; Ottawa, 1940. Hereafter cited as the *Sirois Report*.

8. The term "constitutional conference" denotes meetings called to seek agreement on a domestic procedure for amending the British North America Act. Neither in normal Canadian usage nor in the present work is the term used to suggest a convention to draft a new constitution *au fond*.

9. V. Evan Gray, " 'The O'Connor Report' on the British North America Act, 1867," *Canadian Bar Review*, 18 (1939): 309-37.

10. P. C. 1908. Reprinted in ibid., 9.

11. *Social Credit and the Federal Power in Canada* (Toronto, 1954), p. 140.

12. P. C. 1908, *Sirois Report*, 1: 10.

13. Ibid., 1: 29.

14. Ibid., 1: 36.

15. John W. Dafoe, "The Canadian Federal System under Review," *Foreign Affairs*, 18 (1940): 646-58.

16. Provincial autonomy existed, in the commission's eyes, when a province controlled enough revenue to permit it to carry out its constitutional responsibilities free from any oversight by the central government. *Sirois Report*, 2: 269.

17. Dafoe, "Canadian Federal System," 656.

18. *Sirois Report*, 2: 86, 269-73.

19. Ibid., 2: 273.

20. Ibid., 2: 30.

21. Ibid., 2: 50.

22. Ibid., 2: 51.

23. Ibid., 2: 84.

24. Ibid., 2: 275.

25. The federal government regulated all important railway operations while the provincial governments were responsible for all highway traffic. The problem was complicated during the nineteen-thirties by the indirect competition between governments; the provinces were vigorously promoting highways and road transport, while the federal government was subsidizing transcontinental railway freight.

26. *Sirois Report*, 2: 72-73, 275.

27. The *Report* also suggested that this particular problem might be overcome by constitutional amendment to provide concurrent legislative authority over natural products marketing, which would permit administrative cooperation.

28. J. A. Corry's *Difficulties of Divided Jurisdiction* (Ottawa, 1939) was one of the special research studies commissioned by the investigators. Professor Corry's arguments against conditional grant schemes reappear in the *Sirois Report* itself, 1:257-59; 2: 22-23. His arguments dealt with the friction arising between governments through the supervision of financial and performance standards, and the impossibility of applying sanctions for failure to meet standards.

29. *Sirois Report*, 2: 34.

30. D. V. Smiley, "The Rowell-Sirois Report, Provincial Autonomy, and Post-War Canadian Federalism," *Canadian Journal of Economics and Political Science*, 28 (1962); 58.

31. *Sirois Report*, 2: 276.

32. *Attorney-General of Ontario v. Mercer*, (1883) 8 A.C. 767. The board held in this case that lands escheated to the crown fall to the provinces in which they are situated, and not to the federal government.

33. (1883) 9 A.C. 117. In this case the board held that within the limits set by the B.N.A. Act's distribution of powers, "the local legislature is supreme, and has the same authority as the Imperial Parliament or the Parliament of the Dominion." Ibid., at 173.

34. Objection might be made to this use of the term "sovereign" for some hold that sovereignty cannot be limited legally. Allied to this contention is a dispute as to the existence of sovereignty. Having noted these points, the present study will use the term in the senses indicated by the context.

35. *Liquidators of the Maritime Bank of Canada v. Receiver-General* of New Brunswick, [1892] A.C. 437.

36. Ibid.

37. Ibid. at 441-42.

38. *Abbott v. City of St. John*, [1908] 40 S.C.R. 597.

39. John T. Saywell, *The Office of Lieutenant-Governor* (Toronto, 1957), chap. 1, and authorities there cited.

40. B.N.A. Act, secs. 58-60, 90, and *Maritime Bank* case, 443.

41. W. J. Wagner, *The Federal States and Their Judiciary* ('s-Gravenhage, The Netherlands, 1959), p. 159.

42. Unpublished Ph.D. dissertation, Queen's University, (Kingston, Ont., 1972), 91.

43. Supreme Court of Canada Act, R.S.C. 1952, c. 259.

44. *Attorney-General for Ontario v. Attorney-General for Canada* (Reference case), [1912] A.C. 571. See also the article by a former chief justice of Ontario, N. W. Rowell, "The Place and Functions of the Judiciary in Our Canadian Constitution," *Canadian Bar Review*, 15 (1937): 57-67.

45. "The Nature, Use and Effect of Reference Cases in Canadian Constitutional Law," in W. R. Lederman, ed., *The Courts and the Canadian Constitution* (Toronto, 1965).

46. *The Courts and the Governmental Process*, 205.

47. *In re the Ownership of and Jurisdiction over Offshore Mineral Rights*, [1967] S.C.R. 792, and, *Attorney-General for Manitoba v. Manitoba Egg and Poultry Association*, [1971] S.C.R. 607.

48. Province of Canada, *Parliamentary Debates on the Subject of the Confederation of the British North American Provinces* (Quebec, 1865), 33.

49. *Attorney-General for Ontario v. Attorney-General for Canada (Reference*

case), [1912] A.C. 571 at 581. Lord Atkin brought his predecessor's comment into accord with the Statute of Westminster in 1937: "In totality of legislative powers, Dominion and Provincial together, [Canada] is fully equipped." *Attorney-General for Canada* v. *Attorney-General for Ontario (Labour Conventions* case), [1937] A.C. 326, at 354.

50. *Russell v. The Queen* [1882] 7 A.C. 829.

51. *Attorney-General for Ontario* v. *Attorney-General for the Dominion (Local Prohibition* case), [1896] A.C. 348, and *Toronto Electric Commissioners* v. *Snider,* [1925] A.C. 396.

52. A little more meaning was read into the general clause by the 1947 decision of the Judicial Committee in *Cooperative Committee on Japanese Canadians* v. *Attorney-General of Canada (Japanese Canadians* case), [1947] A.C. 87. It would be difficult, however, to maintain the view that this decision goes very far in restoring the peace, order, and good government phrase to the amplitude of meaning it once had.

53. *Liquidators of the Maritime Bank of Canada* v. *Receiver-General of New Brunswick,* [1892] A.C. 437; *Attorney-General for Ontario* v. *Attorney-General for the Dominion (Local Prohibition* case), [1896] A.C. 348.

54. *The Government of Canada* (2nd rev. ed.; Toronto, 1954), p. 109.

55. Professor Mallory argues that whenever the jurists encountered an attempt by Parliament to control part of the economy, they met it with an outright *laissez-faire* attitude and sought to strike down the offending legislation by finding that it trenched illegally on provincial powers.

56. *Bonanza Creek Gold Mining Co., Ltd.* v. *The King,* [1916] A.C. 566.

57. *Social Credit,* p. 47.

58. *In re the Board of Commerce Act and the Combines and Fair Prices Act (Board of Commerce* case), [1922] A.C. 191.

59. [1925] A.C. 396. See Frank R. Scott, "Federal Jurisdiction over Labour Relations—A New Look," *McGill Law Journal,* 6 (1960): 153-67.

60. *Attorney-General for British Columbia* v. *Attorney-General for Canada (Natural Products Marketing Act* reference), [1937] A.C. 377.

61. "Social Planning and Federalism," In Michael Oliver, ed., *Social Purpose for Canada* (Toronto, 1961), 400-401.

62. *Attorney-General for Nova Scotia* v. *Attorney-General for Canada,* [1951] S.C.R. 31.

63. *P. E. I. Potato Marketing Board* v. *H. B. Willis Inc.,* [1952] 2 S.C.R. 392.

64. *Johannesson v. West St. Paul,* [1952] 1 S.C.R. 292.

65. Cf. Bora Laskin: "Recent Supreme Court cases like [the *Reference* re *Farm Products Marketing Act,* [1957] S.C.R. 198, and *Murphy* v. *C.P.R.* [1958] S.C.R. 626] show that a decided thaw has affected the hitherto frozen federal commerce power, a power which was once referred to as 'that old forlorn hope so many times tried unsuccessfully.' " *Constitutional Law,* 318.

66. *Citizens Insurance Co.* v. *Parsons,* (1881) A.C. 96; *Bank of Toronto* v. *Lambe,* (1887) 12 A.C. 575, and *Caron* v. *The King,* [1924] A.C. 999. The question whether the federal government could levy an indirect tax within a province for provincial purposes was not decided. See also Frank R. Scott, "The Constitutional Background of Taxation Agreements," *McGill Law Journal,* 2 (1955), 1-10.

67. *Forbes* v. *Attorney-General of Manitoba,* [1937] A.C. 260.

68. [1932] A.C. 514.

69. *Constitutional Law,* p. 658. W. P. M. Kennedy and D. C. Wells, *Law of the Taxing Power in Canada* (Toronto, 1931), 152, argued that in principle this power should fall to the provinces under sec. 92.16. Laskin is now chief justice of the Supreme Court of Canada.

70. "Constitutional Background," 3.

71. *In re Taxation Agreement between Saskatchewan and Canada,* [1946] 1 W.W.R. 257.

72. *Van Buren Bridge Co.* v. *Madawaska and Attorney-General of New Brunswick,* [1958] D.L.R. 2d. 763.

73. *Essays in Constitutional Law* (London, 1934), pp. 86-87.

74. "The decisions under this section," says A. H. F. Lefroy, "and under the corresponding section in the . . . Manitoba Act, largely turn upon questions of fact, namely, whether the New Brunswick Common Schools Act, 1871, prejudicially affected rights or privileges of the Roman Catholics in the province with respect to denominational schools which they had by law at the Union." *Canada's Federal System* (Toronto, 1913), pp. 632-33.

75. [1892] A.C. 445.

76. [1895] A.C. 202.

77. "The argument made against the appeal to the Governor General in Council was that the existence of such a right of appeal, involved this result that the legislature could not repeal its own statute, whereby the pre-Confederation system was continued, enacted between 1870 and 1890, creating rights and privileges in the field of education," Varcoe, 150. See also Lefroy, chap. 26.

78. *Canada in Question: Federalism in the Seventies* (Toronto, 1972), p. 31. His discussion of the federal government and education in the pages that follow this comment are unique and invaluable.

79. [1917] A.C. 62.

80. Laskin, *Constitutional Law,* p. 938. See generally, the discussions on the Canadian Bill of Rights in *CBR,* 37 (1959): 1-237.

81. See Frank R. Scott, *Civil Liberties and Canadian Federalism* (Toronto, 1959), and W. F. Bowker, "Basic Rights and Freedoms: What Are They?" *CBR,* 37 (1959): 43-65.

82. [1953] 4 D.L.R., 641.

83. Bora Laskin, "Our Civil Liberties—The Role of the Supreme Court," *Queen's Quarterly,* 61 (1955): 471.

84. *Henry Birks & Sons* v. *Montreal,* [1955] S.C.R. 799.

85. *Switzman* v. *Elbling,* [1957] S.C.R., 285.

86. *Rex* v. *Hess* (No. 2), [1949] 4 D.L.R. 199. The chief justice of Canada had argued similarly in his judgement in *Reference re Alberta Statutes* [1938] S.C.R. 100 at 132-34, but the *ratio decidendi* of this decision partook of too many different interpretations to permit it being of help in clarifying the present issue of the location of legislative authority over civil liberties.

87. [1957] S.C.R. 285 at 328.

88. *The Queen* v. *Joseph Drybones,* [1970] S.C.R. 282. For the general debates, see Professor Smiley's fierce attack on the "entrenchment" approach, "The Case Against the Canadian Charter of Human Rights," *Canadian Journal of Political Science,* 2 (1969), 277-91, and the works cited therein.

89. Richard Simeon, *Federal-Provincial Diplomacy: The Making of Recent Policy in Canada* (Toronto, 1972), chap. 5.

90. Mason Wade, *The French Canadians 1760-1945* (Toronto, 1956), p. 428.

91. *Evolving Federalism*, p. 119.

92. Mallory, pp. 8-9; Dawson, *Government*, p. 154.

93. As Professor Wheare has pointed out, the existence of this power introduces important unitary elements into an otherwise federal constitution. *Federal Government*, pp. 19-21. A third unitary element distinguished by Professor Wheare is the unified system of courts with its bench appointed by the central régime, but, as has been pointed out, this is not so unitary in fact as it sometimes appears.

94. *Sirois Report*, 1: 253; Mallory, *Social Credit*, chap. 2, and Kennedy, *Constitution*, 415-30.

95. "Disallowance: Report of Sir John Macdonald (Minister of Justice)," Canada, *Sessional Papers, 1869* (Ottawa, 1869), no. 18.

96. G. V. La Forest, *Disallowance and Reservation of Provincial Legislation* (Ottawa, 1955), p. 37. See also Eugene Forsey, "Disallowance of Provincial Acts, Reservation of Provincial Bills, and Refusal of Assent by Lieutenant-Governors since 1867," *CJEPS*, 4 (1938): 47-59.

97. *Social Credit*, p. 13. At p. 169, Professor Mallory observes: "One of the most significant facts which emerges from a study of disallowance is that the power has been used primarily against the West. These disallowances fall into two distinct groups. In some instances, disallowance was the result of the unflagging attempt, in the defence of imperial interests and imperial treaty obligations, to minimize the attempts of British Columbians to reduce their Asiatic fellow-citizens to the status of helots in their modern Athens. The remainder of the western disallowances were defensive measures to protect the commercial and financial interests from attack in the western provinces." The table of disallowed statutes reproduced by La Forest as Appendix A to his *Disallowance* shows that more than three quarters of the one hundred and twelve disallowed statutes were passed by the four western provinces.

98. La Forest, *Disallowance*, p. 15.

99. [1938] S.C.R. 71, 83.

100. This was a sentence that the chief justice quoted from an earlier decision he had written for the Judicial Committee of the Privy Council, *Wilson* v. *Esquimalt and Nanaimo Railway Co.,* [1922] 1 A.C. 202, at 210.

101. [1938] S.C.R. 71, at 95.

102. Professor Mallory and others have suggested the wisdom of retaining the legal right as an effective instrument by which the federal cabinet can persuade provincial governments to modify "undesirable" legislation. To similar effect, see Frank R. Scott, "The Special Nature of Canadian Federalism," *CJEPS*, 13 (1947): 13-25.

103. *The Globe and Mail* (Toronto), August 11, 1960.

104. Professor Laskin wrote in 1960 that sec. 91.1 of the B.N.A. Act probably gave Parliament full authority to abolish the reservation and disallowance parts of the constitution—if it wished to do so. *Constitutional Law*, 63.

105. The case is referred to by J. R. Mallory, "The Lieutenant-Governor's Discretionary Powers," *CJEPS*, 27 (1961): 518-22, and by John T. Saywell, "Reservation Revisited: Alberta, 1937," ibid., 367-72.

106. Toronto, 1950.

107. London, 1956.

108. Canada, *Special Committee on British North America Act; Proceedings and Evidence and Report* (Ottawa, 1935).

109. The B.N.A. Act encompasses a number of B.N.A. Acts and amendments, but, for convenience, the most usual singular form will be employed.

110. J. Castell Hopkins, *The Canadian Annual Review of Public Affairs 1935 and 1936* (Toronto, 1936), pp. 448-49.

111. The British North America (No. 2) Act, 1949, 13 Geo. VI, chap. 81 (U.K.).

112. Canada, *Proceedings of the Constitutional Conference of the federal and provincial governments, January and September, 1950* (Ottawa, 1951).

113. Ibid., 46-47, 68-69.

114. These events are most easily followed in Professor Simeon's admirable analysis, *Federal-Provincial Diplomacy.*

115. The exceptions were the policies on medical care, old age pensions, and post secondary education.

116. For details, see Carter.

117. Some debated federal government competence to deal with various forms of pollution control, represented, for example, in the Canada Water Act of 1970 but it was one of the few constitutionally-vulnerable points in Mr. Trudeau's approach to the distribution of powers.

118. "The Dynamics of Federalism in Canada," *Canadian Journal of Political Science,* 1 (1968): 18-39.

119. Ibid., 38.

120. The centralist attitude was well-represented in the pages of *The Canadian Forum,* one of the few publications that turned from the preoccupations of war long enough to examine the *Sirois Report* thoroughly. The compact view is represented in "Faits et nouvelles: Le rapport Sirois," *"L'Actualité économique,* 16(2) (1940): 146-59.

121. See the following discussions in *The Canadian Forum,* 20 (1940-41): Frank H. Underhill, Robert F. Legget, and Dorothy Steeves, "The Sirois Report—A Discussion of Some Aspects," 233-39; "The Sirois Report—Further Discussion," 261-65; "New Governmental Agencies," 302-304, and G. M. A. Grube, "Some Weaknesses of the Sirois Report," 334-36.

122. Robert Rumilly, *L'autonomie provinciale* (Montreal, 1948), p. 123.

123. H. A. Innis, "The Rowell-Sirois Report," *CJEPS* 6 (1940): 562-71.

124. "Report of the Royal Commission on Dominion-Provincial Relations," *Canadian Historical Review,* 21 (1940): 245-53.

CHAPTER 5   THE COMPACT THEORY (pp. 149-71)

1. G. F. G. Stanley, "Act or Pact? Another Look at Confederation," Canadian Historical Association, *Report of the Annual Meeting,* 1956 (cited hereafter as *CHA Report* with date), 2.

2. Frank R. Scott, "French-Canada and Canadian Federalism," in A. R. M. Lower, *et al., Evolving Canadian Federalism* (Durham, N.C., 1958), p. 80.

3. See Louis P. Pigéon, "The Meaning of Provincial Autonomy," *Canadian Bar Review* (hereafter cited as *CBR*), 29 (1951): 1126-35.

4. Robert Rumilly, *L'autonomie provinciale* (Montreal, 1948), pp. 11-12.

5. Stanley, 13.

6. Ibid., 9.

7. Province of Canada, *Parliamentary Debates on the Subject of the Confederation of the British North American Provinces* (hereafter cited as *Confederation Debates*), (Quebec, 1865), 764.

8. Ibid., 15.

9. Ibid., 16.

10. Ibid., 110.

11. See, for example, George-Etienne Cartier at 240, A. A. Dorion at 252, Christopher Dunkin, Cartier, and T. D. McGee at 540 ff.

12. W. M. Whitelaw, *The Maritimes and Canada Before Confederation* (Toronto, 1934), p. 240. In refuting the treaty viewpoint, Whitelaw examined the treatment of the Quebec Resolutions after drafting, and discovered that delegates at Quebec, by specific resolution, did not affix their signatures to an original copy (as they might to a draft treaty) but merely authenticated different printed versions as accurate representations of what had been agreed. This procedure was devised to placate Maritime malcontents. Ibid., p. 261.

13. Jean-Charles Bonenfant, "Les canadiens français et la naissance de la confédération," *CHA Report 1952*, 45.

14. Pierre-Basile Mignault, *Manuel de droit parlementaire* (Montreal, 1889), pp. 224, 288, 333. (*N.V.* Quoted in Quebec, *Report of the Royal Commission of Inquiry on Constitutional Problems* (hereafter cited as *Tremblay Report*), (4 vols., in 5 books; Quebec, 1956), 2: 179.)

15. "La confédération: pacte ou loi?" *L'action nationale*, 34(2) (1949). 275-76. To similar effect, see Premier Duplessis' comments in *Dominion-Provincial Conference (1945), Dominion and Provincial Submissions and Discussions* (Ottawa, 1946), 20; and Wilfrid Eggleston, *The Road to Nationhood* (Toronto, 1946), p. 263.

16. Paul Gérin-Lajoie says: "Actually, up to the 1930's, most writers, politicians, and even the Judicial Committee of the Privy Council had accepted the Confederation Act as embodying a 'treaty' or a 'pact' which Canadians as well as the Parliament of the United Kingdom were bound to respect." *Constitutional Amendment in Canada* (Toronto, 1950), p. 206. Appendix C of Dr. Gérin-Lajoie's work contains a series of quotations from leading figures of the first half of the twentieth century, all evidencing explicit or implicit support for the compact theory. Further evidence establishing the extent of the theory's acceptance was cited in the *Tremblay Report*, 2: 147.

17. Published in translation at Quebec, 1884. Unless otherwise indicated, all quotations are drawn from this source.

18. Quoted in Robert Rumilly, *L'autonomie provincial* (Montreal, 1948), pp. 30-31.

19. Canada, *Report of the Royal Commission on Dominion-Provincial Relations* (hereafter cited as *Sirois Report*), (3 vols.; Ottawa, 1940) 1: 54.

20. Canada, *Dominion Provincial and Interprovincial Conferences from 1887 to 1926* (hereafter cited as *Interprovincial Conferences*) (Ottawa, 1951), 15. The treatise referred to was J. C. Taché, *Des Provinces de l'Amérique du Nord et d'une Union fédérale* (Quebec, 1858). Taché's work was well-chosen for Mercier's purpose. Better than any other, it espoused the prior

rights of the provinces over those of the federal authority. But the scheme proposed by Taché bore some marked differences from any of the projects discussed at Quebec in 1864. Most notable, perhaps, was Taché's view that the existing parliamentary system should be combined with the popular election of the officers of all three branches of government at both federal and provincial levels.

Many verbal differences exist between Mercier's quotations and the original. Compare Mercier, *Interprovincial Conferences,* pp. 15-16 (French text), with Taché, pp. 206, 182, 183. The substance remains the same, however, and the differences may have resulted from the effects of a translation into English for the conference address and a retranslation for the official record.

21. Previous amendments to the B.N.A. Act had been made at Westminster on request of the federal Parliament alone. Quotations from the resolutions are from *Interprovincial Conferences,* pp. 20-25. Commentary may be found in C. R. Biggar, *Sir Oliver Mowat* (2 vols.; Toronto, 1905), 2: 507-508.

22. *Sirois Report,* 1: 55.

23. *Hansard,* 183 (1930): 24.

24. Both letter and memorandum were published *in extenso* in *The Globe* of Toronto, September 20, 1930, and in large part in R. MacG. Dawson, *Constitutional Issues in Canada, 1901-1931* (Toronto, 1933), pp. 23-24. Quotations used here are from Dawson.

25. Gérin-Lajoie, *Amendment,* p. 154.

26. This argument was later adopted by the Tremblay Commission which quoted Lord Carnarvon's introduction of the bill at Westminster: "The local legislatures, he had said then, would have the right to amend their constitutions, but the provisions which govern the Constitution of the Central Parliament would be in the nature of permanent enactments." *Tremblay Report,* 2: 149.

27. *Liquidators of the Maritime Bank of Canada* v. *Receiver-General of New Brunswick,* [1892], A.C. 437; and, *Hodge* v. *The Queen,* (1883) 9 A.C. 117.

28. He wrote to the prime minister: "La Confédération est un contrat, qui a été signé par les différentes provinces canadiennes, après de longues discussions, à des conditions acceptables à toutes les parties contractantes. Je me demande comment un semblable contrat pourrait être modifié sans l'assentiment de toutes les parties." Quoted in Rumilly, p. 171.

29. *Canadian Problems: as seen by Twenty Outstanding Men of Canada* (Toronto, [1933]), p. 248.

30. Rumilly, p. 106.

31. Ibid., p. 108.

32. *L'avenir constitutionnel du Canada* (Montreal, 1935), p. 148.

33. Ibid., pp. 149-50. It is difficult to see how the right of the provinces to be consulted authoritatively could be protected by the method Dr. Ollivier proposed. Although a parliamentary counsel, Dr. Ollivier did not suggest how one Parliament could enact an amending procedure which any succeeding Parliament could not change at its own discretion.

34. "Social Reform and the Constitution," *Canadian Journal of Economics and Political Science* (hereafter cited as *CJEPS*), 1 (1935): 409-54.

35. Gérin-Lajoie, *Amendment,* p. 242, and Ollivier, pp. 155-57.

36. Gérin-Lajoie, *Amendment,* pp. 167-68. The author later became a leading

member of Liberal Quebec governments during the sixties and was a significant architect of his provincial party's constitutional policy.

37. Canada, *Journals of the House of Commons of Canada,* 4 (1871): 254.

38. *Interprovincial Conferences,* p. 67.

39. Ibid., p. 79.

40. *Hansard,* 113 (1914): 614.

41. Quoted in Rumilly, p. 172.

42. Redistribution was carried out in 1946. During the debate on the bill in the Commons, a Conservative lawyer from Calgary West, Arthur Smith, said that the Act of 1867 was a statute that confirmed "a contract made between three people, in which six people later joined." Consequently, he said, the central government, which was "a creature of their making," should seek the provinces' assent to redistribution of Commons membership. Mr. St. Laurent explicitly refuted this statement of the compact doctrine and said that, legally, Parliament did not need provincial approval to have any part of the B.N.A. Act amended. *Hansard,* 251 (1946); 2615-21. For protests made by the province of Quebec on this issue, see Rumilly, pp. 257-59, and the *Tremblay Report,* 1: 157-60. Technical aspects of representation are discussed by Norman Ward, *The Canadian House of Commons* (Toronto, 1950), pp. 19ff.

43. British North America (No. 2) Act, 1949 (13 Geo. VI, Chap. 81 [U.K.]).

44. Both the Ferguson memorandum and the *Tremblay Report* made this point. The extent of possible impingement on local concerns is discussed by Gérin-Lajoie, *Amendment,* introduction; and in the *Tremblay Report,* 1: 160-63.

45. New Brunswick received $63,000 annually for ten years to help balance its budget. Nova Scotia received a similar grant. British Columbia was promised $100,000 annually in perpetuity to induce it to enter the union.

46. Financial considerations were also important to Quebec, but for it, the *key* clauses undoubtedly were the linguistic, educational, and legal provisions.

47. See especially works cited by J. A. Maxwell, Wilfrid Eggleston, A. M. Moore, and J. Harvey Perry.

48. Ontario, *Journals of the Legislative Assembly,* 1869, 34.

49. Text of the resolution is found in Canada, *Journals of the House of Commons,* 2 (1869): 231-32.

50. Ibid., 260. This formal exposition of the compact theory was rejected by a majority that included many of the Confederation Fathers, among them: John A. Macdonald, Cartier, Tilley, Galt, and Tupper.

51. The problem is probed thoroughly in works cited by A. H. Birch, A. E. Buck, Brooke Claxton, the *Sirois Report,* and in the following: H. F. Angus and Roger Brossard, "The Working of Confederation, *CJEPS,* 3 (1937): 335-54; *Canadian Bar Review,* special constitutional law issue of June 1937; *Canadian Problems as Seen by Twenty Outstanding Men of Canada* (Toronto, [1933]); H. McD. Clokie, "Basic Problems of the Canadian Constitution." *CJEPS,* 8 (1942): 24-32; J. A. Maxwell, "Aspects of Canadian Federalism," *Dalhousie Review,* 16 (1936): 275-84; Norman McL. Rogers, "The Constitutional Impasse," *Queen's Quarterly,* 31 (1934); H. Shane, "Canadian Disunion," *Dalhousie Review,* 18 (1938): 157-64.

52. See: British Columbia, *The Governments of Canada Before the Rowell Commission* (Victoria, B. C., 1938), passim.

53. In 1954, Quebec adopted a personal income tax act (2-3 Elizabeth II, chap. 17) which began by enunciating aspects of the doctrine: "whereas it is essential to the survival of the provinces that they have at their disposal the financial resources necessary to exercise their rights and meet their obligations," and, "whereas the Canadian constitution concedes to the provinces priority in the field of direct taxation. . . ." The preamble also recited that the province had sought to work out with Ottawa a fair and suitable fiscal arrangement "consonant with the spirit and letter of the federative pact," but to no avail, and the tax measure had therefore to be enacted.

54. *Tremblay Report,* 3(2): 220.

55. Ibid., 3(2): 229-30.

56. Ibid., 3(2): 233.

57. See British Columbia, *Governments of Canada,* 25-30.

58. Joseph Pope, ed., *Confederation: being a series of hitherto unpublished documents bearing on the British North America Act* (Toronto, 1895), p. 110.

59. *Sirois Report,* 2: 247-59.

60. "In each Province the Legislative may exclusively make Laws in relation to Matters coming within the Classes of Subjects next herein-after enumerated; that is to say . . ."

61. "Nos problèmes constitutionnels," *Revue du Droit,* 16 (1938): 577-99.

62. Rumilly, p. 106.

63. Quoted in Eggleston, p. 18.

64. John T. Saywell, *The Office of Lieutenant-Governor* (Toronto, 1957), p. 26.

65. Quoted in Lionel Groulx, *Histoire du Canada français depuis la découverte* (4 vols.; Montreal, 1950), 3: 75.

66. Quoted in *Tremblay Report,* 1: 92.

67. The Francoeur resolution: "That this House is of opinion that the Province of Quebec would be disposed to accept the breaking of the Confederation Pact of 1867 if, in the other provinces, it is believed that she is an obstacle to the union, progress and development of Canada." A. Savard and W. E. Playfair, trans., *Quebec and Confederation* (Quebec, 1918), title page.

68. Ibid., 113-14.

69. Rumilly, p. 273.

70. Objection had been taken to the formation of the Canadian Bar Association, which Quebec lawyers were advised to boycott. See the speech of Premier Taschereau to the bar association in 1921.

71. Rumilly, pp. 49-50.

72. Canada, *Precis of Discussions, Dominion-Provincial Conference November 3 to 10, 1927* (Ottawa, 1928), 15.

73. *Le Devoir* (Montreal), daily issues, October 2-14, 1961.

74. "The Compact Theory of Confederation," Canadian Political Science Association, *Proceedings of the Annual Meeting,* 2 (1931): 205-30. All quotations by Professor Rogers in this section are from this paper.

75. G. D. Kennedy has discussed the difficulties of assimilating the later provinces (in time of creation) to original partners in the compact in his "Amendment of the British North America Acts in Relation to British Columbia, Prince Edward Island, and Newfoundland," *University of Toronto Law Journal,* 8 (1949-1950): 208-17.

76. This opinion is disputed in Gérin-Lajoie, *Amendment*, chap. 5.

77. If these proposals had been implemented, Professor Alexander Brady says, "the major initiative in social policy would irretrievably shift to the national capital, and provincial independence in finance and manoeuvrability in policy would drastically diminish." In his "Quebec and Canadian Federalism," *CJEPS*, 25 (1959): 265.

78. See his *Essai sur la Centralisation* (Montreal, 1960).

79. "The Theory and Practice of Federalism," in Michael Oliver, ed., *Social Purpose for Canada* (Toronto, 1961).

80. Stanley, p. 16.

CHAPTER 6   THE DUAL ALLIANCE (pp. 173-201)

1. François-Albert Angers, *Essai sur la Centralisation* (Montreal, 1960), 144.

2. "Two Ways of Life: The Primary Antithesis of Canadian History," Canadian Historical Association, *Report of the Annual Meeting, 1943* (hereafter cited as *CHA Report*), 1.

3. *Our Sense of Identity* (Toronto, 1954), ix.

4. *Roots and Values in Canadian Lives* (Toronto, 1961). The concept of "unhyphenated Canadianism" at the time was strongly identified with the then prime minister, J. G. Diefenbaker.

5. John Meisel, *Working Papers on Canadian Politics* (Montreal, 1972), pp. 197-98.

6. "Act or Pact? Another Look at Confederation," *CHA Report, 1956*, 13.

7. Howe to George Moffatt, in J. A. Chisholm, ed., *Speeches and Public Letters of Joseph Howe* (2 vols.; Halifax, 1909), 2: 25.

8. *Hansard*, 29 (1890): 745.

9. In A. R. M. Lower, *et. al., Evolving Canadian Federalism* (Durham, N.C., 1958), p. 61.

10. Quoted in Mason Wade, *The French Canadians* (Toronto, 1956), pp. 427-28, 524-25.

11. This guarantee is limited to the legislative assembly and the courts of Quebec, to the Houses of Parliament, and to federal courts, wherever sitting. *Trustees of the Roman Catholic Separate Schools* v. *Mackell*, (1917) A.C. 62.

12. George V. Ferguson, *John W. Dafoe* (Toronto, 1948), pp. 14-15.

13. The Laurier compromise had resulted in a system of multilingual education, for Manitoba was dotted with Icelandic, German, and French island settlements. The legislature foresaw only chaos under the Laurier arrangement and was seeking to rationalize the school structure with its act of 1916.

14. "The Manitoba Schools and Canadian Nationalism 1890-1916," *CHA Report, 1951*, 57.

15. Quoted in Robert Rumilly, *Histoire de la province de Québec* (32 vols.; Montreal, 1947), 9: 134.

16. "Problèmes d'entente," in Léon Lortie and Adrien Plouffe, ed., *Aux sources du présent* (Toronto, 1960), 108.

17. Henri Saint-Denis, "The Contribution of the French Canadian to Canadian

Unity," in *Canadian Problems: as seen by Twenty Outstanding Men of Canada* (Toronto, 1933), 273.

18. Premier George Drew refused to assent to the federal proposals because he felt they denied Ontario a fair share of the revenues to be split among the provinces.

19. "Réflexions sur la Constitution canadienne," Institut social populaire, *Publication mensuelle*, No. 455 (June, 1952): 11.

20. "Mémoires au gouvernement du Québec," Institut social populaire, *Publication mensuelle*, No. 460 (January, 1953): 1-9.

21. Jean-Charles Bonenfant," "La vie politique du Québec de 1910 à 1935," in Lortie, 25-33.

22. *Statutes of Quebec,* 18 Geo. v (1928), chap. 80.

23. Albert Plante, "Aide fédérale à l'éducation et minorités," *Relations,* No. 157 (January, 1954), 5. In this article Father Plante tried to reconcile the conflict between the two concepts.

24. The loss of language and religion by those of French origin outside Quebec was documented by the Rev. Richard Arès in a series of articles in the Jesuit magazine, *Relations*. His findings are summed up in "Positions du français au Canada: bilan general," No. 165 (September, 1954): 260-63.

25. Falardeau, *Roots and Values,* p. 28.

26. *Roots and Values,* p. 49.

27. See Everett Hughes, "Regards sur le Québec," in Jean-Charles Falardeau, ed., *Essais sur le Québec contemporain* (Quebec, 1953), pp. 217-30.

28. *Canadians et Canadiens* (Montreal, 1955), p. 30.

29. As early as 1955 Professor Frank R. Scott observed that "the currents of constitutional thinking in Quebec suggest that the identification of the government of Quebec with the whole French-Canadian race is greater than ever before." "The Constitutional Background of Taxation Agreements," *McGill Law Journal,* 2 (1955): 10.

30. "Il faut refaire la Confédération," 44 (1954): 15-58.

31. Article quoted by Professor Scott in Mason Wade, ed., *Canadian Dualism/ La Dualité canadienne* (Toronto, 1960), p. 87.

32. Four vols. in 5 books; Quebec, 1956.

33. "Quebec and Canadian Federalism," *Canadian Journal of Economics and Political Science,* 25 (1959): 259.

34. See particularly his "La confédération: pacte ou loi?" *L'action nationale,* 34 (1949) (II)): 194-230, 243-77; and his "Le Fédéralisme: ses principes de base et sa valeur humaine," in Institut social populaire, *Publication mensuelle,* No. 441 (February, 1951): 1-32.

35. Despite the historical account's special viewpoint, scholars outside Quebec should have little quarrel with the presentation of facts. Brady, "Quebec," 267.

36. *Tremblay Report,* 1: 182.

37. Ibid., 2: 5.

38. Ibid., 1: 6.

39. Ibid., 3(2): 284.

40. Ibid., 2: 42.

41. See his *Le fédéralisme canadien; évolution et problèmes* (Quebec, 1954), discussed earlier in this inquiry (chap. 3).

42. *Tremblay Report,* 2: 94.

43. Ibid., 2: 102.

44. Those stressed were: an authoritative distribution of powers, the supremacy of a written constitution, and supervision of the system by an impartial and truly federal court. Ibid., 2: 102-10.

45. Ibid., 3(2): 285.

46. Ibid., 2: 128.

47. "Quebec," 268.

48. The *Massey Report,* which suggested large scale assistance to the arts and letters of Canada from the central treasury, is discussed in chap. 2 of the present study.

49. *Tremblay Report,* 3(2), 293.

50. These recommendations have been discussed in greater detail in chap. 5 of the present study. Further discussion in English may be found in Martin O'Connell, "M. Duplessis' Royal Commission," *Canadian Forum,* 36 (1956): 50-52, one of the few notices taken of the *Tremblay Report* in the English periodical press. See also Roland Parenteau, "Federal-Provincial Relations, III," *Canadian Public Administration,* 1 (1958): 16-25.

51. *Tremblay Report,* 3(2): 292.

52. Ibid., 3(2): 290.

53. Ibid., 3(2): 286-87.

54. Ibid., 3(2): 279.

55. Ibid., 3(2): 302.

56. See his "The United States Supreme Court and Foreign Courts; An Exercise in Comparative Jurisprudence," *Journal of Public Law,* 6 (1957): 478, and, "The Supreme Court and the Bill of Rights—The Lessons of Comparative Jurisprudence," *Canadian Bar Review,* 37 (1959) 39.

57. (1953) 4 D.L.R., 641.

58. *Switzman* v. *Elbling* (The *Padlock* case), (1957) 7 D.L.R. 2d., 337, at 357.

59. "This was a view which scarcely roused a dissenting voice in the Canada of 1867," says Professor Stanley, but many have been the dissents recorded since then. These include the dissents of the centralists, of those who insisted on seeking to fulfil Durham's dream of racial homogeneity, and of those who would permit no single region to delay the material betterment of the whole state. So bitterly opposed have been the centralists and the *Canadiens* that one Quebec historian was led to observe: "Un Canada sans province canadienne-française demeura toujours l'idéal des planificateurs et des centralisateurs. S'ils étaient honnêtes, ils le diraient franchement, brutalement." Michel Brunet, *Canadians et Canadiens* (Montreal, 1955), p. 164. Among those dissenting from this two nations plan of constitutional amendment has been Dean Frank R. Scott, who certainly should not be counted among those wishing to see French Canada disappear. See his "Areas of Conflict in the Field of Public Law and Policy," *McGill Law Journal,* 3 (1956): 29-50.

60. *Montreal Star,* February 8, 45. (*N.B.* Quoted in Dean E. McHenry, *The Third Force in Canada* (Berkeley, Calif.; 1950), p. 232). A similar claim was made in the Speech from the Throne to the Quebec legislature on November 8, 1950: "first and foremost, the Canadian Constitution owes its origin to a compact concluded between two great races." Province of Quebec, *Journals of the Legislative Assembly,* 86 (1950-1951): 4.

61. Stanley Knowles, *The New Party* (Toronto, 1961), p. 62.

62. The Federal Program of the New Democratic Party (Ottawa, 1961), 20-21.

63. All quotations have been taken from a mimeographed copy of the brief supplied to the present writer through the courtesy of Michel Forêt, Montreal, secretary of Le nouveau parti démocratique de Québec. Minor typing errors in the mimeographed copy of the English translation have been corrected in the quotations.

64. "Canadian Unity and the Constitution," partial text of a speech to the Osgoode Hall Legal and Literary Society, Toronto, January 15, 1962 (mimeo).

65. The writer is indebted to Michel Forêt, for a mimeographed copy of this declaration, "Communiqué à la presse," January 26, 1962.

66. "The Future of English Canada," *Canadian Dimension,* 2 (1965): 12, 25.

67. *Egalité ou indépendance,* (Montreal, 1965), p. 72.

68. Ibid., p. 110.

69. Ibid., p. 116.

70. Ibid., p. 118.

71. This and succeeding quotations are found in: *Preliminary Statement by Mr. Daniel Johnson, Former Prime Minister: Confederation of Tomorrow Conference,* (Toronto, 1967), Government of Quebec.

72. A. W. Johnson, "The Dynamics of Federalism in Canada," *Canadian Journal of Political Science,* 1 (1968): 18-39.

73. *Canada and the French-Canadian Question,* (Toronto, 1966), pp. 70-71.

74. *Le Fédéralisme, l'acte de l'Amérique du nord britannique et les Canadiens français,* (Montreal, 1964), 118.

75. See works cited by Martin O'Connell and Alexander Brady, "Quebec"; and D. V. Smiley, "The Rowell-Sirois Report, Provincial Autonomy, and Post-War Canadian Federalism," *CJEPS,* 28 (1962), 54-69; "The Tremblay Report," *Canadian Tax Journal,* 4 (1956): 155-56.

76. Essentially, this would seem to have been Professor Brunet's position during the fifties. He frequently reverted to the two nations idea, cautioned that it must be gauged realistically, and assailed those "dreamers" who hoped to see Canada develop into a truly bilingual and bicultural state. *Canadians et Canadiens,* chap. 1.

77. *Pourquoi je suis séparatiste* (4th ed.; Montreal, 1961), secs. 2 and 4. See also Peter C. Newman, "A Policy Blueprint for the Republic of Quebec," *Maclean's Magazine,* 75(4) (February 24, 1962): 22, and the general literature of the Quebec separatist movements.

78. See his "Areas of Conflicts," (reprinted in Wade, *Canadian Dualism*), "The Constitutional Background," *loc. cit.,* and "French Canada and Canadian Federalism" in A. R. M. Lower, *et. al., Evolving Canadian Federalism* (Durham, N.C., 1958), pp. 54-91.

79. "Dynamics of Federalism," p. 29.

80. D. V. Smiley, *Canada in Question: Federalism in the Seventies,* (Toronto, 1972), pp. 161-66; and Ramsay Cook, *Canada and the French-Canadian Question* (Toronto, 1966), passim.

81. *Democratic Government and Politics* (2nd ed.; Toronto, 1951), pp. 582-83.

CHAPTER 7 THE DEUX NATIONS CONTROVERSY (pp. 203-215)

1. The campaign will not be described speech by speech. Details will be found in Martin Sullivan, *Mandate '68,* (Toronto, 1968), Donald Peacock, *Journey to Power,* (Toronto, 1968), and *Canadian Annual Review.*

2. *Hansard,* Sept. 1, 1964, 7525, and Dec. 18, 1964, 11339.

3. *Hansard,* April 6, 1965, 43-44.

4. Mr. Faribault's text is quoted in Dalton Camp, "Reflections on the Montmorency Conference," *Queen's Quarterly,* 76 (1969): 185-99.

5. Ibid., 199. This resolution is incorrectly given in some of the popular works cited above.

6. Sullivan, p. 169.

7. Unless otherwise cited, all quotations for Mr. Stanfield have been drawn from the mimeographed text for the occasion and kindly supplied to the author by the staff of Mr. Stanfield's Office of the Official Opposition, or by the national headquarters of the Progressive Conservative Party of Canada, Ottawa.

8. Text reported in Newman, pp. 159-60.

9. Thomas Van Dusen, *The Chief* (Toronto, 1968), pp. 69, 79.

10. See, especially, Kenneth McNaught, "The NDP's Special Status Kick," *Saturday Night,* October, 1967.

11. Pamphlet supplied by the New Democratic Party parliamentary research office, Ottawa.

12. John Saywell, ed., *Canadian Annual Review for 1968,* 60-61.

13. Unless otherwise cited, all quotations for Mr. Trudeau are taken from the mimeographed texts of speeches issued by the Office of the Prime Minister, House of Commons, Ottawa.

14. Constitutional Conference, First Meeting, *Proceedings* (Ottawa, 1968), 227-37.

15. See Newman and the issues of the *Canadian Annual Review* for the years 1963 to 1967.

16. In contrast to the English-language mass media, French newspapers, and especially the influential *Le Devoir,* did not like Mr. Trudeau's stance and gave increasing support to the Stanfield position.

17. See: Edward McWhinney, "Canadian Federalism: Foreign Affairs and Treaty Power," *Ontario Advisory Committee on Confederation, Background Papers and Reports* (Toronto, 1970), and, Howard A. Leeson, "Foreign Relations and Quebec," in J. P. Meekison, ed., *Canadian Federalism: Myth or Reality,* (2nd ed., Toronto 1971), 453-66.

18. For detailed exploration of this and other issues, see: John Meisel, *Working Papers on Canadian Politics* (2nd ed., Montreal and London 1973), and especially chap. 2, "Party Images in Canada."

19. Meisel's work, cited above, gives the best possible indication of the low salience which it is probably appropriate to attribute to policy factors in electoral decision-making. See especially chap. 1.

CHAPTER 8 TWO NATIONS OR MORE? (pp. 217-34)

1. *On Liberty and Consideration on Representative Government* (Oxford, 1948), p. 292.

2. One justification for selecting the criteria inductively is our logical expectation that the importance of different issues to the structure of institutions would vary from federation to federation.

3. These phrases and the alternative "centrifugal and centripetal" imply a single plane continuum, either linear or circular, between complete integration and full disaggregation. Both metaphors fail thereby to provide for the locating at similar distances from the extremes of several concepts which differ in structural or other features. While unfortunate, this limitation continues to elude the writer's conceptual abilities.

4. Whether the *Established Programs* (Interim Arrangements) *Act* of 1965 constitutes a minor exception to this point is debatable.

5. That is, not every gain is necessarily somebody else's loss.

6. For one case, see the author's "B.C.—the Politics of Exploitation," in R. A. Shearer, ed., *Exploiting the B.C. Economy* (Toronto, 1968), and reprinted in H. G. Thorburn, ed., *Party Politics in Canada* (3rd ed.; Scarborough, Ont., 1972).

7. "Quebec: Heaven is Blue and Hell is Red," in M. Robin, ed., *Canadian Provincial Politics* (Scarborough, Ont., 1972).

8. An outstanding exception is Ramsey Cook's *Provincial Autonomy, Minority Rights and the Compact Theory, 1867-1921* (Ottawa, 1969).

9. None of the obvious hypotheses of this type seemed satisfying enough to merit burdening the present analysis with it.

10. "The Real Issue is Money," *The Globe and Mail,* Toronto, May 25, 1973, 4.

11. "Continentalism and Quebec Nationalism: A Double Challenge to Canada," *Queen's Quarterly,* 76 (1970): 511.

12. Donald V. Smiley, *The Canadian Political Nationality,* (Toronto, 1967).

13. See Gad Horowitz, "Conservatism, Liberalism, and Socialism in Canada: An Interpretation," *CJEPS*, 23 (1966) 143-71.

14. Richard Simeon, *Federal-Provincial Diplomacy,* (Toronto, 1972), pp. 312, 296.

15. Donald V. Smiley, *Canada in Question: Federalism in the Seventies* (Toronto, 1972) p. 181.

16. See, for example, P. J. T. O'Hearn, *Peace, Order and Good Government* (Toronto, 1965), and Marcel Faribault and Robert Fowler, *Ten to One: the Confederation Wager* (Toronto, 1965).

17. For elaboration, see Edwin R. Black and Alan C. Cairns, "A Different Perspective on Canadian Federalism," *Canadian Public Administration,* 9 (1966): 27-45.

TABLE OF MAJOR CASES

Judicial Committee of the Privy Council decisions

Aeronautics, 151
Bank of Toronto v. Lambe, 249n66
Board of Commerce, 249n58
Brophy v. A.-G. Manitoba, 127-28
Citizens Insurance Co. v. Parsons, 249n66
City of Winnipeg v. Barrett, 127
Fort Frances, 42
Hodge v. The Queen, 103, 254n27
Initiative and Referendum Act, 8
Japanese Canadians, 42, 241n79, 249n52
Labour Conventions, 45-46, 168, 242n1, 248-49n49
Local Prohibition, 8, 124, 249n51
Maritime Bank, 7, 120, 236n10, 239n33, 248n35, 249n53, 254n27
Mercer, 119, 152, 248n32
Natural Products Marketing (1937), 54, 125, 247n27, 249n60
Radio Communications, 58, 126, 240n65, 241n75
Reference, 123, 248n44
Roman Catholic Schools v. Mackell, 128
Russell v. The Queen, 39, 152, 153, 249n50
Toronto Electric Commissioners v. Snider, 124, 125, 249n51
Winner, 240n66

Supreme Court of Canada decisions

Alberta Statutes reference, 250n86
Birks, 130, 250n84
Chicken and Egg, 122, 126, 248n49
Disallowance and Reservation, 133-34

Drybones, 131, 250n88

Farm Products Marketing (1957), 249n65

Johanneson v. West St. Paul, 249n64

Nova Scotia Delegation, 103, 125, 249n62, 246n61

Offshore Minerals, 122, 248n47

Ontario Highway Transport Board, 103

Padlock Act, 130, 188

P.E.I. Potato Marketing Board v. Willis, 103, 126, 249n63

Saumur v. City of Quebec, 130, 188

Switzman v. Elbling, 250n85, 259n58

Taxation Agreement between Saskatchewan and Canada, 243n16, 250n71

INDEX

Abbott, Mr. Justice, 131
Acadians, 197-98
Accountability, 110-11
Act of Union, 25, 150
Administrative decentralization, 230
Administrative federalism, 16, 63-112, 220-21, 227, 242n2; weaknesses of, 108-10
Agricultural marketing, 95
Agriculture, 91, 93-94, 109
Alberta, 81, 84, 88, 93, 134, 165
Allowances: blind and disabled, 78, 142; Family, 51
Amendment, constitutional: 13-15, 52-53, 94, 95, 112, 135-41, 150, 152, 155, 157-58, 178, 188, 190, 191, 221, 237n20, 242n105, 254-nn21,33; procedures for, 17, 135-41; federal-provincial conferences on, 135-41
Amendments to B.N.A. Act. *See* British North America Act, amendments
Angers, Francois-Albert, 170, 180, 257n1
Angus, H. F., 115
Annexation Manifesto, 24
Arès, Richard, 151, 182, 258n24
Assimilation, 23-25, 210
Associate Statehood, 195, 211, 212, 214
Atkin, Lord, 63, 103, 113, 248n49
Atomic Energy, 39
Australia, 21

Bastedo, F. L., 135
Belgium, 204
Bennett, R. B., 45-46, 155
Bernard, Col. Hewitt, 28, 235n1
Bertrand, Jean-Jacques, 209
Better Terms, 55, 161
Bilingualism, xii, 112, 143, 144, 199, 211, 214
Bill of Rights (Canada, 1960), 43, 207
Birch, A. H., 241n88
Bird, Richard, 88
Blake, Donald, 226
Blake, Edward, 35, 161
Borden, Robert L., 159
Bourassa, Henri, 175
Brady, Alexander, 146, 182, 185
British Columbia, 1, 73, 81, 88, 165, 166, 233, 255n45
British North America Act, 7, 22, 57, 114, 166, 187, 188, 240n57; amendments to, 136-37, 169, 255n42; as treaty, 149-71; passage of, 31; preamble, 7, 131; Section 51: 158; S.91: 33-34, 39, 41, 123, 126, 136, 152-53, 166; S.92: 33-34, 152; S.92.1: 120, 124; S.92.10(c): 38, 191; S. 92.13: 33, 40, 47, 129; S. 93: 58, 97, 123, 127-28; S.94: 38, 65, 97, 123; S. 95: 33, 123; S.109: 50, 123, 191; S.132:45, 123, 168; S.133: 52, 128, 129
British North America League, 24-25

Broadcasting: educational, 167;
Radio case, 39, 58; television,
57-58, 194, 223
Brown, George, 32, 37, 150
Browne, G. P., 8, 236n11
Brunet, Michel, 180, 209, 228,
259n59, 260n76
Burns, R. M., 92, 93, 102,
244nn25, 39

Cairns, Alan C., 4, 86, 223,
235n2, 262n17
Camp, Dalton, 261n4
Canada, Inner and Outer, 6
Canada, Royal Commission on
Bilingualism and Biculturalism,
xii, 18, 58, 174, 208; Royal
Commission on Dominion-
Provincial Relations (Sirois
Commission), 33, 46, 86, 89-90,
108, 114-19, 145, 154, 155,
157, 162, 164-65, 252n120-124;
Royal Commission on National
Development in the Arts, Letters,
and Sciences (Massey Commis-
sion), 57, 185, 242n117,
259n48
Canada Assistance Plan, 78, 81,
142, 233
Canada Council, 57
Canadian Broadcasting
Corporation, 167, 179
Canadian Charter of Human
Rights, 131
Canadian Pacific Railway, 37, 222
Canadianism, unhyphenated, 174
Carter, George, 108, 244n22
Cartier, George-Etienne, 27,
32, 204
Centralism, crisis, 40-47; cultural,
56-59, 212, 219; of Macdonald,
28-39
Centralist concept, 15-16, 21-61,
121, 145, 220, 221, 222, 224,
231, 232, 252n120, 259n59
Centralization, 8, 16, 19, 21-61,
51, 107, 111, 146, 184, 185,
191, 239n41, 246n63; devices
of, 33-34, 132-35, 247nn5,25;
finance, 54, 169; influences
toward, 223; planning, 47-52;
popular feeling, 46; tendencies
toward, 9, 221-23; wartime,
41-44

Chaput, Marcel, 197
Charlottetown meeting, 28, 151,
235n1
Citizenship, second class, 207
Civil Code, 181, 187, 190
Civil liberties. See Liberties, civil
Classical federalism, 8, 242n2
Claxton, Brooke, 48, 89, 158
Clokie, H. McD., 236n9
Cohen, Maxwell A., 43, 90
Coldwell, M. J., 50, 241n98,
242n100
Cole, R. Taylor, 8
Communities, provincial, 6, 232
Compact theory, 17-18, 22, 149-
72, 174, 179, 197, 219, 221,
252n120, 253nn12,16,20,
254n28, 255nn42,50
Concepts of federalism: develop-
ment of, 225; time lines for, 225
Concurrent jurisdiction, fields of,
33, 104, 123, 134, 233
Conditional grants. See Grants,
conditional
Confederation: Fathers, of, 4,
28ff, 133, 185, 204; "intentions"
of Fathers of, 4, 31, 38, 44, 150;
moves toward, 24-31; real nature
of, 2-6, 11, 95, 115; and U.S.A.,
1, 27
Confederation Debates, 31
Confederation of Tomorrow
Conference, 193
Conscription crisis, 66, 176, 177
Conservation, 93
Constitution, amendment of. See
Amendment, constitutional
Constitution: and socialists, 47;
new Canadian, 85; salvation by,
231
Constitutional Act, 22, 174
Constitutional conferences, 231;
Ottawa, 210; Victoria, 215
Constitutional crisis, 162, 230
Constitutional law, 7, 84-85
Contracting out. See Opting-out
Contract theory. See Compact
theory
Control, devices of central, 33-34,
132-35
Controls of prices and incomes, 47
Controls, rent, 79
Cook, Ramsay, xii, 195, 199, 262n8

Cooperative Commonwealth
Federation, 47-52, 79
Cooperative federalism, 7, 16, 52,
64, 85, 89, 96, 141, 193
Coordinate federalism, 17, 96, 112,
135, 192, 210, 211, 220, 221,
231; definition of, 113-14
Corry, J. A., 65, 95, 106, 132, 199,
242n2, 244n30, 248n28
Courts, 65, 221, 251n93;
provincial effects on, 121-22
"Creative politics," 227
Creighton, Donald, 28, 39,
237nn6,9, 238n25
Criminal code, 33, 65, 121, 230

Dafoe, John W., 115
Dawson, R. McGregor, 8, 30, 54,
108, 124, 238n30, 254n24
Decentralization, 50-51, 104, 222;
tendencies toward, 9, 221-23
Delegation power, 53, 118-19,
139, 230, 232
Depression, economic, 44-47, 115
Deux nations, 203, 206, 207, 231
Dicey, A. V., 113, 184
Diefenbaker, John G., 56, 87, 97,
134, 199, 204-205, 212, 213,
214, 257n4
Disallowance, 33, 34, 36, 132-35,
155, 251nn97, 102, 104
Distribution of powers, 123;
Tremblay Report and, 163-66
Divorce, 33
Dominion-provincial. See Federal-
provincial
Dorion, A. A., 27
Dorion, J. B. E., 32
Douglas, T. C., 53, 79, 190, 209
Doyle, Sir Hastings, 34
Drew, George, 87, 170, 258n18
Dualism, cultural, 7, 173-201
Dualist federalism, 18, 22, 173-
201, 215, 219, 221, 231
Duff, Sir Lyman, 134
Duplessis, Maurice, 104, 166-67,
178, 179, 181, 188
Durham Report, 23-24, 26,
236n4, 259n59

Economic crisis, 44-47, 115, 162
Economic disparities, 170
Economy, control over, 34, 47-52,
231

Education, 6, 26, 30, 33, 49-50,
57, 91, 92, 94, 95, 101, 112,
117, 127-29, 144, 164, 195;
financing of, 97-98, 128, 143,
245n52; responsibility for, 6,
16-18; technical, 98, 101, 142;
university, 57, 97-98. See also
Schools
Egalitarianism, 19, 86, 222, 232
Egalité ou indépendance, 193
Election, of 1896, 203; of 1968,
203-215
Elites and federalism, 4, 5, 222,
226-27
Emergency power, 41-44, 46
Equality. See Egalitarianism
Equality of provinces, 151, 232-33
Equalization, 53, 66, 69, 86-94,
104, 170, 180, 230
Estates-General, 196
Executive federalism. See
Administrative federalism

Falardeau, Jean-Charles, 173,
180, 258nn25,27
Faribault, Marcel, 204, 212,
261n4, 262n16
Fathers of Confederation. See
Confederation, Fathers of
Federalism, administrative. See
Administrative federalism
Federalism, definitions, 7; legal
view of, 119-32; syndrome of, 10
Federalist vocabulary, 3
Federal-Provincial committees,
94-98
Federal-Provincial conference by
specific year, (1935) 90; (1941)
162; (1945-46) 53, 66, 73,
90-91, 92, 162, 170; (1950)
79; (1966) 97-98; (1971) 94;
generally, 94-96, 118
Federal-provincial conferences of
premiers and prime ministers,
16, 95, 193
Federal-Provincial Continuing
Committee on Fiscal and
Economic Matters, 92, 94
Federal-provincial diplomacy,
85, 229
Federal-Provincial Fiscal
Arrangements Act, 69
Federal-provincial secretariat,
90, 92, 104, 118, 186

Federal regimes, characteristics of, 9-10
Ferguson, G. Howard, 155-57, 168, 177
Ferland, Philippe, 181
Finance dependence index, 87
Financial independence. See Independence, financial
Fiscal autonomy, 12, 17, 153, 162, 219
Fisheries, 30, 91
Foreign relations and provinces, 167
Forsey, Eugene, 199
Fox, Paul, 242n109
France, 204
Francoeur Resolution, 166, 256n67
Free trade, 24
Fulton-Favreau amendment formula, 15, 158, 191, 193, 210-15, 221
Functional cooperation, 64
Functional federalism, 244n24
Fur industry, 93

Galt, Alexander T., 27, 29, 32; and confederal scheme 237n17, 238n32
Gardiner, James G., 178
Gérin-Lajoie, Paul, 135, 158, 178, 253n16
Godbout, Adélard, 160
Gouin, Lomer, 177
Grain elevators, 38-39
Grants, conditional: definition of, 71; generally, 51, 56, 61-86, 108, 142-43, 182, 223, 248n28; and C.C.F., 48; medicare, 80-81; in Sirois Report, 119
Grants, equalization, 86-89, 221
Grants, impact of, 80-84
Grants, National Adjustment, 117-18
Grants, unconditional, 55, 67, 95, 143, 170
Grants-in-aid. See Grants, conditional
Green Book centralism. See Reconstruction conference

Haldane, Lord, 46, 113, 241n73
Hartle, D. G., 109
Health, 78, 91, 93, 95, 100, 102,
117, 142, 198, 222; jurisdiction over, 48, 49
Health services, 54
Highways, 72-74, 79, 94, 95, 102, 103, 121, 142, 240n66, 247n25
Holmes, John, 228
Holton, L. H., 162
Horowitz, Gad, 5, 191, 235n5
Hospital construction, 54
Hospital insurance, 73, 142
House of Commons representation, 158-60
Housing, 94
Howe, Joseph, 24-25, 175, 178, 237n10
Howland, William, 35

Ideology, official, 5, 229
Ideology, party, 1, 3, 5
Immigration, 194, 222
Independence, financial, 12, 16-18, 32, 82-84, 87-88, 108, 170, 219, 257n77
Independence, political, 12, 167, 257n77
Industrial Disputes Investigation Act, 40-41
Inequalities, 11, 86
Innis, H. A., 145-46
Institute of Public Administration of Canada, 92
Intentions. See Confederation, Fathers of
Intercolonial railway, 30, 164
Interdelegation of Powers, 103-105, 232-34
Interest groups, 224
Intergovernmental bargaining, 230
Interprovincial Conferences, political, 101-102, 152-55, 159
Interprovincial cooperation, 66, 101-102

Johnson, A. W., 143-44, 198, 260n72
Johnson, Daniel, 193, 197, 209-14, 240n60, 260n71
Joint Programs. See Grants, conditional
Judicial Committee of the Privy Council, 7, 89, 114, 122, 124, 144, 151, 156, 159, 185

Kennedy, W. P. M., 5, 30, 52, 127, 238n29, 241n74

Kerwin, Mr. Justice, 134
King, W. L. Mackenzie, 6, 40, 44-45, 55, 69, 72, 160, 166, 177, 241n71
Knowles, Stanley, 260n61

Labour, 13, 42, 47-48, 49, 53, 92, 94, 100, 118, 195
L'action nationale, 181
La Forest, G. V., 239n52
Lamontagne, Maurice, 104-105, 107, 111, 184, 246n62
Language rights, 13, 17, 18, 127-29, 131
Laskin, Bora, 38, 103, 126, 130, 240, 246n59, 250nn69, 83
Laurier, Sir Wilfrid, 175, 203, 239n50, 257n13
Leach, Richard, 100, 243n6, 245n50
League for Social Reconstruction, 48-49, 52
Lederman, W. R., 8
Leeson, Howard, 261n17
Lemieux, Vincent, 224
Lesage, Jean, 101, 167, 196
Letellier de St. Just, Luc de, 35-36
Lévesque, René, 208
Lewis, David, 241n92
Liberalism, 5, 209, 218, 228
Liberal Party, 69, 104, 209, 211
Liberties, civil, 13, 17-18, 42-44, 49, 109, 112, 129-32, 165, 187-88, 194, 231, 250n86; and Quebec, 43-44
Lieutenant-governors, 33-36, 65, 120, 155, 166, 239n50
Livingston, W. S., 135, 236n15
London: conference, 30, 151; Resolutions, 28, 161, 164, 238n26
Loranger, T. J. J., 151-53
Loreburn, Earl, 123
Lower, Arthur, 4, 173, 235n4, 236n6, 239n33
Lynn, James H., 71

McCarthy, D'Alton, 58
Macdonald, Sir John A., 5, 6, 27, 41, 90, 123, 150, 154, 175, 204, 235n3, 237n9; and Annexation Manifesto, 24; and centralism, 31-39, 133, 238n25
Macdonald, John Sandfield, 26, 161

Macdonald, V. C., 8
MacKay, R. A., 115
Mackenzie, Alexander, 35, 39, 161
MacKenzie, Norman A., 44, 52, 157, 242n105
Mackintosh, W. A., 66
McNaught, Kenneth, 261n10
McWhinney, Edward, 187, 261n17
Maheux, Arthur, 177
Majorities, 13-15, 26-27, 80, 232; concurrent, 14
Majority, double, 26, 237n14
Mallory, J. R., 64, 115, 125, 133, 239n51, 240n57, 251nn97, 102
Manitoba, 35, 79, 92, 128, 136, 167, 203
Manitoba Act, 159, 176
Manitoba railways, 37
Manitoba schools, 39, 128, 257n13
Manning, E. C., 80
Maritime Marshland Rehabilitation Program, 71
Maritime Provinces, 28-29, 32, 66, 73, 159, 161, 164
Maritime union, 28
Marriage, 30, 33
Marsh, Leonard, 48, 242n101; Marsh Report, 50-51
Massey Report, 57, 185
Maxwell, J. A., 55, 108, 242n114
Medicare, 80, 81, 222, 252n115
Meekison, J. Peter, 261n17
Meisel, John, 59, 174, 242n119, 261n19
Mercier, Honoré, 154, 253n20
Mignault, P. B., 157, 165
Mill, John Stuart, 217
Mines, 102
Minorities, 14, 53, 80, 129-30; religious, 30, 33, 130
Montmorency conference, 18, 204
Morton, W. L., 176
Mowat, Oliver, 29, 35, 37, 154, 238n26, 239n48
Multi-culturalism, 214
Municipal affairs, 32, 195

Nationalism, 1, 7, 19, 58, 209, 222, 228, 232, 234
National Policy, 37
National standards, 16, 50, 51, 80, 145
Nation-building, 6, 15, 21, 25

Natural Products Marketing Act, 45
Natural resources, 50, 95, 194
Negotiations, federal-provincial, 85
New Brunswick, 17, 25, 28, 30, 81, 129, 159, 233, 255n45; and Sirois Commission, 164, 195
New Democratic Party, 64, 189, 200, 212, 213; and "special status," 208
Newfoundland, 28, 84, 88, 134, 138, 167, 193
Newman, Peter, 260n77
Nicol, Eric, 228
North West Territories, 176
Nova Scotia, 17, 28, 30, 154, 159, 211; 255n5; and secession, 161-62

O'Connell, Martin, 259n50
O'Connor, W. F., 238n30
October crisis (1970), 42, 43, 47, 51, 52
Official Languages Act, 129, 213-14, 232
O'Halloran, Mr. Justice, 131
Oliver, Michael, 105, 242n103
Ollivier, Maurice, 157, 242n106, 254n33
Ontario, 17, 73, 81, 92, 154, 155-57, 161, 165, 176-77, 233
Opting-out, 56, 142-43, 230

Pardoning power, 30
Parenteau, Roland, 259n50
Parties, political, and federalism, 55-56, 224
Peace, Order and Good Government, 39, 124
Pearson, Lester B., 56, 64, 97, 104-105, 107, 141, 167, 204, 210, 221, 246n65
Pendulum theory, 221-22
Penitentiaries, 30
Pensions, old age, 54, 72, 91, 97, 252n115
Pépin, Jean-Luc, 64, 107
Planning, provincial, 79
Plante, Albert, 258n23
Pluralism, 11, 59, 144, 180
Police, 92, 153, 244
Policy, intervention, 78-79, 88-89
Policy Limitation Index, 83
Policy-making, provincial, 79-83

Political culture, 3, 44, 218
Political initiatives, 11
Political socialization, 4n
Pollution, 109, 252
Pope, Joseph, 235n1, 237n8, 238n25
Porter, John, 227
Powers, division of, 3, 9, 161, 162
Pre-confederation, 22-31, 237
Prices and incomes controls, 47
Prince Edward Island, 28-31, 78, 159, 167, 193, 233
Principles, political, 3
Privy Council (U.K.). See Judicial Committee
Progressive Conservative party, 18, 56, 69, 204, 205, 237n14
Property and civil rights, 33, 40, 129, 153, 158, 190, 238n26, 241n73; and sec. 94, 37-38, 124, 153, 165
Provincial revolt, 154
Provincial rights, 39, 55, 156
Public accountability, 109-10
Public works, 48, 94; federal take-over, 13, 38

Quasi-federalism, 25-27
Quebec, 1, 17-18, 32, 35-36, 57, 58, 72, 78, 84, 88, 92, 97, 101, 104, 128, 136, 137, 140, 154, 157, 160, 165, 167, 178, 203, 224, 233, 237n14, 255nn42,46, 258n29; Quebec Act, 166, 174; education, 179, 212; foreign relations, 167, 212; language, 173-201; and Sirois Commission, 165; taxation, 68, 178. See also Separatism
Quebec Resolutions, 3, 28, 30-32, 123, 150-51, 161-62, 169, 235n1, 239n32
Quebec, Royal Commission of Inquiry on Constitutional Problems. See Tremblay Report

Racism, 16, 154, 234; and centralism, 58-59, 259n59
Railways, jurisdiction over, 39, 247n25
Rand, Mr. Justice, 103
Reconstruction conference. See Federal-Provincial Conference on Reconstruction

Regina Manifesto, 47-48
Regional development, 48, 79
Regulation 17 (Ontario), 128, 176-77
Religion, 6, 183, 258n24. *See also* Schools
"Rep-by-pop," 27, 159, 255n42
Reservation (of provincial bills), 34, 36-37, 132-35
Residual powers, 14, 29-30, 39, 41, 124, 152-53
Responsible government, 25
Riel rebellion, 223
Rinfret, Thibaudeau, 115, 126, 188
Rivers and Streams bill, 37, 240n55
Robinson, John Beverley, 22
Roblin, Duff, 79
Rogers, Norman McL., 168-69, 241n71
Ross, Malcolm, 173
Rowell, N. W., 115
Rowell-Sirois Report. *See* Canada, Royal Commission on Dominion-Provincial Relations
Rubin, G., 122
Rumilly, Robert, 240n60

Saint-Denis, Henri, 186
St. Laurent, Louis, 52, 54, 69, 137, 160, 181, 255n42
Sankey, Lord, 113
Saskatchewan, 53, 78, 135, 137
Saywell, John, 34, 35, 239n46
Schools, language and, 39, 128, 257n3; minorities and, 189; separate, 26, 39, 176, 128, 250n74. *See also* Manitoba
Schwartz, Mildred, 226
Scott, Frank R., 21, 48, 51, 105, 125, 129, 158, 175, 197, 200, 239n40, 240n59, 241n92, 242n104, 249nn59, 66, 252n2, 258n29, 259n59
Senate, 10, 15, 31, 34, 48, 154, 167, 189; representation in, 29; Senate-House Special Committee on the Constitution, 231
Separatism, 1, 193, 194, 195, 197, 210, 215
Sewell, Jonathan, 22
Sharman, G. Campbell, 121-22, 243n9

Shaw, Walter, 80
Siegfried, André, 58
Single party dominance, 224
Sirois, Joseph, 115
Sirois Report. See Canada, Royal Commission on Dominion-Provincial Relations
Skelton, O. D., 25, 26, 237n12, 238n32
Smiley, D. V., xii, 8, 65, 71, 72, 96, 108, 119, 128, 199, 224, 229, 236n8, 243n8, 244nn24,25, 246n71, 248n30, 250n88, 260n75
Smith, Denis, 241n82
Smith, William (Chief Justice), 22
Social Credit, 134, 166, 240n57
Socialists, 1, 47-53, 59, 170, 224; and dualism, 189, 192. *See also* Party names
Social Planning for Canada, 49
Social welfare, 17, 44, 47, 49, 54, 60, 73, 81, 91, 101, 117, 164, 186, 195, 196
Sovereignty: economic, 6; provincial, 165
Spending power, federal, 34, 84-85, 128, 132
Stanfield, Robert L., 206, 211, 214, 261n16
Stanley, G. F. G., 150, 171, 175, 252n1, 259n59
Statehood, associate, 18, 193-94
Statistics, 30, 94
Status, special, 181, 206, 208, 211, 212, 232
Statute of Westminster, 156
Statut particulier, 18, 196
Stevens, Geoffrey, 227
Subsidies to provinces, 29, 30, 34, 48, 54, 67, 155, 160-62
Sullivan, Martin, 261n1
Supreme Court of Canada, 15, 38, 47, 103, 114, 121, 125, 130, 151, 159, 187, 188, 190, 224, 240n60
Survival and *la survivance*, 1, 5, 104, 107, 150, 167
Switzerland, 204

Taché, J. C., 253n20
Tardivel, Jules-Paul, 175
Tariffs, 6, 116, 194, 223
Taschereau, Alexandré, 157

Tax abatements, 56, 142-43, 230
Taxation, 154, 198; direct, 32,
   67, 126, 163, 185-86; double,
   67; indirect, 127, 249n66; public
   utilities, 69; Quebec, 68, 178;
   sales, 127; in *Tremblay Report*,
   163-64, 169
Tax collection, 12, 66-70, 222
Tax credits, 69
Taxes: collection, 12; estate, 54,
   68; corporations income, 54, 68,
   163-64, 186, 243n11; personal
   income, 54, 68, 81, 142,
   163-64, 243n11, 256n53
Tax rentals, 67-70, 94, 95, 126,
   181, 222, 243nn15,16,17
Tax Structure Committee, 80, 94
Taylor, K. W., 93
Telephone and telegraphs, 39
Thorson, J. J., 129
Trade and commerce, 39, 40, 47,
   125
Trans-Canada Highway, 72-74,
   79, 142
Transport, interprovincial, 39
Treaty of Paris (1763), 174
Treaty power, 46, 109, 168, 196
Tremblay Report, 18, 57, 101,
   163-64, 170, 181, 182, 185,
   190, 196, 200, 254n26

Trudeau, Pierre-Elliott, xiii, 105,
   107, 140, 143, 168, 170, 199,
   209, 211, 214, 261n16; and
   human rights, 131-32; and
   October crisis, 43, 47, 51, 52
Trudeau-Turner amendment
   formula, 15, 17, 140-41,
   158, 221, 232
Tupper, Charles, 29, 32, 161
"Two nations," 18, 64, 97, 177,
   180, 182, 187-96, 203-15, 232,
   259n59, 260n76

Underhill, Frank H., 48
Unemployment, 45, 46, 54, 55
Union Nationale, 213

Veto, central government, 13, 17,
   37, 132-35
Voters, 155; and qualifications, 29

Wagner, W. J., 121, 248n41
War Measures Act, 42-43
Watson, Lord, 7, 113, 120, 124,
   239n33
Watts, R. L., 8, 236n14
Welfare. *See* Social welfare
Wheare, K. C., 113, 218, 251n93
Whitelaw, W. M., 239n34,
   253n12